W9-DFJ-762

ECHOES

Studies in Continental Thought

John Sallis, general editor

ECHOES

After Heidegger

JOHN SALLIS

INDIANA UNIVERSITY PRESS

Bloomington and Indianapolis

The paper used in this publication meets the minimum
requirements of American National Standards for Information
Sciences—Permanence of Paper for Printed Library Materials,
ANSI Z39.48-1984.

Manufactured in the United States of America

Library of Congress Cataloging-in-Publication Data
Sallis, John
Echoes : after Heidegger / John Sallis.
p.   cm. — (Studies in continental thought)
Includes bibliographical references.
ISBN 0-253-35058-1 (alk. paper). — ISBN 0-253-20583-2 (pbk. :
alk. paper)
1. Heidegger, Martin, 1889–1976. 2. Heidegger, Martin, 1889–
1976—Influence. 3. Philosophy, Modern—20th century.
4. Philosophy.
I. Title. II. Series.
B3279.H49S325 1990
193—dc20 —dc20   89-46009
                                                              CIP

1 2 3 4 5 94 93 92 91 90

For André

ὁδὸς ἄνω κάτω μία καὶ ὡυτή.

Heraclitus
Fragment 60

Contents

Acknowledgments

Preliminary versions of some portions of this book have appeared as papers in the following publications: *Continental Philosophy* (Routledge), 1 (1988); *The Collegium Phaenomenologicum*, ed. J. Sallis, G. Moneta, J. Taminiaux (Kluwer, 1988); *Research in Phenomenology* (Humanities Press), 17 (1987); *Heidegger et l'idée de la phénoménologie* (Kluwer, 1988); *Kunst und Technik,* ed. W. Biemel and F.-W. von Herrmann (Klostermann, 1989). I would like to thank the publishers of these volumes for permission to draw upon these papers.

I am especially grateful to three people whose own work and encouragement were decisive for this book: André Schuwer, Jacques Derrida, and David Krell. Thanks also to Nancy Fedrow for her generous assistance. Also to Lauren and Jerry.

Paris
June 1989

References to Heidegger's Texts

Reference is by volume number (where appropriate) and page number (unless otherwise indicated).

GA   *Gesamtausgabe.* Frankfurt a.M.: Vittorio Klostermann, 1975–.

KM   *Kant und das Problem der Metaphysik.* Frankfurt a.M.: Vittorio Klostermann, 1973.

N   *Nietzsche.* Pfullingen: Günther Neske, 1961.

S   *Vier Seminare.* Frankfurt a.M.: Vittorio Klostermann, 1977.

SD   *Zur Sache des Denkens.* Tübingen: Max Niemeyer, 1969.

SG   *Der Satz vom Grund.* Pfulligen: Günther Neske, 1957.

SU   *Die Selbstbehauptung der deutschen Universität.* Frankfurt a.M.: Vittorio Klostermann, 1983.

SZ   *Sein und Zeit.* Tübingen: Max Niemeyer, 1960.

US   *Unterwegs zur Sprache.* Pfulligen: Günther Neske, 1960.

VA   *Vorträge und Aufsätze.* Pfulligen: Günther Neske, 1959.

WD   *Was Heisst Denken?* Tübingen: Max Niemeyer, 1954.

Z   *Der Begriff der Zeit.* Tübingen: Max Niemeyer, 1989.

’Ηχώ

The word bespeaks casting. Also doubling. Voice cast out across a space, only to be returned, almost as if from others, doubled indefinitely. This is how the word speaks: by bespeaking—that is, by an excess of signification, by a signifying that would lie outside or before the signifying of the meaning of the word; as a deed of speech can itself (as deed, in deed) signify something; as deed or speech can foretell something, showing it before anything is said of it, or rather, saying it by showing. The word speaks also by being bespoken, engaged by that from which it speaks.

(a)

And so, first, some stories.

The first an old story, told in late antiquity by Ovid. It is a story that is almost too familiar to bear retelling, a story too in which an overarching purpose or meaning seems too readily discernible, its depth too near the surface, perhaps nothing but surface, like a mirror, lacking the space in which to resound. Yet, suppose one were to listen to it now with ears attuned to its echo across the expanse of two millennia, the space of—almost—the entire history of metaphysics.

It is the story of Echo.

Once Juno had come to the mountains looking for Jove, her purpose being to expose him in his amorous pursuits among the nymphs. However, she was intercepted by the nymph Echo, who chattered away at her until those nymphs who had been in Jove's company had time to flee. Thanks to Echo's speech, Jove's deeds went unexposed. But Echo paid dearly for having tricked the goddess. Juno punished her by depriving her of the power of originating speech. Henceforth:

> She liked to chatter,
> But had no power of speech except the power
> To answer in the words she last had heard.[1]

Henceforth, Echo's speech was limited to merely repeating what someone else had just said. It was as though her voice were no longer her own, as though it were taken over by the words of others, expropriated.

Recounting thus how Echo came to be deprived of living speech, the story then tells of her futile efforts to make love to Narcissus, a design which she could carry out only by repeating to the beautiful youth certain tail-end fragments of his own speech. Narcissus' response was the same as in every other case, the same, finally, as in the case of every other: he repulsed her, retreated before her, withdrew irrevocably into his own self-enclosing gaze:

> But he retreated:
> "Keep your hands off," he cried, "and do not touch me!
> I would die before I give you a chance at me."[2]

All she ever said thereafter was—repeatedly—"I give you a chance at me." Finally, she disappears from sight:

> Her body dries and shrivels till voice only
> And bones remain, and then she is voice only
> For the bones are turned to stone. She hides in woods
> And no one sees her now along the mountains,
> But all may hear her, for her voice is living.[3]

In the end she is nothing but the words of others, a voice that is the death of the living voice.

Or the life of the dead voice. For there is another story about Echo, told a few centuries later by Longus.

Now Echo has come to sing and to play the pipe and the lute. Daughter of a nymph, she had been taught by the Muses and, once she had grown up, she had come to sing with them and to dance with the nymphs. The story tells, then, of how she provokes the

---

1. Ovid, *Metamorphoses,* 3: 359–361. Translation cited is that of Rolfe Humphries (Bloomington: Indiana University Press, 1955).

2. Ibid., 3: 390–392.

3. Ibid., 3: 396–401.

wrath of Pan, who envied her music but was enraged by the way in which she, in love with her virginity, fled all males, whether men or gods, giving him thus no opportunity to enjoy her beauty. The story continues:

> Therefore he sent a madness among the shepherds and goatherds, and they in a desperate fury, like so many dogs and wolves, tore her all to pieces and flung about them all over the earth her yet singing limbs. The earth in observance of the nymphs buried them all, preserving in them still their music, and they by an everlasting sentence and decree of the Muses breathe out a voice.[4]

A maniacal, Bacchic frenzy. Echo, her voice, her music, dismembered—like Dionysus—and dispersed, scattered, disseminated, yet sounding forth still from beneath the earth, unseen.

There is another story, one told from quite a different world, a world remote from the classical culture of the other two stories, a world that would be closer to nature, a world in which one would be more observant of the earth. The story is told in the course of the account that Thoreau gives of his sojourn in the woods, in a cabin that he himself had built, on the shore of Walden Pond. As classical antiquity is quietly allowed to recede ("I kept Homer's Iliad on my table through the summer, though I looked at his page only now and then"),[5] Thoreau heralds the turn from preoccupation with books to "the language which all things and events speak without metaphor"[6]—a move that, by the time of Thoreau, had itself become almost classical, repeating the Cartesian turn to the great book of the world, inverting and yet, in the end, also repeating the Socratic turn.

But now, with Thoreau, it is especially a move within the order of sound. In the chapter of *Walden* entitled "Sounds" he celebrates the undisturbed solitude and stillness of his summer reverie amidst the sounds of the woods. He tells, too, of the intrusive sound of the railroad ["when I hear the iron horse make the hills echo with his

---

4. Longus, *Daphnis and Chloe*, 3: 23. Translation cited is that of George Thornley (London: William Heinemann, 1916).

5. Henry David Thoreau, *Walden and Other Writings*, ed. Joseph Wood Krutch (Toronto: Bantam, 1981), 179. *Walden* was first published in 1854.

6. Ibid., 187.

snort like thunder . . . (What kind of winged horse or fiery dragon they will put into the new Mythology I don't know)"];[7] and he tells how even in his retreat this sound kept him linked to society. Yet, he continues, the trains move on, "and all the restless world with them"; and then, says Thoreau, "I am more alone than ever"—that is, withdrawn still more toward nature. It is then that he hears a different sound coming over nature from society, the sound of bells, "a faint, sweet, and, as it were, natural melody, worth importing into the wilderness."[8] Now a second nature comes over the nature in which he sojourns; a natural melody (Thoreau marks it as being "as it were, natural") sounds forth from the towns into the wilderness, not to intrude upon it, but rather "as if the pine needles in the horizon were the strings of a harp which it swept." The melody imparts itself to the woods by awakening the voices of nature, the "vibration of the universal lyre": what is thus produced Thoreau calls an echo. Hence, the story becomes one of echo, of the echo of nature, in distinction from the Echo of classical culture. Here, then, is the heart of the story:

> There came to me in this case a melody which the air had strained, and which had conversed with every leaf and needle of the wood, that portion of the sound which the elements had taken up and modulated and echoed from vale to vale. The echo is, to some extent, an original sound, and therein is the magic and charm of it. It is not merely a repetition of what was worth repeating in the bell, but partly the voice of the wood; the same trivial words and notes sung by a wood-nymph.[9]

In words somewhat other than those of Thoreau, the story may be said to tell of how the woods receive the sound of the bells and then sound forth the echo of that sound. The echo is said not merely to repeat the sound of the bells but to blend that sound with the voice of the woods. Most remarkably, the echo is said to be an *original* sound, even if only "to some extent," or, more precisely, even if improperly so. For the echo has almost always been taken to be the very opposite of the original, a mere image of the original sound, its difference from the original merely a lack, a falling away

7. Ibid., 191.
8. Ibid., 196.
9. Ibid.

from the properly original, a resounding at a distance. Thoreau's story displaces this classical schema, regarding the difference now as produced by the voice of nature itself, which is itself something original, producing thus an original divergence from the original: the same words and notes sung by a wood-nymph, as Thoreau says, invoking Echo, though not by name, returning echo finally to its classical origin, echoing that origin.

Yet, Echo has sounded not only in the woods but also in the mountains. Hence, still another story, the last one. It is a story of wandering alone in the Alps under a sky so clear that the sunlight has almost the same intense transparency as in Sicily or even Greece, the same burning intensity yet cooled, or rather masked, by the fresh mountain air. The story tells of climbing over a ridge and then down into a high valley. Boulders are strewn here and there, reminders of deafening avalanches; but now only the occasional tinkle of a cowbell is to be heard. Nothing else. It is partly for this reason that listening proves so exceptional here, because there is almost nothing to hear; but also because the valley, encircled by snow-covered peaks, forms a kind of open enclosure into which one's voice can expand and resound. Here monologue and its interiority are unthinkable. Instead, the voice is drawn out into a space which, rather than being simply filled by the sound of the voice, claims it and in a sense takes possession of it. Here there is a spacing that disperses the voice while also giving back its sound, a spacing that multiplies it while also letting its sound echo back as if from other voices. Hearing the echo, one then experiences silence, not as the mere opposite of speech or sound but as the open space of the voice.

Each of the stories tells the story differently, lets a different echo sound forth, a different echo of what before any of the stories would originally have been called Ἠχώ. The Echo of the first story names a displacement of speech from the origin, a certain loss of voice, even though, finally, she is only voice. Hers is a voice that in the contrast to the self-enclosing vision of Narcissus is reduced to empty repetition. The Echo of the second story is still more displaced, indeed dispersed, disseminated; and yet, her voice is not so much removed from an origin as it is, rather, sheltered by the earth. Thoreau's echo is an original sound, a sound that diverges originally from the original precisely insofar as the original is sheltered by the earth, that is, received and resounded by the voice of nature. The final story transports echo back to the mountains from which she once came, releasing the voice into the open enclosure provided by the earth.

Nonetheless, there is a trace of coherence in these stories, even the possibility of tracing a certain coherent progression in them, as I have just done. Let me, then, speak of *the figure of echo*, stipulating that the definite article and the singular form refer, not to unity or singularity, but to the trace of coherence among the echoes of the stories; even though these echoes, themselves echoes of a withdrawn original that would have been named Ἠχώ, are also irreducibly plural, since all of them—or, rather, what one would otherwise call echo as such, the concept of echo—would name the operation of indefinite doubling, the pluralizing of speech. But there could be a *concept* of echo only at the cost of unaccountable reduction. I will speak, instead, only of the *figure*, suspended between one and many.

Figure is, first of all, representation. Echoing *figura*, which translates σχῆμα, it echoes also *Schema* and thus represents as neither concept nor particular but as an image suspended between the two. What does the figure of echo thus represent? Presumably, the figure represents echo. But what is echo apart from the representing, apart from the image(s), the figure(s), produced in the stories? Is it an original, Ἠχώ, that the images would only represent from afar, nonoriginally? Or, shifting from history to nature, is it an acoustical phenomenon that would be schematized, if not conceptualized, by the representation? Presumably, the figure of echo can also represent something else, something other than echo, by way of what is usually called metaphorical representation, representing, for example, the condition of human speech by way of the acoustical phenomenon of echo. And yet the line between literal and metaphorical will prove difficult to draw: human speech is itself acoustical; speech itself echoes, echoes even itself—indeed, literally, one would like to say.

Figure is, thus, also figure of speech. Even if the pluralizing figure of echo threatens to blur the lines on which the theory of rhetoric has always relied.

The figure of echo is also the bodily shape or form of Echo. The first of the stories tells how her body, repulsive to Narcissus, dries and shrivels until there remains only voice and bones; how the bones turn to stone, so that finally she is only voice, a figure never to be seen but only heard. On the other hand, the second story tells of her virgin beauty and of how her flight from Pan led to her dismemberment. The other stories tell also of a certain shape or form, that of the space of echo, a space of nature, an open enclosure into which the voice is cast and recast.

Figure is, thus, also geometrical. Yet, the figure of echo, that is, the space within which echoes resound, has neither the linearity nor the center possessed by the classical geometrical self-representations of metaphysics. In order to accord with the third story, the representation would have to begin with at least two lines, parallel and yet, like two vectors, opposite in direction, thus positing origin both above and, though differently, below. Or, as in the final story, the figure would be that of an open enclosure, a transformation of a very classical, though not merely geometrical, figure. For a cave is also an open enclosure. More precisely, the space of echo is represented in the single figure of open enclosure by assembling the two parts of the classical representation, the enclosure within the cave and the openness outside.

Yet, what of the echo itself in the figure of echo? Is the figure a figure of echo or of Echo? Is it a matter of a proper name, of a name that would name the thing proper, the thing itself, τὸ πρᾶγμα αὐτό? Can there be an echo *itself,* especially considering that echo is represented, echoed, in various stories belonging to a history? Can there be an echo *proper,* considering that an echo is precisely something always also improper, something that is never simply itself but an echo of something else, of something different from it; considering that it is even a certain return of the other to the proper, or rather, a blending, as the sound of the bells is blended with the voice of the woods. If there were a convenient graphic device for doing so, one would do well to write the name in a way that would leave it undecided, suspending it between Echo and echo.

And yet, can one not say straightforwardly what an echo is? Can one not, finally, put the stories aside? Is this not what philosophy has always done, has always had to do, namely, to turn away from stories and from those who merely tell stories, to turn toward the things themselves, addressing them with its question: τί ἐστι?

Let it be said, then: an echo is a reflection of sound from a solid surface. Yet, it is not just any kind of reflection. There must be a sufficient interval between the sounding of the original and the production and audition of the echo; otherwise there is only reverberation, prolonging or altering the originating sound but lacking the distinctness of an echo. Furthermore, if it is to be an echo, the reflection must to some extent preserve the quality of the originating sound, reproducing it. An echo must be an *image* of the originating sound, like the shadow that a thing casts on the opposite wall. And like a shadow it is an image produced naturally, without need of human artifice; even in those instances where there is an echo in art—for example, an echo within an architectural space or an echo in music—its possibility is linked, if not reducible, to what is natural in such art (stone, space, sound), and it remains always something of an imitation of the natural echo, an echo of an echo.

One might say, then, that an echo is a naturally produced sonorous image. Or, if one wanted to stress the reception of the image, one might call it an acoustical image. Or, if one wanted to stress the preeminence of vocal sound, taking the voice as representative of sound, one might then call the echo an image of voice.[10] But one

---

10. John Hollander draws attention to the following lines from Wordsworth's poem "The Power of Sound":

Ye voices, and ye Shadows
And Images of voice—to hound and horn
From rocky steep and rock-bestudded meadows
Flung back, and, in the sky's blue caves, reborn—
On with your pastime! til the church-tower bells
A greeting give of measured glee;
And milder echoes from their cells
Repeat the bridal symphony.

As with Thoreau, it is a matter of the echo in nature and the echo of bells, though now distinguished and contrasted rather than blended. Hollander calls special attention to Wordsworth's description of the space of echoing as "the sky's blue cave": "that cave is itself a rebirth of Echo's 'airy Shell' in *Comus* even as Milton had opened

would then have slipped into metaphor, representing a whole by a part; one would have slipped away from the thing itself or would have let the thing itself slip away.

Let me return, then, to the naturally produced sonorous image. If the originating sound is sufficiently brief in duration, if its duration is no greater than the delay that separates the originating sound from the echo, then the echo will return the entire sound with relative clarity, even though always with an element of what according to the classical schema would be called distortion. If, on the other hand, the originating sound continues beyond the interval required for the echo to return, then it will interfere with the echo, which will then be heard only in confusion with its source. Until the originating sound ceases, there will be confounding of image and original, neither being heard distinctly. Only after the originating sound ceases will the echo be heard distinctly; then it will be so heard for a duration equal to the delay between source and echo. As a result, the echo will return only the last part of what it echoes; only the final fragment of an extended sound will be heard distinctly in echo. Echoes return only fragments, tail-end fragments, as in Echo's responses to the words of Narcissus.

Sonorous images are much more prone to proliferation than are visible images. An echo is frequently reechoed in such a way that a series of echoes is produced, each echo decreasing in intensity until the series finally trails off. If the reflecting surfaces are complex, as for instance in a cave, the echoes may themselves sound in confusion and give the impression of a lurking vocal presence, a disembodied voice haunting the concavity. It is likewise, though with less confusion, in that other place that is privileged with regard to echoes, that natural space of echoes, namely, the mountains: here the distances between the reflecting surfaces make the echoes seem to be distinct, disembodied voices.[11] As always with

out the echo-haunted forest caves into the openness, rather than the hollowness, of the cosmos" (*The Figure of Echo: A Mode of Allusion in Milton and After* [Berkeley: University of California Press, 1981], 19). Here one could speak, too, of open enclosure, as in the last of the stories.

11. Hollander notes that, for instance, in the Homeric Hymn to Pan, Echo's place is in the mountainous and Olympian realm ("Then do the nymphs of the mountain accompany Pan. . . . Echo makes moan round the tops of the mountains"). Ovid, on the other hand, transports her from the mountains to the woodland caves:

images, there is the appearance of originality, the seeming to be an original rather than an image, a voice rather than an echo. And because of this seeming there is always the danger of confusing image with original, the danger of taking the image to be an original, a danger for action and a danger for theory. And yet, imagination will always transform this danger into delight or ecstasy, blurring the distinction, hovering between image and original, and drifting into metaphor.

(b)

Now, *after Heidegger*, can one not drift into metaphor?

Can one evade the drift into metaphor? Can one somehow escape it? Should it be evaded? Or now, after Heidegger, can one perhaps give in to the drift? Is one now somehow warranted in drifting along in the drift? But is the drift—now, after Heidegger— a drift into metaphor? Can one perhaps no longer drift into *metaphor*? But then, into what?

Now, *after Heidegger*. What senses does *after* have—after Heidegger? Can one assume that its senses remain intact, delimited beyond the reach of questioning? Can one assume even that the sense of sense is so delimited once and for all—even after Heidegger? Does the *after* remain intact even after the radical displacement to which Heidegger's work submits the concept of time that for more than two millennia has determined the sense of the *after*, the concept of time that, in the absence of utmost vigilance, will continue to determine the *after* in the very questions of how matters stand after Heidegger.

One thing is indisputable. Now, after Heidegger, the hunt begins. Indeed it has already begun. The hunt, for instance, for the remains of metaphysics that contaminate Heidegger's text and prevent it from leaving metaphysics behind. The hunt also for signs of reinscription in his text, of textual debts owed, at least according to a very classical economics that could hardly have withstood the

"Ovid's story of Echo's hopeless love for the autoleptic youth follows the spurned nymph into the woods and, finally, into what will be thenceforth her canonical domain, rocky caves" (*Figure of Echo*, 7–9).

Erschütterung brought on by Heidegger's work. The hunt in his texts for traces too of his biography, of the concrete life of the man Martin Heidegger. The hunt especially for traces of his political misadventure of 1933–34; as though the relation of life to thought had ever been clear, least of all after Heidegger; even as though a tribunal could now, after Heidegger, be established to judge—and no doubt condemn—the thought on the basis of the life.

Let it be said at once: I do not intend to contest the legitimacy of this hunt, though I could hardly avoid questioning its limits and have indeed already begun to do so. After Heidegger there are more traps than one would ever have thought possible, and the hunters will be able to elude them only in one way: by thinking.

My concern is not with seeking out any such alien remains in Heidegger's text. I am concerned, rather, with Heidegger's text *itself*, with hearing what it *itself* can say, now, after Heidegger. And yet, now, after Heidegger, one cannot continue to speak in the same way of the *itself*, of the proper, as though Heidegger's work had not submitted the proper to a radical rethinking, as though his work had not revealed within language itself, within language proper, an operation of impropriety. Because echoes belong to language itself, every text is exposed to the possibility of differing from itself. Even Heidegger's text itself, bespeaking the echoes of language, is exposed to this possibility and, as I shall attempt to show—not, of course, without running the same risk—does not always avoid submitting to it. Thus, in turning to Heidegger's text itself, one must be attentive to the phantoms that haunt it and that reproduce within it precisely what the text would submit to *Destruktion* or commit to overturning. These spirits need to be exposed, not in order to reenclose Heidegger's text in itself, not in order to expose lacunae within it, but rather to let it say what it can, to let it echo language itself, to let its echoes resound, now, after Heidegger.

The drift into metaphor has already begun. Always, perhaps. But surely as soon as one begins to speak of the echoes of a text. For a text is something written, something visible. Even to speak of its phantoms is already to drift from one order of visibility to another very different order. To speak of its echoes is to drift a great deal further: from the sphere of the visible to that of sound. Or, rather,

it is to drift from the sonorous phenomenon, the naturally produced sonorous image, into some metaphorical sense of echo appli-
cable to written texts. Perhaps the drift cannot be evaded. In any
case, why should one not give in to it? Is there really anything
wrong with speaking of the echoes of a text? At least as long as one
is aware of having thus drifted into metaphor, as long as one keeps
distinctly in mind the difference between the metaphorical sense
and the literal sense, as long as one does not risk confounding
image with original, the figure of echo with the thing itself.

And yet, after Heidegger, can one avoid that risk? Can the drift
into metaphor be itself controlled by a schema that would be im-
mune to the effects of that drift, as though drift and metaphor
were not already themselves adrift in metaphor; and especially as
though Heidegger had never written that there is metaphor only
within metaphysics ("*Das Metaphorische gibt es nur innerhalb der
Metaphysik*" [SG 89]). If, after Heidegger, thinking has been twisted
free of the opposition between intelligible and sensible, then the
delimitation of metaphor as the application of something sensible
to the description of something not merely sensible, something to a
degree intelligible, cannot but be disrupted. One will not be able by
this means to control the difference between the echo itself and the
figure of echo. If, in addition and on the basis of Heidegger's
work,[12] the opposition between the sensible and the linguistic, the
opposition that would allow one to distinguish a simply prelinguistic perception—if this opposition is deconstructed, then it will
become even more difficult to control and secure the difference
between the echo itself and the figure of echo. Whatever the drift
and whatever the securities, one will not be able to secure the drift
as a drift into metaphor.

It will be a matter, then, of a reading adrift among various sorts
of echoes. There will be, of course, as always, textual echoes, that is,

12. The relevant result is indicated in Heidegger's remark that when one walks
through the woods one walks through the word *woods* (GA 5: 310). It is gathered
also, of course, in the utterance at the beginning of the "Letter on Humanism":
"Language is the house of Being" (GA 9: 313). In *Being and Time* this result is already
in force by virtue of the role given to *Rede* in the constitution of the *Da* of Dasein
(SZ §34).

echoes of semantic or syntactic elements within a text or between texts. But there will also be echoes among the things themselves, that is, among *die Sachen* that are to be thought; most notably, certain echoes between Being and its meaning that prove even to interrupt the thinking of the meaning of Being. There will be echoes belonging to language itself, and there will be echoes of metaphysics in thinking at the end of metaphysics. There will be, most provocatively, echoes of a doubling and a return, of a return that doubles just as an echo doubles a sound in returning it—hence, echoes of echoes. This doubling return will be neither simply present in nor simply absent from Heidegger's text; but it will prove to figure decisively in that text.

The figure of echo also echoes several decisive shifts that are irreversible after Heidegger. First of all, a shift from that fullness of vision of which metaphysics never ceased to dream, a shift to speech, to the voice, to a voice detached from intuition, from the preservation and recovery of presence, from the dream of presence. Not the voice, then, of transcendental philosophy, which could never echo but in whose interiority the echo-effect would be utterly reduced. Rather, a voice cast into space, a voice as detached from subjectivity and from origin as the disembodied echoes returned to it across the open enclosure in the mountains. A voice listening beyond itself, ecstatically.

A shift also from the condition of vision, light, to that of an echoing voice, namely, the open enclosure, what Heidegger will call clearing (*Lichtung*). A shift too from time, measured, above all, by the coming and going of light, by the course of the sun, to a mixing of time and space in the resounding of an echo across an open enclosure, within the clearing.

A shift also toward the limit of presence, toward what would announce itself without appearing as such. As an echo sounds out the limit of the space in which it sounds.

My concern will be, then, to reinscribe several of Heidegger's texts so as to draw them toward the limit, to mobilize the figure of echo in order to free those texts to say what they can say, now, after Heidegger. It will be a matter of drawing the Heideggerian text out along several lines, lines defined by the questions of—to give the merest titles—time, the sensible, imagination, mortality, understanding, poetry, and translation. It will be a matter especially of listening along all these lines, in all these spaces, for echoes of a doubling return that would itself echo what the Greeks thought as the sameness, the togetherness, of the upward and the downward ways.

Nonphilosophy

Nonphilosophy cannot but be drawn back toward philosophy itself. First of all, in being so named, that is, by the torsion between what would be named *nonphilosophy* and the name itself. For it is named simply by opposition; and, as a result, the content by which the name would determine that which is named *nonphilosophy* is none other than that of the concept of philosophy itself, simply submitted to negation. If *nonphilosophy* were its proper name, the name proper to it—that is, if there were no torsion—that which is named *nonphilosophy* would prove not to be nonphilosophy at all, being, rather, governed by the concept of philosophy—which is to say that *nonphilosophy* is not its proper name, that there cannot but be torsion. Even more so, granted that philosophy governs not only the content but also the form, i.e., opposition, which not only is determined within philosophy but also belongs to the very determination of philosophy. Thus, what it is named (non*philosophy*) as well as how it is named (*non*philosophy) are governed by philosophy, which to this extent draws to itself not only that which would be named *nonphilosophy* but also the very tracing of the torsion (for example, through its reference to the opposition between form and content).

As soon as it is named *nonphilosophy*, what would be thus named is drawn back not only toward but into philosophy. Hardly even an echo.

Is there any other alternative short of twisting the thing free of the name by a counterthrust that could not but set everything adrift? How is nonphilosophy to be named if not simply as *non-*

philosophy? How is the other of philosophy to be addressed if not simply by way of opposition?

Listen to the philosophers, to what some of them have said about philosophy and nonphilosophy. Listen to the voices—echoed across the space of historical and linguistic differences—with which philosophy has addressed its other, has attempted to say itself by saying its opposition to its other.

Parmenides, received by the goddess:

> It is necessary that you shall learn all things, as well the unshaken heart of well-rounded truth as the opinions of mortals in which there is no true belief.[1]

Plato—or rather, Socrates, alluding to Homer, speaking to Theodorus on the occasion of meeting the Stranger from Elea:

> However, I fancy it is not much easier, if I may say so, to discern this kind than that of the gods. For these men—I mean those who are not feignedly but really philosophers—appear disguised in all sorts of shapes, thanks to the ignorance of the rest of mankind, and visit the cities, beholding from above the life of those below, and they seem to some to be of no worth and to others to be worth everything. And sometimes they appear disguised as statesmen, and sometimes as sophists, and sometimes they may give some people the impression that they are altogether mad.[2]

Hegel, introducing his and Schelling's *Critical Journal of Philosophy* in 1802:

> Philosophy is by its nature something esoteric . . . ; it is philosophy only by being opposed to the understanding and therefore still more to common sense . . . ; in relation to the latter the world of philosophy is in and for itself an inverted world.[3]

Finally, Merleau-Ponty, just before his death, in his last course "Philosophy and Non-Philosophy since Hegel":

---

1. Parmenides, I, 28–30. Translation cited is that of Leonardo Tarán, *Parmenides* (Princeton: Princeton University Press, 1965), 9.

2. Plato, *Sophist,* 216 c–d. Translation cited is that of H. N. Fowler (London: William Heinemann, 1921).

3. G. W. F. Hegel, "Einleitung. Ueber das Wesen der philosophischen Kritik überhaupt und ihr Verhältnis zum gegenwärtigen Zustand der Philosophie insbesondere," in *Jenaer Kritische Schriften,* ed. Hartmut Buchner and Otto Pöggeler, vol. 4 of *Gesammelte Werke* (Hamburg: Felix Meiner Verlag, 1968), 124f.

True philosophy is non-philosophy,—which is to enter into the profundity of "experience."[4]

What of experience? Philosophy has always appealed to it, to its depth, to a more profound experience to which the philosopher would always have been converted through the inversion of common sense. Or else, the appeal to experience has become the empiricist appeal to the element of nonphilosophy, to an element posited outside philosophy, as the outside *of* philosophy, an element that philosophy will always already have begun to draw into itself, to appropriate. Could one ever persist in nonphilosophy, effectively resisting that true nonphilosophy that would be, finally, indistinguishable from philosophy itself? How could the experience into which nonphilosophy would enter (the entrance into which would determine nonphilosophy) be set beyond the appropriative reach of philosophy? To what operation would one refer by writing: "experience"? What displacement would be marked by the quotation marks? Could one ever persist in both philosophy and nonphilosophy *at the same time* and *for an indefinite time,* disrupting the appropriative orientation that would, even if only in the telos, reduce the double to the single of philosophy? In that case, to write that true philosophy is nonphilosophy would be to say—in the *is*—not an identity or subsumption but a doubling.

Would one not need, then, also to double the inversion, to make it a circling, to add a circling back to nonphilosophy that would confirm its irreducibility rather than preparing its appropriation? What of the guises and disguises in which the philosopher would circle back to the city, returning to the profundity of "experience" concealed there from the rest of mankind, concealed also from the philosopher who is unwilling to assume another shape, the shape of an other, and go down into the city? But if one goes down there, one cannot but *risk* being mistaken: mistaken by others for others, for statesmen, sophists, or madmen, perhaps for all three as they tend to coalesce in the figure of tyranny; also mistaken oneself, misled by what is seen (even still) from above of the life of those

4. Maurice Merleau-Ponty, "Philosophy and Non-Philosophy since Hegel," tr. Hugh J. Silverman, *Telos,* no. 29 (Fall 1976), 75.

below; misled by the very element of nonphilosophy, to which the resources of philosophy would never be sufficient; led astray in the opinions of mortals in which there is no truth, led astray from the heart of truth, outside its sphere. Nonphilosophy is the risk of being astray outside. The philosopher returns to the city only at the risk of infamy and death.

(a)

In *Being and Time* nonphilosophy is prephilosophy, the preontological, which remains continuous with philosophy, essentially, structurally continuous. Indeed, what structures and guarantees the continuity is nothing less than the very determination of Dasein, its essence (or its "essence," to mark thus the very transformation of essence in which *Being and Time* is engaged): in that very comportment to Being by which Dasein is, first of all, determined as such, Dasein *is,* preontologically, the question of Being, the question definitive of ontology, of philosophy as such: "But the question of Being is then nothing but the radicalization of an essential tendency of Being [*Seinstendenz*] that belongs to Dasein itself, the preontological understanding of Being" (SZ 15). To take up again, philosophically, the question of Being is to make explicit Dasein's always already operative understanding of Being. Or, more precisely, it is to listen in on [*abzuhören*] Dasein's own recovery of its understanding of Being; it is to interpret Dasein's own self-disclosure: "Such interpretation takes part in this disclosure only in order existentially to raise to a conceptual level [*in den Begriff*] the phenomenal content of what has been disclosed" (SZ 140). The continuity thus prescribes the methodological character of the analysis of Dasein, even though much of what emerges from the analysis—most notably, Dasein's entanglement in self-concealment and, at the level of tradition, submission to a *Vergessenheit* that must now be countered by *Destruktion*—serves to show just how complex and how demanding the transition from prephilosophy to philosophy is.

Derrida has drawn special attention to this continuity, especially to the form that it assumes when, at the outset of *Being and Time,* Heidegger examines the formal structure of the question of Being.

Here it appears as the coincidence of questioner with questioned: the structure is such that the questioner is to take up the question by interrogating a being (Dasein) with which it coincides. That coincidence, expressed in the Heideggerian discourse by the "we"— Derrida of course draws the comparison with Hegel—is what guarantees the possibility of the analysis of Dasein that opens onto the question of Being, the possibility of carrying that analysis through in a rigorous manner, phenomenologically.

Everything depends on what I am calling—in order to mark the necessary caution—the *coincidence* of questioner with questioned; it determines not only the possibility and structure of the analysis but also the range of the horizon within which that analysis can prove to be inscribed. Coincidence is not, of course, mere identity, for there must always have opened up a field across which interpretation can occur, a space within which a phenomenal content can be raised to a conceptual level. Such an opening would not as such displace Heidegger's analysis in the least from the sphere of philosophy, no more than in the case of Hegel's *Phenomenology of Spirit*. To this extent one would be tempted to repeat what Derrida says in *one* moment of his reading of Heidegger: "this *we*—however simple, discreet, and effaced it might be— inscribes the so-called formal structure of the question of Being within the horizon of metaphysics."[5]

Heidegger would perhaps not object. One should not forget how forcefully, in *The Basic Problems of Phenomenology*, presented only months after the publication of *Being and Time*, Heidegger himself placed the project of fundamental ontology within the horizon of metaphysics: the project undertakes finally to fulfill "the latent goal and constant and more or less evident demand of the whole development of Western philosophy" (GA 24: 106). Not only by recovering in its depth the question most fundamentally definitive of metaphysics but also by radicalizing the regress that has always been carried out from the question of Being to the analysis of the subject (in the broadest sense), *Being and Time* would bring

---

5. Jacques Derrida, *Marges de la philosophie* (Paris: Les Éditions de Minuit, 1972), 149.

metaphysics to the point of its fulfillment, would think it through to its end, would move finally to that very center that would always have determined metaphysics.

And yet, this could not be the last word. For in its very radicality that way to the center would be also the way to the outermost limit of metaphysics. In *The Basic Problems of Phenomenology* such a duplicity is marked in several specific connections. Heidegger declares, for instance, that ancient ontology "can never be overcome, because it represents the first necessary step that every philosophy as such has to take." And yet: "We not only wish to but must understand the Greeks better than they understood themselves" (GA 24: 157). Again, with respect to Hegel's alleged disssolution of ontology into logic: "Hegel must be overcome by radicalizing the posing of the question [*Radikalisierung der Fragestellung*]; and at the same time he must be appropriated" (GA 24: 254). The duplicity is marked in a more general form in Heidegger's way of relating the Greek determination of Being to production (*Herstellen*), specifically to the anticipatory sight that governs production by intuiting in advance the look of what is to be produced. As a result of this orientation to production, intuition (*Anschauung*) became, from ancient ontology on, "the ideal of knowledge, i.e., the ideal of the apprehending of beings in general" (GA 24: 167); and beings in general came to be determined as what presents itself to an intuition, even if to a superior kind (seeing with "the mind's eye")—that is, their Being came to be determined as what Heidegger will call *Vorhandenheit*. The double gesture is explicit: precisely in repeating ancient ontology, recovering it in its depth, Heidegger's project would call into question the ancient determination of Being as *Vorhandenheit*, determining Dasein and, in a sense, even what are called things (as *zuhanden*) outside the Greek determination, breaking with the orientation to production. Within the horizon of metaphysics indeed, but also at its limit, effacing, extending the limit.

What, then, of the value of presence? Even if confirmed in the "we," is it not also, from the very outset, withdrawn by the formal determination of Dasein as that being that comports itself to Being? This determination serves to submit Dasein's self-relation to its comportment to (especially) its own Being, which is to say that

Dasein's relation to itself could never be a matter of undivided self-presence; Dasein's presence to itself would always already have been breached by its comportment to its own Being. As a matter of being given back to itself from—to take the most explicit moment—the possibilities upon which it projects, Dasein's self-relation would not be even simply mediated presence but rather would occur in a giving no longer thinkable as a mode of presence.

I would want, then, to underwrite another moment in Derrida's reading of Heidegger. Referring to the question of the "we" in Heidegger's text as "the most difficult," he continues: "it is not a matter here of imprisoning [*d'enfermer*] all of Heidegger's text in a closure that this text has delimited better than any other."[6] Yet, I would underwrite this precisely by reformulating the schema of closure and delimitation as that of the double gesture and by attempting to show that such a gesture is constantly in play in Heidegger's text, even where Heidegger's own formulations tend to reduce the duplicity, a doubling within and yet also beneath Heidegger's text.

On the one hand, then, the continuity between philosophy and nonphilosophy (as preontological) remains intact in *Being and Time*. However complex and demanding the transition might be, there would be no rupture. Nonphilosophy would always already be philosophy to some degree. Philosophy would always already have commenced.

Yet, on the other hand, Heidegger's text moves to the limit; indeed it does so in inscribing *that very comportment to Being* that would also have guaranteed the continuity. However formal, reduced, incomplete this move may remain in *Being and Time* and the other Marburg texts, it nonetheless broaches *another nonphilosophy,* a nonphilosophy that would begin at the limit of philosophy.

In the later texts—the texts after 1930, foregoing for the moment any further discrimination—it is this other nonphilosophy that is primarily at issue. Now there is a boundary, a limit, to be transgressed. Now the other of philosophy does not lie before philosophy. Or, rather, the other that does precede philosophy is *either* so continuous with philosophy that it is always already determined,

6. Ibid., 147.

assimilated as the prephilosophical, its otherness cancelled; *or* it prefigures the breach that philosophy will take to the limit, that will take philosophy to the limit and broach the other nonphilosophy. Either the one or the other—or, rather, both the one and the other.

Now the other of philosophy lies *after* philosophy. One must pass through philosophy on the way to this other, but not as one passes through the preontological in the project of fundamental ontology. Now it is a matter of rupture, of transgression. Now it is a matter of the end of philosophy and the task of thinking.

(b)

The opening sentence of Heidegger's late text "The End of Philosophy and the Task of Thinking" needs to be taken with utmost seriousness: "The title names the attempt at a reflection that persists in questioning [*im Fragen verharrt*]" (SD 61).

Let it be said at once, all at once, even though its unfolding is indispensable: it is not only a matter of simply persisting, of continuing to pose questions ever anew, thus refusing to close interrogation; it is also a matter of compounding this persistence, of questioning the questioning in the sense of interrogating its structure and its possibility. But in questioning about its possibility, about that which precedes and sustains it, one would retract that absolute privileging of the question that would legitimate simply persisting in the question, that would legitimate even the simple compounding of the question (why the why?). One would prove to have persisted in the questioning to the point of exceeding the questioning, or, rather, letting the questioning exceed itself toward that which calls it forth.[7]

The opposition of philosophy to the other nonphilosophy is expressed in the title of Heidegger's text, along with the suggestion

---

7. This may be read as tracing a certain recoiling of the question that Derrida introduced at the conference on Heidegger at the University of Essex in 1986 (see "On Reading Heidegger," *Research in Phenomenology*, 17 [1987], 171–185) and that he took as one of the *fils conducteurs* in *De L'Esprit: Heidegger et la question* (Paris: Galilée, 1987), see especially 24f., 147–154 n. I have discussed this at length in a review article on *De L'Esprit:* "Flight of Spirit," *Diacritics* (1989).

of a transition from the former to the latter; likewise in the two questions posed at the end of the opening section of that text and adopted as headings for the two principal sections of the text:

1. To what extent has philosophy in the present age entered into its end?
2. What task is reserved for thinking at the end of philosophy? (SD 61)

The title and these two questions suggest a very simple schema: philosophy has recently come to an end or is now about to end; then, after the end of philosophy, something else is to begin, something called thinking. One could presume that Heidegger's text is to fill out this schema by considering the manner in which philosophy has ended or is about to end and the character of the new beginning then to be made, of the task to which it will be addressed, the task of what is called thinking.

And yet, for Heidegger's attempt at a reflection to proceed in such a manner would be precisely *not* to persist in questioning. It is imperative not to detach such a schema from Heidegger's text, not to employ it as a grid for reading that text, not to close off the questions that it could so easily close off, including that of its own appropriateness. In order to persist in questioning, thus reenacting in reading the text the very persistence that the text demands of itself, it is necessary to question, above all, those questions that give the appearance of being utterly secure as questions, those questions that seem only to need answers.

So, then, some questions about the question of the end of philosophy and the task of thinking.

To begin: What is an end? What is asked about in asking about the end of philosophy? What sense of end—assuming for the moment that a range of senses could be delimited—is appropriate? Is the end of philosophy simply the point at which philosophy ceases to occur, its termination? But then, is not this very representation—of a point in history, in time, at which philosophy ceases—itself thoroughly determined by philosophy? Are not the very means by which the end of philosophy would thus be represented drawn precisely from philosophy? Would one not need to ask: Can philosophy represent or delimit its own end? Do its means suffice for

determining the very limit of those means? Or, is the end of philosophy something quite different, perhaps its completion, fulfillment,
perfection rather than its termination? Could philosophy not, then,
perhaps remain intact in its end, persist in its final state?

Assuming, still, that a range of senses could be delimited, would
not all of them have been determined by philosophy, within that
very history that is now said to be coming to its end? Could they,
then, remain simply intact at the end of philosophy? Could they
remain simply available—as if fallen from heaven—as means by
which to represent that end that cannot but be also somehow their
end? Could it be their end without producing a certain displacement of these senses, without eroding the range of senses of end?

Could questioning ever end? One must persist, asking also
about the beginning that would seem to be both conjoined and
opposed to the end? What about the opposition if indeed philosophy could continue, even in its most perfect form, alongside thinking? Is thinking the proper name of that other nonphilosophy, fully
coincident with it, assuming that nonphilosophy could have something *proper* to it, something fully coincident with it? Could the
opposition, the otherness of thinking, ever be expressed within
philosophy? Under what conditions? In what guise or disguise?
Would the very saying of the *non* of nonphilosophy be already
transgressive? Would it already have entered into the beginning?

What is, then, this beginning? Is it simply opposed to end? Is it
temporal? Is it a time that would follow the end of philosophy? Or
could one hear in it an echo of ἀρχή, of origin? Could the beginning of thinking be, not some time of commencement, but rather
that by which, from which, thinking would originate, that which
would give thinking its task (*Aufgabe*), to which thinking would be
given up (*aufgegeben*), given over? Is this perhaps why Heidegger
names his attempt as he does: the end of philosophy and the *task* of
thinking? Is it also perhaps why the attempt thus named must be
one that persists in questioning?

One must persist in questioning.

Even in turning now to Heidegger's text, especially now, doubling and yet not merely doubling the persistence in questioning
that the text demands of itself.

At the outset, in the brief, untitled introduction, Heidegger provides a certain indication of how the text is to persist in questioning. The attempt named "The End of Philosophy and the Task of Thinking" is placed within a larger context, a more comprehensive attempt, which is described thus: "It is the attempt undertaken again and again ever since 1930 to shape the question of *Being and Time* in a more originary fashion [*die Fragestellung von* Sein und Zeit *anfänglicher zu gestalten*]" (SD 61). The attempt is—literally—to shape the *Fragestellung,* that is, the way in which the question is posed, set up, deployed; and to do so in a way that is *anfänglicher,* more originary. To persist in questioning would be to sustain this attempt to shape the *Fragestellung* more originarily, to deploy the question in a way that is more in accord with what is called origin.

How is the more originary deployment to be carried out? The introduction to Heidegger's text gives a further indication: it is a matter of an attempt "to subject the point of departure [*Ansatz*] of *Being and Time* to an immanent critique," that is, to pose to the deployment of the question as carried out in *Being and Time* what Heidegger now calls "the *critical* question." Or, rather, to pose it again, to repeat it; for that earlier deployment is itself, in turn, a certain repetition of the question in which the definitive turn of critique would be constituted. Echo and reecho of Kant, of the Kantian turn from objects to what conditions their possibility as objects, the possibility of their appearing as objects. Taking such conditions to be found in the subject, Kantian critique is deployed as a turn to the subject. As such, the Kantian turn would, in turn, repeat the turn that Heidegger finds carried out throughout the history of ontology (the turn from the question of Being to the analysis of the subject) and which he would finally carry out most radically. A turn almost endlessly reechoed in the history of metaphysics. Repetition almost without limit.

Being and Time, too, would repeat the turn, though not of course without releasing certain counterforces.[8] It would be a matter of

8. The connection is drawn out in the first chapter of *The Basic Problems of Phenomenology* (GA 24: 35–107) and in the final section of *Kant and the Problem of Metaphysics* (198–239). In both cases a certain element of the problematic of *Being and Time* (an element opening, too, upon what one would like to call the whole of that problematic) is generated precisely by radicalizing the Kantian turn, by a *Wiederholung* (as Heidegger says) of the Kantian project of a critique of reason.

turning to what is now to be called Dasein, of turning to it in such a way as to uncover the operation of that understanding of Being, the genuine a priori, that makes it possible for beings to show themselves. That operation will prove to be—in the very briefest formula and restricting it, for the moment, to a single level of the analysis—what is called *Erschlossenheit* (disclosedness), the operation in which is opened a space, a world, in which beings can present themselves. One could, then, say—again with the restriction to a single level—that disclosedness proves to be *die Sache des Denkens* in *Being and Time, die Sache* to which the thinking ventured in that text—at least a ~~thinking~~ of philosophy—proves to have turned.

One could generalize the critical question, then, as the question of *die Sache,* as the question of that to which thinking would turn in its turn from beings toward their possibility. To shape the deployment of this question more originarily, to subject the critical question as deployed in *Being and Time* to an immanent critique would mean, then, to carry through the critical question itself more persistently, to engage in the question of *die Sache* with greater persistence in questioning. Now it would be a matter of persisting even to the extent of letting a difference open up between *die Sache* and Dasein, of questioning the assumption that *die Sache* is an operation of Dasein, even the operation constitutive of Dasein. Now it would be a matter of no longer assuming, of no longer resuming (even if more radically, even if most radically) that regress to the subject that Heidegger finds common to the entire history of metaphysics and that in the project of *Being and Time* he still proposed to resume. Now *die Sache* is to be allowed more persistently to become questionable, its very site and identity coming now into question: "Thus it must become clear to what extent the *critical* question, of what *die Sache des Denkens* is, necessarily and continually belongs to thinking" (SD 61). It is a matter of persisting in questioning *die Sache,* of letting its utter questionableness come into play. To do so is to grant a certain distance between Dasein and *die Sache,* between— to mention only one possible formulation, one that Heidegger in fact eventually abandons—self-understanding and the understanding of Being. It is to let a differential space open up at that point where *Being and Time* inscribed what I called a coincidence of questioner with questioned; such an opening cannot but divide more decisively that presence of questioner to questioned that was already breached in *Being and Time*.

It is to begin to grant to *die Sache* a certain withdrawal. It is also to risk letting questioning exceed itself in the direction of what precedes it and makes it possible.

But what is it that makes a more originary shaping of the *Fragestellung* necessary? What is it that inscribes a distance between Dasein and *die Sache*? What is it that requires that *die Sache* be granted a certain withdrawal? How is it that one must persist in questioning? Why not rather do as common sense and metaphysics would prescribe: leave the question behind as quickly as possible for the sake of getting on to the answer? Why not—in a more properly metaphysical formulation—move on to a ground, even to a final ground in which questioning would reach its end?

Heidegger would answer: because questioning—metaphysical questioning—has reached its end—that is, it is precisely the end of metaphysics that generates the need for redeploying the question more originarily. It is the end of metaphysics that would release the distancing, the withdrawal of *die Sache*, that would disrupt the metaphysical drive to ground. It is in the wake of the end of metaphysics that one must persist in questioning.

For metaphysics is—in the very schematic conception to which Heidegger limits himself in this text—precisely the drive to ground, that is, the turn from beings back to their Being, which is taken to have the character of presence (*Anwesenheit,* παρουσία) or ground (ἀρχή): "What characterizes metaphysical thinking, which investigates the ground for beings, is that such thinking, starting from what is present [*vom Anwesenden*], represents it in its presence [*Anwesenheit*] and thus exhibits it as grounded by its ground" (SD 62).

But what, then, is the end of metaphysics? Is it simply termination, as if the futility of the drive to ground had finally become apparent, vindicating now a kind of utter positivism, confirming somehow the empiricist appeal to an outside of philosophy, to a nonphilosophy that, if it were possible, would be simple exteriority? Or is it final perfection, the fulfillment of the drive in a manner that would make any resumption superfluous? Heidegger insists that it is a matter neither of termination nor of perfection but rather of completion (*Vollendung*) in the sense of a certain kind of gathering, a certain kind of place of gathering: "The end of philosophy is the place, that place in which the whole of philosophy's history is gathered into its most extreme possibility. End as completion means this gathering" (SD 63). The end of metaphysics is the gathering of the history of metaphysics into its most extreme possibility.

What happens, then, in the end of metaphysics? How is it announced concretely?

It is announced as the reversal, the inversion, of Platonism. Heidegger refers to the decisiveness of Plato's thinking: "Metaphysics is Platonism" (SD 63). This decisiveness consists in the way that Platonism established the difference between beings and Being (ground, presence), the way in which it established the circuit, as it were, within which metaphysics turns. The end of metaphysics comes with Nietzsche's reversal of Platonism. In a text in which he reflects on Nietzsche as "the last metaphysician," Heidegger explains: "But then what does it mean, 'the end of metaphysics'? It means the historical moment in which *the essential possibilities* of metaphysics are exhausted. The last of these possibilities must be that form of metaphysics in which its essence is reversed" (N II 201). The end of metaphysics occurs as that form of metaphysics in which its essence is reversed, in which the difference that marks out its circuit is inverted. This form of metaphysics is the *last* possibility of metaphysics, the possibility with which it is exhausted, the possibility which withdraws all further possibilities, the extreme possibility. Heidegger's reading of Nietzsche, *almost* the entirety of that massive undertaking, would demonstrate that this extreme possibility, the end of metaphysics, *has occurred*.

And yet, Heidegger insists: in being gathered into its most extreme possibility, metaphysics does not simply terminate. It does not simply give way to positivism, if for no other reason than that the inversion has the effect of displacing that very order of alleged positivity that would remain, opening within it a certain economy:

> The end of metaphysics that is to be thought here is but the beginning of metaphysics' "resurrection" in altered forms; these forms leave to the proper, exhausted history of fundamental metaphysical positions

the purely economic role of providing raw materials with which—once they are correspondingly transformed—the world of "knowledge" is built "anew." (N II 201)

Though its essential possibilities are exhausted, metaphysics in its end remains intact and continues to operate in a kind of compulsive repetition.

Heidegger would expose also another side: metaphysics not only continues in this purely repetitive way but also asserts itself elsewhere still more forcefully: "As a completion, an end is the gathering into the most extreme possibilities. We think in too limited a fashion as long as we expect only a development of new philosophies of the previous style" (SD 63). Heidegger refers to the relation of philosophy to science, to the way in which sciences develop within the field opened up by philosophy, finally separating themselves from philosophy. The end of philosophy occurs as the completion of such separation, that is, as the triumph of science and technology. One could say that metaphysics dissolves into science and technology, which are thus its outcome, its final possibility. And yet, it is a matter not merely of dissolution but also of completion. One would need, then, to ask: What is it about metaphysics that science and technology bring to completion? A detour through other texts—such as "The Question concerning Technology"—would, of course, supply something like an answer: it is a matter of carrying to the extreme a certain concealment that belongs intrinsically to metaphysics. But one would need also to insist on a certain reticence, at least to wonder whether thinking this answer—thinking the concealment that, despite all their powerful claims to have brought enlightenment, science and technology are said only to bring to completion—would not require a certain transgression of the very limit it would establish. The question is whether one can delimit the end of philosophy without already having taken up the task of thinking. One must persist in questioning. For instance, in questioning how it is that science and technology are both philosophy and nonphilosophy (still another nonphilosophy), both the completion and the dissolution of metaphysics.

The first section of Heidegger's text, governed by the question of the end of metaphysics, concludes at the limit, concludes with a question about a certain operation of the limit: "But is the end of philosophy in the sense of its evolving into the sciences also already the complete actualization of all the possibilities in which the thinking of philosophy was posited?" (SD 65). The question inscribes another: What is "the thinking of philosophy"? What must be the character of the limit dividing philosophy from thinking if thinking also somehow belongs to philosophy? How can the other of philosophy, nonphilosophy, belong also to philosophy? Heidegger continues:

> Or is there a *first* possibility for thinking apart from the *last* possibility which we characterized (the dissolution of philosophy in the technologized sciences), a possibility from which the thinking of philosophy would have to start, but which as philosophy it could nevertheless not experience and adopt? (SD 65)

It would not be a matter of opposition and of transition between opposites, from philosophy to nonphilosophy, but rather of a limit, of a "first possibility" that would be the limit of philosophy, a limit whose operation would delimit philosophy such that philosophy, commencing only this side of the limit, could never experience the limit. Philosophy would always have been delimited by a certain operation of nonphilosophy, and the transition from the end of philosophy to the task of thinking would be a transgression of this limit.

(c)

Everything would depend on the transgression, on crossing the limit in the way called for by *die Sache*.

Suppose—as if the supposition did not already broach transgression—that the limit of philosophy delimits the circuit in which metaphysics turns in its turning from beings as they present themselves to Being as the ground which makes such self-presentation possible, as the presence which lets beings come to presence. Transgression, then, would involve, first of all, asking what remains unthought in that turning. It would involve regress to that which must be already, though concealedly, in play whenever such turning commences.

The second part of Heidegger's text is thus devoted largely to sketching this regress. It may be regarded as involving two stages. The first has as its point of departure the movement from the presentation of beings, their shining in such a way as to show themselves, to Being as that which, shining in and through them, makes it possible for them to present themselves as the beings they are. The regress itself—its first stage—is, then, expressed by Heidegger thus: "Such shining [*Scheinen*] occurs necessarily in a brightness [*Helle*]. Only through brightness can what shines show itself, i.e., shine" (SD 71). Thus, the first stage of the regress is from the shining-showing of beings in their Being to that brightness, that light, which any such shining-showing requires. Echoes of Plato. The regress still short of the limit.

Then comes transgression:

> But brightness in its turn rests in something open, something free [*in einem Offenen, Freien*] which it might illuminate here and there, now and then. Brightness plays in the open and wars there with darkness. Wherever something present [*ein Anwesendes*] encounters something else present . . . , there openness already rules, the free region is in play. (SD 71)

The regress, the transgression, is to the openness, the free region; ever since *Being and Time* Heidegger will have called it *Lichtung* (clearing), which is to be rigorously distinguished from light. Indeed that distinction *is* the transgression: "Light can stream into the clearing, into its openness, and let brightness play with darkness in it. But light never first creates the clearing. Rather, light presupposes the clearing" (SD 72).

What, then, is the nonphilosophy to which the transgression would lead? What is thinking?

Let it be said at once, before there is time for the saying to be interrupted by its conditions, for the inevitable doubling of self-determination to come into play.

Thinking is *of the clearing.*

Differentiation is called for immediately: thinking is not *of* the clearing in the sense that intuition may be said to be *of* something that appears or in the sense that knowledge is *of* a being. Thinking is not *of* the clearing even in the sense that understanding can be *of* Being, say, as εἶδος. How, then, is thinking *of* the clearing?

In two ways. First, as the thinking *of philosophy*. Such thinking, which turns from beings to Being, is *of the clearing* inasmuch as this turning occurs within the clearing. Yet, as a turning to Being as presence, the thinking of philosophy is incapable of what one might call—leaving open still even its very possibility—thinking the clearing. The clearing is the unthought site of the thinking of philosophy, a site even unthinkable for the ~~thinking~~ of philosophy, for that turning whose very condition is that the site be concealed as such and, along with it, the belongingness of thinking to that site.

The other way is that of thinking at the end of philosophy, the way of nonphilosophy. How is thinking *of* the clearing at the end of metaphysics? Does such thinking simply turn to the clearing, to what remains unthought in metaphysics? Does it thus commence by turning once and for all away from metaphysics, away from the circuit of shining-showing by which metaphysics is determined? Does it commence by turning decisively to the clearing, by installing itself unequivocally and irrevocably in an orientation to the clearing?

One cannot but be suspicious of the prospect of such a new immediacy and of rhetoric that appeals to such a prospect. Heidegger's discourse is not entirely innocent of such rhetoric, neither in the present text nor, for instance, in the text "The Overcoming of Metaphysics," however rigorously such texts may, on the other hand, insist that metaphysics is not simply to be left behind.[9]

Even if the nonphilosophy of thinking could go unchallenged by that nonphilosophy in which philosophy is completed and dissolved (i.e., technology), would it not, even then, fall short of that utter freedom of which one might dream? Could one not discern, in the regress that Heidegger's text outlines, the necessity of the return? Is not that regress governed, in a decisive way, by the reference to philosophy? Not only in that philosophy, the circuit of the

---

9. The very title "The Overcoming of Metaphysics" exemplifies such rhetoric, even though Heidegger begins this text by noting that the title could give rise to "many misunderstandings" and then goes on to say explicitly: "For the metaphysics that is overcome [*die überwundene Metaphysik*] does not disappear" (VA 71–72). His reference is, however, primarily to the way in which metaphysics, in its completion and dissolution, persists as technology.

shining-showing of Being/beings, is the *terminus a quo* of the regress; but also in that, even in its finally transgressive stage, the regress remains structurally undifferentiated from a transcendental regress, a kind of imitation, more generally, of the metaphysical regress from beings to Being, a mimesis that would be carried out not in a pregiven sphere—tracing there certain lines already traced in another sphere, that of philosophy—but rather in a space that would first be opened up by the mimesis. Nonphilosophy is not pregiven but only begins in imitation of philosophy.[10]

Heidegger's text alludes to this involvement: "For every attempt to get a look [*Einblick*] into the supposed task of thinking finds itself

10. In *De L'Esprit* Derrida concludes his discussion of Heidegger's *Gespräch* with Trakl by imagining a scene, an exchange, between Heidegger and certain Christian theologians. The latter are made to say to Heidegger: "But what you call the arche-originary spirit and what you pretend is foreign to Christianity is exactly what is most essential in Christianity." Heidegger's imagined response: "But in affirming that the *Gedicht* of Trakl—and all that I say with him—is neither metaphysical nor Christian, I am not opposing anything, especially not Christianity, nor all the discourses on the fall, the curse, the promise, salvation, resurrection. . . . I am trying solely, modestly, discreetly to think that *from* which [*ce* à partir de *quoi*] all that is possible." Derrida extends the Heideggerian response: it is a matter of repetition, of a withdrawal (*retrait*) toward the most originary, of a move that, as repetition, thinks "nothing other, no other content, than that which is there, even as the promise of the future, in the legacy of the metaphysical. . . . But if in objecting to or reproaching Heidegger, one were to say to him that this repetition adds nothing, invents nothing, uncovers nothing . . . , Heidegger, I imagine, would respond: on what you call the path of repetition that adds nothing . . . , the thought of this *Frühe à venir,* in thus advancing toward the possibility of what you believe you recognize, proceeds toward what is completely other than what you believe you recognize. It is not a new content in effect. But access . . . to the *possibility* of the metaphysical . . . opens onto something completely other than what the possibility renders possible. What you represent as a simple ontological and transcendental replica is completely other. . . . The completely other announces itself in the most rigorous repetition" (178–184).

I am proposing to think this *répétition,* this *Wiederholung,* also as mimesis, as a mimesis that would open its own space and only as such differentiate itself, a mimesis to that degree itself set at the limit of metaphysics.

Whatever Heidegger may be made to say in Derrida's imagined scene, he does, in fact, say—or, rather, write—the following, referring to the thinking that would follow the way back (*Rückgang*) into the ground of metaphysics: "This thinking proceeds, specifically as still regarded from metaphysics [*noch von der Metaphysik her gesehen*], back into the ground of metaphysics. But when it is experienced from out of itself, that which thus still appears as ground [Heidegger added here a marginal comment: "Sein als Nichtgrund, Grund"] is presumably something other and something still unsaid, in the same way as the essence of metaphysics is something other than metaphysics" (GA 9: 367).

directed to a look back [*Rückblick*] into the whole of the history of philosophy" (SD 66). Thinking ahead into the clearing, the look into that to which thinking is to be given over, is also a thinking back toward philosophy, a look back into its history. Thinking at the end of metaphysics remains in the transition that one might otherwise mistake as the way to a new immediacy, beyond philosophy, simply nonphilosophy. But there can be no simple nonphilosophy, rather only a never completed transition that would be such as to displace its very sense as something to be completed. Thinking at the end of metaphysics is a thinking at the limit of metaphysics.

Even at its end, when, as in death, it is gathered into its most extreme possibility, even when it is thus deprived of living speech— even if at the very moment of its most rigorous self-enclosure— philosophy still sounds, even if its words are no longer really its own. Even if a final madness leaves its voice dismembered, it continues to echo, to ring out into that open enclosure that Heidegger calls clearing.

Nonetheless, the mimetic opening of the clearing—the opening to nonphilosophy—carries out a more originary deployment of the question. As in *Being and Time,* the movement would be one beyond Being, that is, a movement toward that which makes possible the shining-showing of Being. In *Being and Time* this beyond—what Heidegger called there the meaning of Being (*der Sinn vom Sein*)— was determined as temporality and its locus taken to be Dasein.[11] But in "The End of Philosophy and the Task of Thinking" this beyond of Being is to be thought as the clearing. The later text thus asks—even if with a certain rhetoric of deferral—whether temporality, ecstatic time, is not to be regarded as possible only within the

---

11. Matters would be more complex if one proceeded in terms of Heidegger's entire project as sketched in the introductory chapters rather than in terms of the two published Divisions. One would then need to distinguish between *Temporalität,* the meaning of Being as such, and *Zeitlichkeit,* the temporality of Dasein. The published portion of *Being and Time* provides almost no means for developing this distinction. In *The Basic Problems of Phenomenology,* on the other hand, Heidegger does address, though briefly, the level of the problematic designated by the term *Temporalität* (GA 24: 429–445). See below, chap. 4; also, my *Delimitations: Phenomenology and the End of Metaphysics* (Bloomington: Indiana University Press, 1986), chap. 10.

clearing: "Accordingly, we may suggest that the day will come when we will not shun the question whether the clearing, the free open, may not be that within which alone pure space and ecstatic time and everything present and absent in them have the place which gathers and shelters everything" (SD 72f.). Furthermore—and more assertorially—the beyond is no longer to be taken as having its locus simply in Dasein, not even in the sense of constituting—as existence, as disclosedness, as temporality, depending on the level of Heidegger's analysis—the very essence of Dasein. The beyond would not be a condition within Dasein, something on the side of Dasein's understanding or thinking, that would make it possible for Dasein to understand or think Being.[12] Rather, as clearing, the beyond of Being precedes both thinking and Being in such a way as to make possible the very presencing of thinking and Being to one another. The beyond is to be thought "as the clearing which first grants Being and thinking and their presencing [*Anwesen*] to and for each other." The clearing is to be thought as the place "from which alone the possibility of the belonging together of Being and thinking, that is, presence [*Anwesenheit*] and apprehending, can arise at all" (SD 75). If clearing first grants thinking, then thinking cannot be a representational activity of a subject that would take the clearing as the object of thinking. Thinking is not the subject of, but rather is subject to, the clearing—even in the case of a thinking that mimetically opens the clearing. The same must be said, finally, of questioning: it can break into the clearing only at the cost of submitting itself—and of proving to have submitted itself always already—to the clearing, only by relinquishing its claim to autonomy. And yet, this would be precisely to persist in questioning, in letting what is questionable emerge as such.

Yet, how is it that the opening to nonphilosophy, even if a more originary deployment of the question, is such as to let the full questionableness of *die Sache* come into play? Is it not—however much it may echo mimetically what has sounded from philosophy—simply a regress to a more originary origin, to the clearing beyond Being and

12. This differentiation is explicit already, for example, in the 1949 Introduction to "What Is Metaphysics?" (GA 9: 373–374).

time, to the clearing that is a still more originary origin than Being or time? But in this case how is it that a previously unheard-of questionableness comes into play? How is it that the clearing is more questionable and that thinking, which is of the clearing, is thus required to persist in questioning? How is it that thinking persists in questioning precisely by breaking into the clearing?

In the regress to the clearing there sounds the echo not only of philosophy but also of another, an older voice. It is, says Heidegger, one "which still today, although unheard, speaks in the sciences into which philosophy dissolves" (SD 74), a voice which thus echoes in philosophy and in the nonphilosophy in which philosophy is completed and dissolved. The voice is itself responsive to something heard, something to which it responds. The voice is that which speaks in Parmenides' poem; what is heard and then said is the following:

> . . . Χρεὼ δέ σε πάντα πυθέσθαι
> ἠμὲν ᾿Αληθείης εὐκυκλέος ἀτρεμὲς ἦτορ
> ἠδὲ βροτῶν δόξας, ταῖς οὐκ ἔνι πίστις ἀληθής.

> Fragment I, 28ff.

Heidegger's German translation:

> du sollst aber alles erfahren:
> sowohl der Unverborgenheit, der gutgerundeten, nichtzitterndes Herz
> als auch der Sterblichen Dafürhalten, dem fehlt das Vertrauenkönnen auf
> Unverborgenes. (SD 74)

Again the English translation already cited:

> It is necessary that you shall learn all things,
> as well the unshaken heart of well-rounded truth
> as the opinions of mortals in which there is no true belief.

Thus was the clearing, even if unthought by philosophy, named in the beginning of philosophy, named ἀλήθεια, named in response to the words of the goddess, who is none other than ἀλήθεια itself (cf. GA 54: 6–7). Certainly not a naming in which a subject bestows a designation upon an object; rather, a naming in which one would submit to what is heard from beyond Being, to a voice that echoes silently from the open enclosure, opening that enclosure to the responsive speech that, sounding forth into it, would name it.

But ἀλήθεια is not truth, Heidegger insists in "The End of Philosophy and the Task of Thinking," responding to Friedländer's criticism[13] and now distinguishing rigorously between ἀλήθεια as named in Parmenides' poem (Heidegger translates: *Unverborgenheit*—in English: unconcealment) and ἀλήθεια as ὀρθότης (correctness), now granting that even among the early Greeks the latter sense was dominant. The effect is to deny that there was ever any pure prevailing of ἀλήθεια as unconcealment, any speaking and thinking immediately open to it; rather, ἀλήθεια "was experienced only as ὀρθότης" (SD 78). It is no more a matter of immediacy at the beginning than at the end of metaphysics.

But, then, ἀλήθεια would never be simply present as such. This is why the opening to it could never be simply a regress to a more originary origin but rather one in which the very determination of origin—as ground, i.e., presence, to be itself brought to presence in metaphysics—is eroded, reinscribed as ~~Grund~~ (GA 9: 367; also n. 10). What would come decisively into play in the opening to nonphilosophy is concealment:

> Only what ἀλήθεια as clearing grants is experienced and thought, not what it is as such. This remains concealed. Does this happen by chance? Does it happen only as a consequence of the carelessness of human thinking? Or does it happen because self-concealing, concealment, λήθη, belongs to ἀλήθεια, not just as an addition, not as shadow to light, but rather as the heart of ἀλήθεια? (SD 78)

Λήθη at the heart of ἀλήθεια would make it the very element of questionableness. In the clearing questionableness would no longer be determined by subordination to, or even in correlation with, one who would question but rather as the element of questioning, as preceding it and making it possible, as drawing it beyond itself by the very attraction of the λήθη at the heart of ἀλήθεια, as drawing it along in the withdrawal, questioning become ecstatic.

---

13. An extended account of the exchange between Heidegger and Friedländer is given by Robert Bernasconi, *The Question of Language in Heidegger's History of Being* (Atlantic Highlands: Humanities Press, 1985), chap. 2. I have dealt with it, more briefly, in *Delimitations*, chap. 14.

(d)

Heidegger turns again to Parmenides at the end of a seminar held in Zähringen in September 1973. From the seminar only a protocol is available.[14] In the seminar Heidegger reads from a text written during the winter of 1972–73, a text devoted to a saying by Parmenides. Echoes within echoes.

Heidegger's turn to Parmenides, the turn back (*Rückkehr*) to the beginning, is, he says, a roundabout way that is necessary for the turn into (*Einkehr*) the experience of the clearing. He continues:

> The turn back takes place in the *echo* [*Echo*] of Parmenides. It takes place as that listening that opens itself to the word of Parmenides from out of our present-day era, from out of the epoch of the dispensation [*Schickung*] of Being as *Ge-stell*. (S 132)

Not only does Heidegger repeat, at a very critical juncture of the seminar, that what is said occurs in "the echo of Parmenides" (S 134), but also he forestalls mistaking such discourse as mere appropriation of what Parmenides said. He is concerned not only with seeing how a certain matter "has shown itself for Parmenides" (S 133) but even with hearing it "with a Greek ear" (S 135).

The theme of the text that Heidegger reads in the seminar is: the heart of ἀλήθεια. He begins by citing from "The End of Philosophy and the Task of Thinking" the passage (cited above) in which the question is raised whether concealment is the heart of ἀλήθεια. Then he comments: "What is said here is not so; Parmenides says no such thing" (S 133). Thus the question is to be reopened: what is to be heard in Parmenides' saying about the heart of ἀλήθεια, about ἀληθείης εὐκυκλέος ἀτρεμὲς ἦτορ? It is to this question that the text read in the seminar is addressed. That text is itself primarily a reading of a series of Parmenides' sayings.

Heidegger establishes, first, that in Parmenides' saying that ἀλήθεια is εὐκυκλέος one is to hear—instead of the usual rendering "well-rounded"—"the well-encompassing, the appropriately

14. I am grateful to Kenneth Maly for calling my attention to the importance of this text in a seminar that he conducted near ancient Elea during the 1985 session of the Collegium Phaenomenologicum.

encircling [*das Wohlumfangende, schicklich Umkreisende*]" (S 134). But what, then, of the ἀτρεμὲς ἦτορ, the unshaken, unwavering heart that would thus be appropriately encircled by well-encompassing ἀλήθεια?

Heidegger cites from Fragment 6: "ἔστι γὰρ εἶναι" and translates: "*Ist nämlich Sein.*" It is this unheard, unheard-of, scandalous saying (*dieses unerhörte Wort*)—that Being is—that marks "exactly how far from familiar thinking Parmenides' extraordinary way is" (S 135); it is what Heidegger insists must be heard "with a Greek ear." Heidegger continues: "The name for what is addressed in this matter sounds thus [*lautet*]: τὸ ἐόν, which is neither a being nor simply Being, but rather τὸ ἐόν" (S 135). Then he adds, in direct apposition to τὸ ἐόν: "*Anwesend: Anwesen selbst.*"

What is to be heard in these words, these echoes within echoes? What is to be heard if one listens to them from out of the orientation given by "The End of Philosophy and the Task of Thinking"?

The "unwavering heart" to which Parmenides' *unerhörtes Wort* is addressed is not a being. Nor, Heidegger says, is it simply Being (*noch lediglich das Sein*). And yet, in a sense it is Being; it is, as he says, "*Anwesen selbst,*" or, still more explicitly, "*Anwesenheit selbst.*" It is presence, i.e., Being, not simply but rather as coming to presence. For coming to presence is precisely what presence, i.e., Being, simply does not do, does not do simply. Rather, for the most part, as in common sense, it merely shines unobtrusively through beings in such a way that these beings themselves shine so as to show themselves, to come to presence. Metaphysics would of course invert common sense and direct itself to Being; yet, in turning merely within the circuit of Being/beings, it cannot but turn Being into a being in the very process of bringing it to presence.[15] What is at issue in the remote sayings of Parmenides is another coming to presence: Being would come to presence in being set back within the clearing, that is, in being appropriately encircled by ἀλήθεια.

15. See especially the discussion of errancy as the counteressence to the essence of truth (*das wesentliche Gegenwesen zum anfänglichen Wesen der Wahrheit*) developed in "On the Essence of Truth" (GA 9: 196–198); and that of the metaphysical releasing of *das Sein* into *die Seiendheit* in such a way as to give priority to *das Seiende* (N II 486).

But, then, ἀλήθεια too must be thought in the direction of τὸ ἐόν: "Ἀλήθεια is not an empty openness, nor an unmoving chasm. It is to be thought as the disclosure [*Entbergen*] which appropriately encircles the ἐόν . . ." (S 136). He adds: "This, presencing coming to presence [*das Anwesend-Anwesen*], itself permeates [*durchstimmt*] the encircling unconcealment which appropriately discloses it" (S 137). The clearing is not simply a beyond of Being; it is not the promise of a new immediacy at the end of philosophy. The clearing is, rather, the clearing *of* Being, of Being as τὸ ἐόν; that which the clearing encircles permeates it, sounds, resounds, echoes, throughout it.

Nonphilosophy would not, then, install itself beyond philosophy, in a beyond of Being, but rather must endure being stationed at the *limit*. Indeed it would cross the limit, but not in a simple movement of transgression; rather in a movement simultaneously in both directions, a double movement. It would think what metaphysics was to have thought, Being as Being, but would do so only by crossing over to the clearing that encircles Being. And yet, it would think the clearing only by returning to what is encircled, to what shines within the space of ἀλήθεια, to what sounds throughout the open enclosure.

The text on Parmenides that Heidegger reads in the Zähringen seminar, one of his very last texts, perhaps comes closest to openly announcing the necessity of the return from beyond Being and thus the schema of doubling at the limit.

Is this schema ever really announced? Perhaps one could never finally decide, never find in Heidegger's text the schema itself, the schema as such, assuring oneself that at a certain point one would no longer hear merely echoes of the schema in Heidegger's text. Perhaps, then, the schema remains undecidable in Heidegger's text. Perhaps even one could mount an assault against Heidegger, a critique (as it is called), for his not having announced the necessity of the return, almost as if he could never entirely cease dreaming of the beyond of Being, which would also be beyond the city, beyond ethics, and beyond politics.

Perhaps.

And yet, perhaps undecidability is not so intolerable as one might have supposed, nor the gesture of what is called critique so innocent as one might have thought.

Perhaps even schematizing the schema as a doubling in which is added to the move beyond Being a certain return from beyond—perhaps even this cannot with utter assurance be taken to represent the schema as such, considering how thoroughly the *as such,* determinate being, is put into question in the question of Being, considering too that it is a matter of persisting in questioning.

Suppose, then, that one were to listen as the schema echoes—as indeed it does—throughout Heidegger's texts. To listen, not in order to evade the rigor of questioning, but rather in order to begin to enact and to say a doubling that recoils upon questioning, dividing it from itself, making it exceed itself. In order precisely to persist in questioning.

In order also to begin thinking whether this schema is perhaps what, most provocatively of all, echoes after Heidegger.

It has echoed unmistakably in the reading that I have ventured of "The End of Philosophy and the Task of Thinking." Most unmistakably at the point where the move beyond Being is first traced, indeed in the very sentence that bespeaks the transgression: "But brightness [*Helle*] in its turn rests in something open, something free [*in einem Offenen, Freien*], which it might illuminate [*erhellen*] here and there, now and then" (SD 71). On the one hand, thinking would move from the brightness required for the shining-showing of Being/beings to the clearing, the open space of illumination; it would think illumination as a lighting within the clearing, *Licht* within *Lichtung.* Yet, on the other hand, wherever ("here and there") and whenever ("now and then") the lighting illuminates precisely the clearing, then thinking would retrace that reversal, returning from beyond to the illumination of the beyond, its illumination this side—or, at least, from this side—of the limit of philosophy.

The doubling return is also echoed in other moments of that text, even if less openly. Thus, in that deferred question that would eventually refer space to the beyond, to the clearing, a certain linguistic constraint serves to add the double to the movement beyond: for not only does the very schema of the beyond metaphorize and, hence, lead back to the very space that would be referred beyond but also the relation of space to that beyond—the clearing as the within-which (*worin*) of space—equally metaphorizes space, again broaching the return.[16]

Much the same can be said of that mimesis, that connection of *Einblick* to *Rückblick*, of *Einkehr* to *Rückkehr*, to which the move beyond, otherwise structurally undifferentiated from transcendental regress, would be bound. To begin in imitation of philosophy is to double back to philosophy in the very move toward the beyond of philosophy.

Echoes of the schema proliferate in Heidegger's text. It will not be easy, perhaps not even possible, to schematize this proliferation. Not even by returning from Heidegger's last texts.

In the text on Parmenides, one of Heidegger's last, he reopens the question of the unwavering heart of encircling ἀλήθεια. No longer is λήθη declared—even interrogatively—the heart of ἀλήθεια; rather, now the unwavering heart that ἀλήθεια would encircle is said to be Being itself as it resounds within ἀλήθεια. What is to be said, then, about the thinking that would return from ἀλήθεια? Can that return be said to be governed no longer by concealment but by something else, by this newly (and most anciently) proclaimed heart of ἀλήθεια? Certainly the return is now declared a return toward Being as it echoes within the clearing. Certainly, then, this proclaimed heart of ἀλήθεια governs a certain moment of the return. And yet, it must be said to govern the return in a way that concealment never could have; for concealment is precisely that to which one cannot simply turn or return, that which escapes every effort simply to turn to it, diverting and repulsing every such effort, prompting a return only by

16. It is in this connection that I would underwrite, even if in another direction, the following moment in Derrida's reading of Heidegger: "And if Heidegger has radically deconstructed the authority of the *present* over metaphysics, he has done so in order to lead us to think the presence of the present. But the thinking of this presence can only metaphorize, by a profound necessity from which one does not escape by a mere decision, the language that it deconstructs" (*Marges*, 157). It goes almost without saying that in referring to a metaphorizing I am employing the language of metaphor strategically, not to say metaphorically. Derrida has shown, as indeed Heidegger already declared, that the rhetorical concept of metaphor cannot remain simply intact in a discourse at the limit of metaphysics. See *Marges*, 247–324; *Psyché: Inventions de l'autre* (Paris: Galilée, 1987), 63–93.

turning thinking back away from itself. The question is, then, whether, at the end, in this late text on Parmenides, Heidegger would orient the return toward one rather than the other, toward Being rather than toward concealment. Or whether thinking would not *turn toward Being*, returning to think the shining, sounding, showing within the clearing (what one might call—cautiously, under erasure—a certain positivity), precisely *in being turned away from concealment*, from the negativity of ἀλήθεια. Turning toward the one in being turned away from the other, two interwoven moments.

Return from ἀλήθεια, also from its negativity, its concealment, even from an ἀλήθεια indistinguishable, as in the age of technology, from that negativity, that concealment. Return to what? To the shining, sounding, showing of that which ἀλήθεια would encircle. A place of return.

Heidegger's very last text, written only a few days before his death, addressed to his friend and *Landsmann* Bernhard Welte, concludes: "For there is need to deliberate whether and how, in the age of technologized homogeneous world-civilization, there can still be a homeland [*Heimat*]" (GA 13: 243).

TWO

Time Out . . .

It suspends the flow of time, stops the incessant drive into the future, and yet keeps the clock running. It clips the wings of temporal ecstasy, but only temporarily, only by a certain deferral, a postponement. It can suspend time only by being itself a definite, carefully regulated interval of time, time at a standstill even while remaining time, almost a kind of space of time inserted into time, suspending time, almost as if it were a bit of eternity. Also, then, an intense time, a time of intense preparation, a time of decision.

(a)

Heidegger arrived in Marburg in the autumn of 1923. Gadamer tells of the summer evening's celebration that had preceded Heidegger's departure from Freiburg: friends, colleagues, students invited to Todtnauberg, a bonfire, Heidegger's speech beginning with the words, "Be awake to the fire of the night."[1] Heidegger was to remain in Marburg for five years, years unmatched, it would seem, by any others in their intensity. These were the years in which *Being and Time* was prepared and published. In 1928 he returned to Freiburg, writing to Gadamer at the time that only when he began "to sense the power of the old ground" did he realize how—in the project of fundamental ontology—"everything began to get slippery."[2] The time of that project would prove to have been a temporary suspension, a certain postponement of the abysmal drive of

---

1. Hans-Georg Gadamer, *Philosophical Apprenticeships*, trans. Robert R. Sullivan (Cambridge: MIT Press, 1985), 47f.
2. Ibid., 50.

questioning. And yet, also a time of intense questioning, a postpone-ment of questioning effected only by a certain intensification of questioning. A way of persisting in questioning.

Less than a year after he arrived in Marburg, Heidegger pre-sented a lecture to the Marburger Theologenschaft. To this lecture, "The Concept of Time" (July 1924),[3] there have been repeated references. First of all, by Heidegger himself in a footnote in *Being and Time*, remarking that certain of the analyses there being presented—the note occurs near the beginning of the Second Chap-ter of the Second Division—were communicated in the 1924 lec-ture (SZ 268). Then by Gadamer, who describes the lecture as the "original form" (*Urform*) of *Being and Time*.[4] Also by Michel Haar, who (with Marc de Launay) has translated the lecture into French and who calls it "a first epitome, already very complex, of . . . *Being and Time*."[5] Also by Thomas Sheehan, who provides a precise ac-count of the lecture, concluding that it is "an essential but partial step along the way to the writing of *Being and Time*."[6]

The lecture is indeed an essential step, the decisive moment in which a certain prehistory is gathered from out of, and into, the unity of the future project. Recall some moments of that prehistory, some of the texts of the early Freiburg period. For instance, the review of Jaspers' *Psychology of World-Views*, begun by Heidegger in 1919 though published only much later:[7] here one finds an engage-ment with the analysis of death; also Dasein characterized as having one's own self in a way quite irreducible to immanent acts of con-sciousness; an insistence, too, in criticism of Jaspers, on developing the problem of access to Dasein, on what is already termed herme-

---

3. In addition to its separate publication (here cited), the lecture is to appear as an appendix in a volume of the III. Abteilung of the *Gesamtausgabe* entitled *Der Begriff der Zeit.*

4. Gadamer, "Martin Heidegger and Marburg Theology," in *Philosophical Her-meneutics*, trans. David E. Linge (Berkeley: University of California Press, 1976), 199.

5. Michel Haar (ed.), *Heidegger* (Paris: L'Herne, 1983), 36.

6. Thomas J. Sheehan, "The 'Original Form' of *Sein und Zeit*: Heidegger's *Der Begriff der Zeit* (1924)," *Journal of the British Society for Phenomenology*, 10 (1979), 83.

7. "Anmerkungen zu Karl Jaspers 'Psychologie der Weltanschauung,' " in *Karl Jaspers in der Diskussion*, ed. Hans Saner (Munich: R. Piper, 1973), 70–100. Reprinted in Heidegger, *Wegmarken*, GA 9: 1–44.

neutics.[8] Then, the lecture course (winter semester 1920–21) "Introduction to the Phenomenology of Religion," in which one finds developed the questions of facticity and of primordial temporality.[9] The essay sent to Natorp in Marburg in support of Heidegger's nomination there: a philosophical interpretation of Aristotle introduced by an analysis of the "hermeneutic situation."[10] And the course just preceding his departure from Freiburg, "Hermeneutics of Facticity": by this time a number of the characteristic terms of *Being and Time* have appeared (*in-der-Welt-sein, Alltäglichkeit, Bedeutsamkeit, Vorhandenheit*); also the threefold articulation (*Welt, In, Wer*) that will structure the First Division of *Being and Time;* and, throughout, a call for a certain return to the Greeks, coupled with a demand for the destruction of tradition.[11]

And yet, it seems that it is only after the move to Marburg, specifically, in the lecture "The Concept of Time," that this prehistory crystallizes into a systematic presentation of what is to become the project of *Being and Time.*[12] A year later (summer semester 1925) the lecture course *History of the Concept of Time*[13] presents in

8. See David Farrell Krell, *Intimations of Mortality* (University Park: Pennsylvania State University Press, 1986), chap. 1.

9. These questions are developed in relation to the original Christian experience expressed in St. Paul's Letters to the Thessalonians. See Thomas J. Sheehan, "Heidegger's 'Introduction to the Phenomenology of Religion,' " in *A Companion to Martin Heidegger's "Being and Time,"* ed. Joseph Kockelmans (Washington, D.C.: Center for Advanced Research in Phenomenology and University Press of America, 1986), 40–62.

10. See Thomas J. Sheehan, "Heidegger's Early Years: Fragment for a Philosophical Biography," in *Heidegger: The Man and the Thinker,* ed. Thomas J. Sheehan (Chicago: Precedent Publishing, 1981), 11f.; Gadamer, "Martin Heidegger and Marburg Theology," 200f.; Gadamer, *Philosophical Apprenticeships,* 46f. A copy of this essay has recently been discovered; it has been published in *Dilthey-Jahrbuch* (1989).

11. Now published as GA 63. See Sheehan, "Heidegger's Early Years," 13.

12. A degree of reservation is required here, since many of the texts of the early Freiburg period are not yet available. There is even, at the present time, some uncertainty regarding the list of Heidegger's courses during this period. See Theodore J. Kisiel, "Heidegger's Early Lecture Courses," in *A Companion to Martin Heidegger's "Being and Time,"* ed. Joseph Kockelmans, 22–39.

13. *Prolegomena zur Geschichte des Zeitbegriffs,* GA 20. Recently it has been discovered that in the months after he delivered the lecture "The Concept of Time" Heidegger used it as the basis for an essay with the same title but several times the length of the lecture. The circumstances of its composition are described in detail by Theodore Kisiel, "Why the First Draft of *Being and Time* Was Never Published," *Journal of the British Society for Phenomenology,* 20 (1989).

almost fully developed form what will become the First Division of *Being and Time*. In the following year the book—its first two Divisions—is completed. In 1927 *Being and Time*—all that Heidegger was ever to publish of it—appears.

The 1924 lecture marks, then, the beginning of the Marburg period. Perhaps also something more. Perhaps the text in which Heidegger will have begun to write not only *Being and Time* but also the texts of those courses that immediately follow, in which the slippage of the project will, even if almost imperceptibly, have begun to operate.

"The Concept of Time" begins in a manner appropriate to the theological audience by referring time to eternity—or, rather, by introducing such a referral only to disavow it. In the abrupt disavowal there is not only a decision regarding the ground of time but also a question of the very appropriateness of grounding to time.

The question is: What is time? It is as a way of broaching the problem of access to time that Heidegger begins with the opposition between time and eternity. If the meaning (*Sinn*) of time lies in eternity, in a being out of time, utterly outside of time, then time must be understood on the basis of eternity, from out of eternity. Thereby a way out (*Ausgang*) into the investigation, a point of departure, is prescribed: from eternity to time. The difficulty is that philosophy, unlike theology, can make no claim to understand eternity. This difficulty cannot be removed for the philosopher: "If the philosopher questions about time, then he is resolved *to understand time from out of time* [*aus der Zeit*]" (Z 6). The philosopher would understand time not by taking time out of time toward an eternity from which it would be understood. Rather, he would understand time out of time in precisely such a way as to forego referring it to anything else, would understand it from out of itself. Only the slightest move is required to convert this resolve into the project of understanding time without reference to infinity—that is, the project of understanding the radical finitude of time (see SZ §65).

Heidegger is emphatic: the considerations voiced in "The Concept of Time" are not theological. From a theological point of view, they are considerations that can only serve to make the question of eternity *more difficult*.

Indeed, he adds with equal emphasis, they are not even philosophical. For they do not claim to give a general systematic determination of time; such a determination "would have to question back behind time into the involvement of other categories in it" (Z 6). Over against such a philosophical consideration of time, Heidegger poses his as belonging to forescience (*Vorwissenschaft*). It is the concern of such forescience to consider, for example, how time shows itself for physics, that is, what kind of self-showing is operative in the way that time is preunderstood in physics as clock-time. More generally, forescience undertakes to demonstrate whether "an investigation is in touch with its matter [*bei ihrer Sache ist*] or is nourished by some traditional and worn-out word-knowledge" (Z 7). Heidegger draws a curious—not to say ominous—analogy: forescience is like the police force at the parade of the sciences.

Here, too, it is a matter of investigating time from out of time, that is, of not questioning back behind time to something else, as would allegedly be required of a philosophical determination. Rather, what is to be undertaken is to attend to the way in which time shows itself, to enforce the bond of the sciences to their *Sachen*. Need it be said: forescience is nothing other than phenomenology.

Moving quickly past Einstein's theory of time, back to Aristotle's, from which it is not fundamentally different, Heidegger observes how both regard time as essentially linked to measurement and, hence, as determined from the now-point. The question is: What about the now? The question is the one asked by Augustine: What about the relation of the now to spirit? Is spirit time? Am I the now? In a more precise and differentiated formulation: "Am I myself the now and my Dasein time? Or is it, in the end, time itself that provides the clock in us?" (Z 10). The question is that of the *identity of time and Dasein*. In raising the question Heidegger is also introducing a difference between time as determined by the now (clock-time, but also what *Being and Time* will call *die besorgte Zeit*) *and* time itself. The sense of the identity will prove to require such differentiation: it is an identity of Dasein with time itself, not with the now, not with the clock that time itself provides us for measuring everything in time. This question of the identity of time and Dasein will prove, in a sense, to have been the sole question of Heidegger's lecture.

The development of the question requires that Dasein be characterized. Heidegger begins with a general character: Dasein is the being that each of us ourselves is, the being that each of us touches upon in the basic assertion "I am." The question of time has quickly become a question not of *what* time is but of *who* it is; more closely, it has become a question not only of how we—say, as spirit—are time but of how I am time, of how I am myself as time, of how I am time as myself, of how I am my time. I am myself from out of time, and I am time from out of myself—"*in der Jeweiligkeit als meiniges*" (Z 11).

The characterization is expanded, Heidegger enumerating eight basic structures of Dasein: (1) Dasein is *Being-in-the-world*, in distinction from a subject of the sort that would need somehow to escape from its own immanence into the world; Dasein is in-the-world in the sense of dealing with it (*umgehen*), as concern (*Besorgen*). (2) Dasein is *Being-with-one-another* (*Miteinandersein*), a being with others in the same world. (3) Dasein's being in the world with others occurs for the most part in *speaking* (*Sprechen*). (4) Dasein is a being for which the "*I am*" is constitutive; Dasein is my own. (5) Yet, in its everydayness, Dasein is not itself but is the nobody that is called "*das Man.*" (6) This being is such that its *Being is at issue* (*ein solches, dem es in seinem . . . In-der-Welt-sein auf sein Sein ankommt*); all its concernful dealings in the world are such as to be, at the same time, a matter of concern with its own Being. (7) In everydayness Dasein does not reflect on the I and the self but rather *finds itself* (*befindet sich*) there in its dealings in the world. (8) Dasein is not something that we can observe or prove but rather something that we *are;* thus to speak interpretively about the self is merely one way, though a distinctive way, in which Dasein itself is (Z 12–14).

Thus Heidegger assembles in the lecture most of the existential structures that will be elucidated in the First Division of *Being and Time*, assembles them in much the same language that will be in play there. In the final term of the enumeration—in contrast to the others—it is a matter not so much of an existential structure as of the distinctive methodological structure of the analysis of Dasein, of the precise way in which such analysis itself belongs to Dasein as a distinctive possibility. It is not a matter of observing Dasein, of analyzing it as though it were something other than the one carrying out the analysis. Rather, the interrogator and the interrogated are the same, and everything depends on the remarkable relatedness back and forth between them.[14] In being Dasein I have always already understood and interpreted myself; the analysis of Dasein would, then, draw out that already operative self-disclosure, would, as it were, listen in on it and elevate it to the level of conceptual comprehension.[15]

The posing of the question of primordial access to Dasein, the development of this question and of a strategy responsive to it—it is perhaps this complex of issues opening the Second Division of *Being and Time* that the lecture will have unfolded most rigorously. The opening paradox will already have been in place: How is it possible ever to get access to Dasein as a whole, since as long as it has not reached its end, it is still incomplete, whereas once it reaches that end, it is no longer Dasein at all? The paradox leads to an analysis of Dasein's *end*, that is, death. Heidegger will prove almost already to have written, in the lecture, the existential analysis of death: Death is Dasein's ownmost possibility, a possibility that is extreme (*äusserste*), impending (*bevorstehende*), certain yet indefinite.

One formulation responds to the question: What is it for Dasein to have its own death? What is this having? Heidegger answers: "*It is Dasein's running-ahead* [Vorlaufen] *to its goneness* [Vorbei] *as its extreme possibility, which impends with certainty and complete indefiniteness*" (Z 17).

---

14. Thus, in *Being and Time* Heidegger will refer to "a remarkable 'relatedness backward or forward' which what we are asking about (Being) bears to the questioning itself as a mode of Being of a being" (SZ 8). This is, of course, what I have discussed in the more extended context of chapter 1 as the coincidence of questioner and questioned.

15. Thus, in *Being and Time:* "Like any ontological interpretation whatsoever, this analytic can only, so to speak, listen in [*abzuhören*] to some already disclosed being regarding its Being. And it will attach itself to Dasein's distinctive and most far-reaching possibilities of disclosure, in order from these to get information [*Aufschluss*] about this being. Phenomenological interpretation must give to Dasein itself the possibility of primordial disclosure and, as it were, let it interpret itself. Such interpretation takes part in this disclosure only in order to raise existentially into the concept the phenomenal content of what has been disclosed" (SZ 139f.).

To have its own death, to comport itself to its own death, is, then, to be toward its own goneness, *das Vorbei.* When I comport myself to *dem Vorbei,* there is, Heidegger says, a certain uncovering. One could say: *das Vorbei* is such that, when I cast ahead toward it, there is reflected back from it a certain self-disclosure. Specifically, it reveals my Dasein as at some point no longer there (*als einmal nicht mehr da*), no longer there with such and such things and with these and those persons. In short: "*Das Vorbei* draws everything along with it into the nothing" (Z 17). It is, then, not some event that befalls me, not a "what" (*Was*) at all but rather a "how" (*Wie*); it is, in the end, as the proper end, the authentic "how" of my "there" (*da*).

To have its own death is, then, to run ahead to *das Vorbei,* to run up against one's own goneness. Such movement is authentic Being-toward-death and, as such, is the authentic future. As authentic future it involves, in turn, a return to past and present, and thus forms, unfolds, time itself: "Being-futural gives time [*Zukünftigsein gibt Zeit*], forms the present and lets the past [*Vergangenheit*—not yet *Gewesenheit*] be repeated in the how of its being-lived" (Z 19).

Death is the end, the final possibility, the most extreme possibility, the possibility beyond which one cannot cast oneself, *das Vorbei.* It is, one may say, the suspending of time, of the time as which I am myself. It is *a future that will never be present,* that will never have become present: "As the authentic future, *das Vorbei* can never become present" (Z 21). With death my time will have stopped, come to a standstill; death is as much out(side) of my time as is eternity. And yet, it is precisely from, out of *das Vorbei* that authentic time is formed, that is, proper time, time itself, or, rather, the time that I myself am. Death, *das Vorbei,* suspends time and yet grants time, lets it unfold. It is not something other than time but is, rather, something that one might almost call a time out of time; it is the limit of time, itself neither time nor not time, the limit too of the *itself,* as well as of my *own* self. It is a limit that delimits without being simply delimitable, an elusive and self-effacing limit—impending with certainty and complete indefiniteness.

Indeed, when *das Vorbei* ceases to be elusive, that is, when—always already—one begins to arm oneself against its complete indefiniteness by bringing measure to bear on the not-yet onto which one is thrown back in running up against death as possibility, then it ceases even to be future, becoming only a past measured from the present (the goneness of the no-longer-present). One says now: the past is what is gone, what is irretrievable, so that *das Vorbei* comes to name the past rather than the future. It is with precisely this gigantic ambiguity that the word occurs in Heidegger's lecture. One might well wonder whether the disappearance of the word in *Being and Time* does not have to do with precisely this ambiguity, that is, with the difficulty that one all too easily regards what is gone as the mere opposite of what is present, thus taking *das Vorbei* as an absence that would be only the privation of *die Gegenwart*. But death is a future that can never be present—that is, the task is to think death as absolute, as absolved from being determined by opposition to presence, as the most extreme limit of presence.

The past too is to be won back, thought in its "how" and not just as what is gone. It is to be thought by casting *das Vorbei* in(to) the future, casting oneself toward it, running ahead. In the language of Heidegger's lecture: the possibility of access to history is grounded in the possibility of being-futural. That, Heidegger says, "*is the first principle of hermeneutics*" (Z 26).

Without that casting, time is determined from the now of the present, from the "what" of the present rather than the "how" of the future, from what is present, from the now of the things with which it is presently concerned. Time becomes empty, becomes *langweilig*, a long and boring while that must be filled up with the ever new. Another suspending of time by time, by setting time out of time, by drawing out the now of presence, engaging it in what is present. Or, rather, a suspending of time by inserting into it a now of presence, a definite, carefully regulated, measurable time, almost a kind of space of time, an empty space that one cannot but seek to fill up. Yet, even in this interval, this time out, one keeps the clock running.

The lecture culminates in the assertion of the identity: Dasein is time. Or, in Heidegger's formulation: "Dasein, comprehended in its most extreme possibility of Being, *is time itself*, not *in* time" (Z 19). One could add: only because Dasein is time is there open to Dasein the authentic and inauthentic limiting of time, the suspending of time in a certain time out of time.

The lecture concludes by turning back to the initial question—What is time?—and making explicit the transformation that the question has undergone as a result of the analyses. It has become: Who is time? Then: Are we ourselves time? Then: Am I time? And finally: Am I my time? The transformation is also one by which a question of "what" becomes a question not only of "who" but of "how." This final turn exhibits the interplay of question and *Sache* that will prove methodologically distinctive in *Being and Time* and that effectively fills out the merely preliminary concept of phenomenology: formulation of the question leads into disclosure of *die Sache,* that disclosure, in turn, reflecting back upon the question so as to require its reformulation.

But what of the future already projected, the future from which there will have been a return, the future in the return from which the lecture text will have been written? To what extent will Heidegger in the 1924 lecture text already have written the two Divisions of *Being and Time* that will be published in 1927? To what extent will he also have begun writing the texts of those courses in which a certain torsion will, quite unobtrusively, begin twisting the project out of shape, in which the slippage of the project will begin coming into play, in which perhaps already, even if still almost imperceptibly, everything will have begun to get slippery.

The lecture culminates in the assertion of the identity: Dasein is time, time is Dasein. In *Being and Time* this identity will be opened up, difference inscribed in it; it is such difference that will not yet have been written in in Heidegger's writing of the lecture text. Indeed, he will insist in *Being and Time* that time is not anything other than Dasein; thus the identity will remain, as such, intact. But it will come to be expressed with a certain differentiation: *time is the meaning of the Being of Dasein.* The words thus inscribed, *meaning* and *Being,* serve to indicate what will come to mediate (I use this word cautiously, eraser in hand) the identity of time and Dasein. *Being and Time* will bring to the determination of the identity, on the one hand, an ontological reflection establishing the difference between Being and beings, hence, the difference between Dasein and the Being of Dasein (i.e., care); on the other hand, a significational reflection establishing the difference between a being (or Being) and its meaning (*Bedeutung* or, more broadly, *Sinn*), meaning as *das Woraufhin* of a certain operation of projective understanding. In the lecture these differences will not yet have been inscribed in the identity.

Time remains thus identical with my Dasein, with what could be called each individual Dasein, were it not that such a designation tends to neutralize the mineness, the ownness, of Dasein and its time, thus broaching the inauthentic suspending of time. Time, which will prove to be original dispersion, is dispersed among what could— granted the reservation—be called the multiplicity of individual Daseins. Time will not yet have been, within the identity, sufficiently differentiated from Dasein to function as a meaning-horizon not simply dispersed among Daseins. In the words of the lecture: "Insofar as time is ever mine, there are many times. Die *Zeit ist sinnlos*" (Z 26). It will have been (in this text) meaningless (*sinnlos*) because dispersed; it will be (in *Being and Time*) meaningless because it proves to be the meaning-horizon within which, from which, everything else becomes meaningful, comes to have meaning.

But it is from another future that Heidegger will have begun writing about understanding time (from) out of time. Taken in the most radical sense, such a project would involve understanding time without referring it to a being, without, for example, grounding it in a being. Indeed, in the project of *Being and Time*, time will be taken as that to which all beings are referred, as the meaning of Being (*Sinn vom Sein*)—hence as beyond Being (ἐπέκεινα τῆς οὐσίας), in the phrase that will recur in the texts immediately following *Being and Time* (GA 24: 400–402; GA 26: 237). The question will be: How is one to think together the character of time as beyond Being *and* its being brought back to a being, Dasein, with which it would be identical? A question of doubling and of return. Thus, the apparently simple identity of time and Dasein—their identity with one another, not their self-identity, which is anything but simple, proving even in the lecture to be subject to suspensions and interruptions—will prove to be extremely complex and recurrently questionable. Thus is anticipated in the lecture a twisting of the identity, the move beyond Being turning, as it were, against the move back to Dasein—preparing a certain twisting loose, a slippage, a separation that will no longer be merely differentiation.

(b)

Yet, *Being and Time* will meanwhile have confirmed the identity, establishing it in its open, more extended form: time is the meaning of the Being of Dasein.

The confirmation comes in and as the most decisive transition in the Second Division, the transition from those analyses that would prepare the basis for an originary interpretation of Dasein to that interpretation itself. The basis for the interpretation is the analysis of authentic care (of the authentic Being of Dasein, in which Dasein is disclosed to itself as a whole) *as* what Heidegger calls *vorlaufende Entschlossenheit.*[16] On this basis the originary interpretation then addresses the question of the *meaning* of care, that is, the question of the meaning of the Being of Dasein. It is to be a matter of unfolding this meaning from that originary mode of Dasein's self-disclosure that has been analyzed as *vorlaufende Entschlossenheit.*

Yet, what is meaning (*Sinn*)? What is being asked about in the question of meaning? The question of this question has in fact already been answered and, at the threshold of the transition to the originary interpretation, needs only to be recalled and supplemented. For in the preparatory analysis in the First Division, meaning was determined precisely as the "upon-which [*Woraufhin*] of the projection from which something becomes understandable as something" (SZ 151). That determination arose through the analysis of equipment (*Zeug*) in which it was demonstrated phe-

16. The Macquarrie-Robinson translation is: *anticipatory resoluteness.* If one is to use this translation, precautions must be taken to avoid understanding *anticipation* as *expecting* or *awaiting*, for Heidegger is careful to distinguish *Vorlaufen* from *Erwarten*, the latter designating a certain orientation toward the actualization of the possible in contrast to the comportment to possibility as such that is to be designated by *Vorlaufen* (cf. SZ 261f.). To translate *Entschlossenheit* as *resoluteness* is to lose both the essential connection with *Erschlossenheit* (*disclosedness*) and the sense of nonclosure that the word assumes when *Ent-* is taken as privative.

nomenologically that an item of equipment becomes understandable as such only in being projected upon a certain referential structure, only from that structure, which is also called significance (*Bedeutsamkeit*), worldhood (*Weltlichkeit*), or, more generally, meaning (*Sinn*). The meaning upon which understanding projects is equally that which makes it possible for the equipment to be what it is, to be just the sort of equipment it is. And so, when Heidegger, at the threshold of the decisive transition, recalls the earlier determination of meaning, he adds: "To expose the upon-which of a projection amounts to disclosing that which makes possible what has been disclosed" (SZ 324). Likewise, when at this stage he restates the earlier determination, he modifies the earlier statement to include a reference to making-possible: "Meaning signifies the upon-which of the primary projection from which something can be conceived [*begriffen*] in its possibility as that which it is." As if by way of explanation, he continues: "Projecting discloses possibilities, that is, that which makes possible [*solches, das ermöglicht*]" (SZ 324).

But what about this supplement by which meaning, the upon-which of understanding, becomes also that which makes possible what is projected, becomes the condition of its possibility? Is this perhaps too closely linked to the analysis of equipment? Is it certain that in projecting upon its own possibilities Dasein is projecting upon *conditions* of possibility, upon that which makes possible? Do possibilities make possible? Or, are they not, rather, precisely what is *made possible*? Does this conflation not, in turn, expose the analysis to the danger of drifting, more than Heidegger would ever have authorized, in the direction of a transcendental analysis? As mimesis always risks conflation with what it would double.

It is a matter of unfolding the meaning of care, that is, the upon-which of its projection, the upon-which of the projection that underlies the interpretation of Dasein in the existential analysis itself: "To set forth the meaning of care calls, then, for following up the projection that underlies and guides the originary existential interpretation of Dasein, following it up in such a way that in what is projected its upon-which becomes visible" (SZ 324). It would be a matter of retracing the projection of the Being of Dasein as care, drawing the projection out toward its upon-which, reversing in a sense the understanding of care from the upon-which that must have been implicitly operative, moving now from care to its upon-which. One cannot but wonder, still, whether Heidegger's introduction of a discourse of making-possible does not risk reducing the complex structure of this move, reducing it to a generalized regress to conditions of possibility.

Just as the move, the originary interpretation, is about to commence, Heidegger reinscribes the identity: "The meaning of the Being of Dasein is not something free-floating that is other than and 'outside of' itself [*ein freischwebendes Anderes und 'Ausserhalb' seiner selbst*] but rather is self-understanding Dasein itself" (SZ 325). The meaning of the Being of Dasein is just Dasein itself as originarily disclosed to itself. Since it is time that is about to be determined as the meaning of the Being of Dasein, the identity is the same as that put forth in the 1924 lecture, extended indeed, yet essentially intact.

Then, in the move, it is almost as though the reinscription of the identity had resolved the ambivalence of the move from care to its meaning, resolved it in favor of the discourse of making-possible. One cannot but wonder whether the determination of the upon-which as condition of possibility does not serve, in the end, to keep the identity intact, to insure that the meaning is drawn within the sphere of Dasein, that it not prove other and outside.

Indeed, when the originary interpretation finally proceeds, the resolution is almost fully in force. It is a matter of asking what makes possible (*ermöglicht*)—to take the first moment—authentic Being-toward-death, i.e., *Vorlaufen*. Projecting upon death as its ownmost possibility, sustaining that possibility as possibility, thus understanding itself from that possibility—in both moments of the projection (in both moments at once, together, joined by a certain sliding of the *itself*) Dasein comes toward itself in its ownmost possibility.[17] What makes this possible? Heidegger's answer carries out the transition:

17. Heidegger's analysis of death is discussed in some detail in chapter 5. On the structure of projective understanding, see *Delimitations*, chap. 9.

Suchlike is possible only in that Dasein *can, in general,* come toward itself [*auf sich zukommen*] in its ownmost possibility and sustain the possibility in thus letting itself come toward itself—that is, exists. This letting-itself-*come-toward*-itself, sustaining the distinctive possibility, is the originary phenomenon of the *future* [*Zukunft*]. (SZ 325)

The transition is much the same with respect to the other two moments. For Dasein to take over Being-guilty, that is, to take over thrownness, signifies its being authentically as it always already was (*wie es je schon war, eigentlich sein*). Its being as it always already was is its *Gewesen*—that is, *Gewesenheit*[18] is what makes the second moment of (authentic) care possible. In turn, the third moment, the disclosure of the situation, thus opening the encounter with what is present in the environing world, is only possible in a presenting of these beings. Such presenting (*Gegenwärtigen*) is the originary phenomenon of the present (*Gegenwart*).

The transition is essentially completed, though it will still be necessary to broaden the move by showing that the phenomena just delimited constitute the meaning not just of authentic care but of care as such; and to consolidate what has been attained by the transition, delimiting in a rigorous manner that time that has proven to be the meaning of care. Beyond this transition—the most decisive in the Second Division—and the broadening and consolidation still needed, it will be primarily only a matter of return from this originary order to an originary interpretation of phenomena that are not of its order. From the point of view of the project of fundamental ontology, one could even say that this transition is the most decisive in the entire published part of *Being and Time,* for it is in this transition—and, within the text as published, *only* here—that the move is made from Being to the meaning of Being, the move that, especially after 1930, Heidegger will think more and more as an overcoming of metaphysics, as a transgressive move.

The consolidation begins: in their unity the three phenomena reached by the transition (*Zukunft, Gewesenheit, Gegenwart*) constitute *temporality:*

18. In view of the distinction on which Heidegger insists between *Gewesenheit* and the ordinary German word for past, *Vergangenheit,* it is difficult to translate the former otherwise than by recourse to some neologism such as "beenness."

Coming back to itself futurally, resoluteness brings itself into the situation in making present. Beenness [*Gewesenheit*] arises from the future, and in such a way that the been (or better, beening) future [*die gewesene (besser gewesende) Zukunft*] releases from itself the present. This phenomenon, which has the unity of a future that makes present as beening, we call temporality [*Dies dergestalt als gewesend-gegenwärtigende Zukunft einheitliche Phänomen nennen wir die Zeitlichkeit*]. (SZ 326)

Straining thus the resources of the languages, the formulation reminds one of the *apologia* that Heidegger has given in advance for the harshness of expression: for such analyses as are required of fundamental ontology, "there are lacking not only most of the words but, above all, the 'grammar' " (SZ 39).

Broadening the scope of the analysis to care as such, Heidegger proceeds, finally, to a series of determinations of temporality. First: "Temporality 'is' not a *being* at all. It is not, but it *temporalizes* itself [*zeitigt sich*]" (SZ 328). In this statement the quotation marks serve to mark the bind that the statement cannot escape: it *must be said* that temporality *is* ("We cannot avoid saying: 'Temporality "is"—the meaning of care.' "); and yet, it *cannot be said* that it *is*, since it is not a being at all. Heidegger defers explaining the necessity of the "is" until after "the idea of Being" has been clarified—that is, he defers it to the never published Third Division. The bind will remain in force, threatening Heidegger's discourse, turning it against itself. It threatens also the identity that was reinscribed at the threshold of the decisive transition. The question is—writing now without the proliferation of marks, which serve to mark the bind without in the least undoing it: How can temporality be identical with that being called Dasein if it is not a being at all? If it is not a being at all, if it is not, then how can it avoid being other than and outside of that being called Dasein? Can temporality be both the beyond of Being and the meaning of the Being of a being?

The second determination proceeds from the specific characters of the three originary phenomena that constitute temporality, their characters as "toward-oneself," "back to," and "alongside," respectively. These characters serve to make temporality manifest as "*das* ἐκστατικόν *schlechthin.*" Hence the determination, its import marked by italics, the formulation echoing Hegel, preparing that scene in which Hegel will finally appear near the end of the Second Division (§82): "*Temporality is the originary 'outside-itself' in and for itself* [*Zeitlichkeit ist das ursprüngliche 'Ausser-sich' an und für sich*]" (SZ 329). The three phenomena, future, beenness, and present, are thus to be called the *ecstases* of temporality.

In the discourse of ecstasis, commencing here at the heart of *Being and Time*, the binds will multiply, twisting the discourse in ways that will make it ever more questionable and yet that will allow it to begin to say what previous discourse, shaped by an orientation ontologically insufficient, could never have said.

The *is* must again be erased: temporality, *if it were a being*, would be the originary "outside-itself" in and for itself. *In and for itself*—can temporality be either? much less both? Can it be *an sich* without being substance? Can it be *für sich* without being subject? Can it be *an und für sich* without being substance appropriated to subject, that is, *aufgehoben?* What kind of displacement would already have to have been announced in "the originary outside-itself" in order for the determination of temporality as in and for itself not to re-inscribe Heidegger's discourse in the ontology of *Vorhandensein?*

What, then, about this *outside,* this being—but not being—outside itself? Is it not most remarkable that a discourse seemingly so determined by reference to space is brought into play at the point where it is precisely a matter of expressing the constitution of originary time? Is the spatial orientation of such language an acci-dent, as Heidegger himself asked well in advance of the present context?[19] Could the reference to space have been eliminated and the discourse replaced by one more proper to time? Would it not seem even that the discourse on temporality would have to remain uncontaminated by spatial meanings in order for the goal of funda-

19. "Is it an accident that proximally and for the most part significations are 'worldly', sketched out beforehand by the significance of the world, that they are indeed often predominantly 'spatial'? Or is this 'fact' existentially-ontologically neces-sary? And why?" (SZ 166). "The phenomenon of Dasein's dissemination in space is seen, for example, in the fact that all languages are shaped primarily by spatial meanings. This phenomenon can be first explained only when the metaphysical problem of space is posed, a problem that first becomes visible after we have gone through the problem of temporality (radically put, this is the metontology of spatial-ity . . .)" (GA 26: 174).

mental ontology to be attainable, in order for temporality to be exhibited as the meaning of Being and as founding, most notably in this regard, Dasein's spatiality?

And yet, space, long since subordinated to world and hence even more rigorously to temporality, *does in fact return* at the very heart of *Being and Time;* it does in fact return in metaphorized form at the very point where it is a matter of expressing the constitution of temporality.

Outside of temporality there would be (if it were a being): temporality. Not just time out(side) of time, time out, but time become temporality precisely in being (if it *were* at all) this outside-itself, this exceeding of itself, this standing out beyond itself. But what of this *itself?* What of the itself of something so utterly improper that its very being (if it were a being) would consist in its exceeding itself? Could one ever determine an *itself* of something that is originarily outside itself? Heidegger insists indeed that the *itself* is not that of a (determinate) being: temporality is not, prior to the ecstases, "a being that first emerges from *itself,* but rather its essence is temporalizing [*Zeitigung*] in the unity of the ecstases" (SZ 329). The question that remains (and that will prove decisive in the slippage of the project in the courses immediately following the publication of *Being and Time*)[20] is: How and where is the unity of the ecstases to be marked?

Drawing the distinction, as in the 1924 lecture, between time as ordinarily conceived and originary time, i.e., temporality, referring also to a certain primacy of the future in the temporalizing of the ecstases, Heidegger proceeds to the last of the determinations of temporality, namely, its determination as *finite*. That time is finite does not signify merely that time somehow stops (for one, at one's death, though going on for others, after one's death). Dissociating the determination from the ordinary conception of time that such a supposition would have presupposed, Heidegger links the finitude of temporality to the ecstatic character of the future, specifically to the peculiar negativity of that most extreme possibility upon which one openly projects in authentic care: death as unsurpassable, as

20. This will be discussed in chap. 4.

taking away all possibilities. That ecstatical character that renders temporality finite consists in a certain closing: "The ecstatical character of the originary future consists in this: that it closes Dasein's being-able-to-be [*dass sie das Seinkönnen schliesst*], that is, is itself closed . . ." (SZ 330). The import of the introduction here of closure is to be measured in reference to the value accorded to openness in the discourse of *Entschlossenheit* (the *Ent-* being read at least also, if not exclusively, as privative): as authentic disclosedness it is the most radical openness of Dasein to itself, to others, and to the world. In the determination of temporality as finite, Heidegger is thus installing at the very heart, as it were, of radical openness, an originary closure, which, furthermore, is itself closed—the negativity of self-concealing concealment, λήθη at the heart of ἀλήθεια.

(c)

Afterward it is a matter of return. After the decisive transition to temporality, it could only be a matter of return from that most originary level, the most originary, at least, reached in the published Divisions of *Being and Time*. There are three such returns, and their execution occupies, in turn, the three final chapters of the Second Division. The first is a return to the level of everydayness that was so extensively analyzed in the First Division, a return that would take up again (*wiederholen*) the earlier analyses, but now in their temporal meaning. The return is to have a double effect on the earlier analyses: on the one hand, it is to make those analyses clearer, eliminating (*aufheben*) whatever seemed accidental and arbitrary in them, thus completing them, rounding them out; and yet, on the other hand, the return is to dispel fully the apparent obviousness (*die scheinbare 'Selbstverständlichkeit'*) of those earlier analyses, thus reopening them, removing whatever would have served to close them off. At the same time, the return is also to confirm (*bewähren*) what has been established through the transition to temporality, to confirm it by reference to those essential structures of Dasein's constitution to which the return is made. And yet, it will not be a matter only of confirming subsequently and externally something already definitively established; for, through the return, "the problematic contained in temporality" is to come to light (SZ 332). The return will also double back upon that from which it returns.

Likewise with the other two returns. The return to the question of the self will bring about a more originary insight into the structure of Dasein's temporalizing as historicality (*Geschichtlichkeit*). The final return, too, the return to that time *in* which beings within the world can occur, to the temporal character of such beings—the character that Heidegger calls *Innerzeitigkeit* (within-time-ness)—is to demonstrate that such time "arises from an essential kind of temporalizing of originary temporality" (SZ 333). Not only does this return thus double back disclosively upon the originary temporality from which it returns, but also it shows that the time to which it turns is a genuine phenomenon of time and not, as Bergson would have it, a turning of time into space.

And yet, will space—even if metaphorized—ever cease to return in Heidegger's analyses? Will it not already have returned in the very designation *Innerzeitigkeit*? Can the *within* be thought without space?

Let me concentrate on this final return. Not only because it combines certain elements of the other two returns, but also because it is, most purely, a return from time to time, most decisively a doubling of the time from which it returns. To say nothing of the fact that it is with this return that *Being and Time*—all of it that Heidegger was ever to publish—stops.

The return is to what Heidegger calls *die besorgte Zeit.* This time of concern, to translate it thus, is, on the one hand, the time that belongs to the sphere of concern; it is the time of Dasein's concernful, circumspective dealings with the ready-to-hand (*das Zuhandene*) within the world, the time in which those beings are *innerzeitlich.* On the other hand, it is the time with which Dasein can be concerned, to which Dasein's concern can be directed, the time with which Dasein reckons.

It is a matter, then, of retracing, at the level of existential analysis, the return from originary time to the time of concern, that is, of determining how, in its essential structure, the time of concern arises from temporality, how time arises out of time. It will not go unnoticed that such a discourse on constitutive genesis will from the outset have been a discourse linked—even if metaphorically—to that very time that the genesis would serve to constitute. For instance, by the very language of genesis. To say nothing of the space of a discourse that would draw time out of time.

As in the other returns in which temporality is worked out, it is a matter, as Heidegger himself says, of getting "for the first time a relentless insight into the entanglements [*Verwicklungen*] of an originary ontology of Dasein" (SZ 333).

Nonetheless, the character of the constitutive genesis that the final return would retrace can be stated simply and at once: *the time of concern is self-interpreted temporality.*

Let me outline as directly as possible the structure of this constitutive self-interpretation and the structural moments of the time of concern that is thus constituted. As directly as possible—that is, assuming the narrative of the existential analysis, with only minimal interruptions.

In the world of concern Dasein deals circumspectively with the things of this world,[21] the ready-to-hand, interpreting them from the meaning that they are understood to have within the world, speaking of them, expressing in language the articulation of that meaning. Yet, in interpreting these things, in speaking of them as they are encountered circumspectively within the world, Dasein also interprets and expresses its own being-alongside those things; in interpreting them it interprets also itself, indeed in such a way that this self-interpretation is integral to the interpretation of the things of concern. As soon as one says "Now I need that tool over there," one has expressed one's being-alongside the things of con-

---

21. In *Being and Time* Heidegger systematically avoids the word *Ding* (thing) on the ground that "in addressing these beings as 'things' (*res*), one tacitly anticipates their ontological character," taking it for granted in all its indefiniteness, taking for granted, in the end, the determination handed down by the ontology of *Vorhandenheit* rather than reopening the question of the ontological character of what would otherwise have been called things (SZ 67f.). In later texts, on the other hand, he comes to use the word so decisively that it even serves to entitle some of those texts, for example, *Die Frage nach dem Ding* (*Vorlesung* presented in 1935–36) and "Das Ding" (*Vortrag* first presented in 1950). The story of this return of *das Ding* remains to be told.

cern, expressed it in the *over there* and in that *now* when one is to do something.

Such self-interpretation Heidegger refers back to that which makes it possible, to the condition of its possibility: "And this, in turn, is possible only because—in itself ecstatically open—it is for itself always already disclosed . . . (SZ 408). Always already disclosed to itself, Dasein can then disclose itself interpretively, can interpret itself, in its dealings with the things of concern.

Let me interrupt in order to note that here there is virtually the rigorous order of an a priori, which, as Heidegger himself insisted, is unthinkable apart from time[22]—hence another entanglement. To note also the juxtaposition: *in itself* ecstatically open—*for itself* always already disclosed. One suspects that Hegel's role is not limited to that scene that Heidegger makes for him and with him in the penultimate section of Division Two.

It is as temporality that Dasein would be ecstatically open and would be always already disclosed to itself. Thus, if the identity of Dasein and originary time is again brought into play, one may say that temporality is both that which interprets and that which is interpreted—that is, that what underlies and is originarily in play in Dasein's self-interpretation is a self-interpretation of temporality. And yet, the scene of this self-interpretation—at least (in that phrase that orients so many of Heidegger's analyses) proximally and for the most part (*zunächst und zumeist*)—is the world of concern. Temporality as it comes to be interpreted in its appearance on this scene is what is called and recognized as time. Such time, the time of concern, is recognizable and familiar, even if the origin that temporalizes itself therein (*der in ihr sich zeitigende Ursprung*) remains quite unknown (SZ 408).

In order to determine the character of the time of concern, it is

22. This is most directly and rigorously stated in *The Basic Problems of Phenomenology:* "It is only because ontological propositions are temporal propositions [*temporale Sätze*] that they can and must be *a priori propositions*" (GA 24: 461). In his discussion of the a priori within the context of phenomenology (in *History of the Concept of Time*), Heidegger stresses a certain entanglement: the clarification of the sense of the a priori "presupposes the understanding of what we are seeking: *time.*" He adds: "The a priori to something is that which already always is the earlier" (GA 20: 99ff.).

necessary to consider, first, the specific mode of temporality that interprets itself in this instance and, second, the way in which it here interprets itself. The mode of temporalizing of temporality that is involved here in self-interpretation is that mode that, in the earlier return to everydayness, was identified as the temporality of circumspective concern. In this mode temporality temporalizes as a presenting (*Gegenwärtigen*) that awaits (*gewärtigen*) and retains (*behalten*). It is an awaiting, which is toward the system of involvements; a retaining of what is thus involved, the equipment; and a presenting in such a way that Dasein is absorbed in its equipmental world, engaged with the ready-to-hand (SZ 352ff.). How, then, does this mode of temporalizing get interpreted? What is the horizon, the assemblage of meanings, within which it gets interpreted and expressed? The horizon can only be that one that serves for all interpretation in everyday concern, namely, the world; Dasein interprets its temporality from the world, in connection with those things and events of concern within the world. Specifically, Dasein interprets the present (i.e., presenting) as a *now, that* . . . ; the future (i.e., awaiting) as a *then, when* . . . ; and beenness (i.e., retaining) as a *formerly, when.* . . .[23] A typical example: *Now that* one reaches for the hammer, so that the shoes will be finished *then when* someone comes for them, one finds it as it was *formerly when* one used it for a similar purpose. Such an interpretation is called an assigning of time (*Zeitangabe*): Dasein assigns its originary time (i.e., temporality) to its factical Being-in-the-world, *and,* by bringing time into the world, Dasein gives time to itself, gives it to itself as something with which it can be concerned, can reckon. The interpretation is also called a dating: "Interpreted time has always already been given a dating on the basis of those beings that are encountered in the disclosedness of the there [*Da*]: now that—the door slams; now that—my book is missing, and so forth" (SZ 408). Hence, the time of concern has the structure of *datability:* "Every 'then,' however, is, *as such,* a 'then, when . . .'; every 'formerly' is a 'formerly, when . . .';

23. It should be clear that, here as well as in the syntactically similar citation below, the ellipses do not mark an omission of words from Heidegger's text but rather, occurring in that text, mark the omission of the specific worldly connections, that is, of precisely what Heidegger is engaged in showing can *not* be omitted.

every 'now' is a 'now that. . . .' We call this seemingly obvious relational structure of the 'now,' the 'formerly,' and the 'then' datability" (SZ 407). This is the first of the structural moments of the time of concern.

The second moment is broached as follows: "If awaiting, which understands itself in the 'then,' interprets itself and thereby, as presenting, understands that which it awaits on the basis of its 'now,' then in the assigning of the 'then' there already lies the 'and now not yet' (SZ 409). Here again it is a matter of the self-interpretation of temporality within the world of concern. In this self-interpretation, awaiting (the future ecstasis) interprets itself as *then, when* . . . ; and presenting (the present ecstasis) interprets itself as *now, that.* . . . Yet, in the temporalizing of temporality there is—in a way that will not remain unproblematic, that will even interrupt what is to be said of time—a unity among the ecstases, a unity that, in the return to the question of the self, has been worked out as Dasein's being ecstatically stretched along (*ekstatische Erstrecktheit*) between birth and death (SZ 374). Thus, in the self-interpretation of temporality, the unity of the ecstases, Dasein's connectedness, *also* gets interpreted. In the assigning of time, this connection is also assigned: "In the assigning of the 'then' there already lies the 'and now not yet.'" That is, there is an assigning of an *until then*, an *in-between*, a *during*, which, in turn, can be articulated through the assignment of additional *thens*. This *in-between*, this duration, that belongs to time as interpreted constitutes its character as *spanned:* "This duration [*Dauern*] is, in turn, the time that is manifest in the self-interpreting of temporality; in concern this time thus gets understood unthematically as a 'span'" (SZ 409). This is the second of the structural moments of the time of concern.

The third structural moment lies in the *public* character of the time of concern. Since that world in which time is assigned is never merely Dasein's own but rather a world in which one is always *with* others, since, then, it is a public world, the time assigned in it will likewise have a certain public character. However, the full public character of time is determined by something further: that there is a privileged way of dating, within which all other dating occurs. This privileged dating originates in response to Dasein's thrownness, specifically, to Dasein's having been delivered over to the need for sight, hence, for light; also to the alternation between day, which gives the possibility of sight, and night, which takes away that possibility. Thus, Heidegger: "In its thrownness Dasein has been delivered over to the alternation of day and night. Day with its brightness grants the possibility of sight; night takes this away" (SZ 412). The point is that Dasein assigns time in terms of the possibility of sight, that is, in terms of what grants and withdraws that possibility, that is, in terms of the rising and setting of the *sun.* Thus arises the "most natural" measure of time, the *day;* this span, in turn, gets divided up, though its division is no mere quantification but rather a dating in terms of "the journeying sun." Such a dating is distinctively public: it introduces a publicly available measure, the sun, a "natural clock," which then motivates the production of clocks in the usual sense.

It is thus that Dasein's reckoning with time is, first of all, neither environmental nor mathematical but rather astronomical, solar, taking its measure from the sky.

And so Dasein will say: "Then—when it dawns—it is time for one's daily work" (SZ 414). Thus, the time of concern, first taking its measure from the sky, is also worldly. In each of its interpreted ecstases, as a *then,* a *now,* a *formerly,* it is a time *for* something, a time that is appropriate or not appropriate for something. Since, in turn, every such *for which* occurs within a referential complex oriented finally to what Heidegger calls a *Worumwillen* (a for-the-sake-of-which), time is bound up with significance, that is, with the worldhood of the world. The time of concern has a worldly character; it is, says Heidegger, "world-time." This character constitutes the fourth (and last) of the structural moments.

Thus is the time of concern constituted in and through the self-interpretation of temporality, constituted as datable, spanned, public, and worldly.

Let me simply mention how Heidegger goes on to retrace the way in which still another time, the now-time of the ordinary conception, arises from the time of concern; how he refers to the peculiar comportment involved in the use of clocks as decisive for this further removal of time from its origin; how in this removal the ecstatic character of time, even as interpreted, gets levelled off so that time is conceived then as a mere sequence of nows; how time also is removed from Dasein, infinitized; and how, once time has been severed from what would be called the subject, there can then arise the problem of explaining the way in which the subject can be in time, the way in which spirit can fall into time.

The scene is thus set for the encounter with Hegel. On that scene it cannot but be a matter of undoing the genesis that has just been retraced, retaining from it only a single word, or, rather, a double, a phantom, a spirit of that word, marked by placing it in quotation marks: " 'Spirit' ['*Geist*'] does not first fall into time, but rather it *exists as* the originary *temporalizing* of temporality" (SZ 436). And yet, this is not nothing, this spirit of spirit. Even though *Being and Time* then moves quickly to its end or, rather, stops by exploding into questions, fragmenting into questions.

For originary time would double itself in the time of concern and then eventually redouble itself into the now-time of the ordinary conception. As though there were an *itself* of originary time, as though temporality were not originary *outside-itself*, hence both presupposing and disrupting the *itself*, an originary that would be—if it were at all—the displacement of origin. Originary time will always already (in an order no longer detachable from time) have begun to double itself, will always already have been contaminated by an outside, drifting toward something like the time of concern, perhaps even toward the now-time of its self-concealment. Such doubling and contamination will always already have commenced when the project of fundamental ontology turns toward originary time for the sake of redetermining the meaning of Being. If time is out, then the project will already have run out of time before the question of the *Temporalität* of Being can be broached.

(d)

There is eventually another lecture on time. It comes nearly forty years after the lecture in Marburg. It would be difficult to overestimate the complexity of the shifts that occur even between *Being and Time* and this later lecture "Time and Being." And yet, the very title, reversing that of the 1927 text, makes it imperative to address those shifts, even if without fully gauging their complexity. Even more so if one recalls that the title "Time and Being" was originally proposed for the crucial Third Division of *Being and Time* that was never to appear.

Let me mark, then, two shifts, mark them as directly as possible and yet in such a way as to begin opening the space in which their complexity unfolds.

In *Being and Time,* at the point where Heidegger has just sketched, but not yet undertaken, the return from temporality to everydayness, the self, and the time of concern, he indicates that even after these further tasks are carried out there will remain still a further venture. The temporal analysis of Dasein will remain incomplete and fraught with obscurities as long as the idea of Being in general (*Idee von Sein überhaupt*) has not been clarified, as long as the *is* of everything of which we say that *it is* has not been illuminated (SZ 333). It is toward this same task that Heidegger orients the questions that conclude the Second Division of *Being and Time:* "Does a way lead from originary *time* to the meaning of *Being*? Does *time* itself manifest itself as the horizon of *Being*?" (SZ 437). This is not, however, the question of "Time and Being." In place of the question of the *es ist*, the lecture takes up the question of the *es gibt.* This is the first of the shifts.

It is closely linked to the other shift. Whereas the 1924 lecture was addressed to the identity of time and Dasein, the identity that came to be extended yet preserved in the published Divisions of *Being and Time*, the later lecture is addressed to the question of time and *Ereignis.* This shift shows that the beyond of Being (the ἐπέκεινα τῆς οὐσίας, thought initially—and, in a sense, still—as time) is no longer to be thought by being brought back to a being, Dasein, with which it would be identical. The move beyond Being has, to this extent, been twisted loose from the return to a being. Indeed, in *Being and Time* it *should* have been twisted, to an extent, free in the transition that is addressed by those final questions: from originary time to the meaning of Being, from *Zeitlichkeit* to *Temporalität.*

Thus, in place of the identity of time and Dasein, which in *Being and Time* was expanded into the series time-meaning (of)-Being (of)-Dasein, "Time and Being" undertakes to say another series. And though this text says the series in many ways—in sayings that cannot in the text remain unproblematic, that must also somehow be unsaid—let me write it thus: time-clearing-*Ereignis*.

As in the 1924 lecture and in *Being and Time*, time in its originary guise is to be differentiated from time in the disguise of the ordinary conception, time as a sequence of nows. The differentiation turns now on the difference between presence (*Anwesenheit*) and present (*Gegenwart*): time proper (the proper of time: *das Eigene der Zeit*) is to be determined by reference to presence, which does not simply exclude what has been and what is to come, in contrast to the now-time determined by the present (SD 11). In an initial formulation: time as constantly passing remains as time, does not disappear, that is, it has a certain presence that is not reducible to that of the present. It has a certain presence in something like the sense in which one speaks of the presence of guests (SD 11): *die Zeit anwest.* As such, however, it is determined by Being as presence, no less than, as the earlier texts would have it, Being is determined by time. There will no longer be a simple ordering by which time would be, irreversibly, the horizon for the understanding of Being, that is, the meaning of Being. In a sense there will perhaps never have been any such ordering; for even in *Being and Time* time as the meaning of the Being of Dasein proved to be nothing different from the Being of Dasein, nor even from Dasein itself.

In "Time and Being" the differentiation does not proceed by drawing time back toward an identity with Dasein. It would no longer be even a phantom of that regress to the subject that during the Marburg period Heidegger regarded as recurring throughout the history of metaphysics. Now time is to be thought in the direction of the clearing; it is to be thought out toward the clearing as an outside that would no longer be an outside-itself. Time out—in the clearing. Time allowed to echo in the open enclosure of the clearing.

In the course of "Time and Being" Heidegger recalls the old identity: philosophy has always linked man and time. Now Heidegger says that man can be man only insofar as he stands within (*innesteht*) that time thought out as the clearing. No doubt there is more to be said: in the seminar devoted to the lecture "Time and Being," Heidegger says that in the lecture "the role of the essence of man with respect to the clearing of Being remains deliberately left out [*ausgespart*]" (SD 30); likewise with the relation between man and Being, which is not expressly discussed, even though "it belongs essentially to every step of the question of Being" (SD 37). Nonetheless, despite all retrospective supplements, Heidegger does *in fact* venture in the lecture to think time, Being, and the clearing *without* developing the reference to *man*. Such a venture would have been simply unthinkable in *Being and Time*.

In the lecture time is not other than the clearing but rather, in being differentiated from now-time, is thought out toward the clearing. Indeed much of the lecture is devoted to naming and thinking time as the clearing, as the open (*das Offene*), as the clearing in which what Heidegger calls *der Zeit-raum* opens up—*Zeit-raum* neither in its usual sense as an interval of time nor as some mixture of time and space; but rather as a prespatial *Ortschaft* that would first grant space in the usual sense, *even though*—one should add—it is precisely such space (*der uns gewöhnlich bekannten Raum*) that gets metaphorized in all these namings, returning thus to that from which it would originate.

There are still other names that serve for thinking time out toward the clearing. For example, the four-dimensional extending (*Reichen*), in which is most directly transformed what *Being and Time* called ecstatical temporality (with its three ecstases *and* their unity).

Yet if what I am calling time out toward the clearing is said in many ways in the lecture, that which the lecture ventures finally to say can, it seems, not be said otherwise. Or, rather, as soon as it is named *Ereignis*, one has already named it otherwise, already represented it as *something present* (SD 20). Even if one were somehow to elude this trap, going on then to formulate the decisive question, the question that philosophy will always formulate, the question "What is *Ereignis?*"—one will only have stumbled on into another trap. For in asking about the "what," about the essential Being of *Ereignis*, one asks about that which is now only to be determined from *Ereignis*, almost as if one wanted to derive the source from the stream (*den Quell aus dem Strom herleiten*) (SD 20–21, 24).

What remains, then, to be said this side of the traps? Heidegger: "Only this: *Das Ereignis ereignet*" (SD 24). Yet even then, having thus said *Ereignis,* Heidegger cannot but conclude the lecture with a reference to the insufficiency of the saying: "It has spoken only in declarative propositions [*nur in Aussagesätzen*]" (SD 25).

Indeed, the difficulty, the insufficiency, the traps involved in saying what the lecture ventures to think and to say do not emerge only at the end when it is *Ereignis* that is to be said; rather, from the very outset Heidegger explicitly calls attention to the peculiar danger to which the saying is exposed. For example, the danger that immediate intelligibility (*unmittelbare Verständlichkeit*) will be demanded of it, a danger against which Heidegger takes precautions by means of his introductory references to Klee's painting, Trakl's poetry, and Heisenberg's physics; also by way of the advice that he gives his listeners at the end of that introduction: "It is a matter not of listening to a series of declarative propositions but rather of following the path of a showing" (SD 2). And on that path, long before *Ereignis* comes to be said, the difficulty of saying is brought explicitly to attention: for example, that in thinking the threefold extending of time, one cannot say—and yet, somehow must say in order to break with the ordinary conception—that the future, beenness, and the present (*Gegenwart*) are at once present ('*zugleich*' *vorhanden*) (SD 14).

What is to be said, then, of such a way of saying? What is to be said after one has followed this path of showing?

It is a way that takes up again (*wiederholen*) the saying of Parmenides ἔστι γὰρ εἶναι, that resays it as *Es gibt Sein* (SD 8). It is a way that would say the *Geben* by saying the clearing-concealing extension (*lichtendverbergende Reichen*) that is also the *Geben* of *Es gibt Zeit* (SD 16); but that cannot say it without also withdrawing that saying, refusing, for example, to say that the three extendings of time are at the same time or that they are present. It is a way that leads on to a saying of the *Es* of the *Es gibt,* which names *Ereignis* and yet cannot do so without also withdrawing from the representation that would have turned what would be named *Ereignis* into something present. It is a way that leads on to the question "What is *Ereignis?*" only to withdraw it, referring it back to philosophy, from the beyond of Being back to Being, maintaining thus the differentiation, prohibiting all talk of *Sein als Ereignis,* granting a withdrawal of *Ereignis* from *Sein*. And so: "*Das Ereignis ist weder, noch gibt es das Ereignis*"—or, rather, more precisely, one is *not to say* either the one or the other, either the *es ist* or the *es gibt*. One is to say only: *das Ereignis ereignet;* to recall then perhaps another ancient name, reinscribing it as ἀ-λήθεια; and then, finally, to unsay even these sayings, to unsay all that the lecture would have been able to say "only in declarative propositions" (SD 24f.).

On this way the unsaying, the withdrawal of saying, is a way of granting the withdrawal of *die Sache,* its withdrawal from Being, from presence, from philosophy. The unsaying is a way of saying— while unsaying—*Entzug.*

The way is that of a saying that also knows (in an unheard-of way) how not to say.

Heidegger advises that one follow the way.

And yet, a certain differentiation needs to be observed. One may follow the way in such a way that the saying/unsaying would fall away, finally, in favor of a new saying. The lecture broaches such a way of following the way (though without quite suppressing all resistance to such a way), broaches it in the words that immediately follow the saying *das Ereignis ereignet: Damit sagen wir vom Selben her auf das Selbe zu das Selbe.* In the Zähringen seminar, likewise attending to the echo of the Parmenidean ἔστι γὰρ εἶναι, Heidegger calls such saying: tautological thinking (S 137).

Or, one may follow the way in such a way that the unsaying remains in play, that is, in such a way that it will always be necessary to continue unsaying, in the face of the same, the difference that saying opens, the difference between, on the one hand, what would be originary (were it not the very withdrawal of origin) and everything nonoriginary to which the saying of the originary cannot but return.

Does Heidegger decide between these alternatives? Are they simply alternatives? Is it not remarkable that "Time and Being," issuing in tautology (*das Ereignis ereignet*), continues on to a final unsaying of all that has been said? And that the Zähringen seminar, declaring tautological thinking, sounds also the return toward Being?[24]

24. See above, chap. 1 (d).

Never, it seems, does it simply cease being a matter of unsaying and of return.

And yet, at the beginning of "Time and Being" Heidegger's proposal is "to think Being without beings" (SD 2), that is, without determining Being from beings, without granting—and, hence, also having to unsay—a return of the thinking of Being to beings. Heidegger insists, even, that without such thinking of Being without beings "there is no longer any possibility of bringing genuinely into view the Being of what today *is* all around the globe" (SD 2). Only a return, then, *après coup*, from a rigorously a priori, a return that one would not be called upon to unsay.

The formula recurs very near the end of "Time and Being," as the demand to think Being without looking back to metaphysics: "To think Being without beings means: to think Being without looking back to metaphysics [*ohne Rücksicht auf die Metaphysik*]. But such a look back governs also the intention to overcome metaphysics. Therefore, it is a matter of letting go of the overcoming and of abandoning [*überlassen*] metaphysics to itself (SD 25). Heidegger, it seems—here, at least—would have it be a matter of proclaiming the end of metaphysics, the end of the history of Being (see SD 44), so that if any overcoming were still to be required it would be, not an overcoming of metaphysics, but a coming over to a saying of *Ereignis* from out of and in regard to itself (Heidegger says: "*um Es aus ihm her auf Es zu*"—SD 25). And—most remarkably—it would be a matter of "unrelentingly overcoming the obstacles that easily make such saying insufficient" (SD 25).

Is it a matter of obstacles, as though one could, finally, erase the entire text except for—and for the sake of—*das Ereignis ereignet*, finally even erasing these final words? For the sake, finally, of *die Sache*? Or—perhaps—in order to wait in silence? Would such a final suppression of all return lead to tautological thinking? Would one thus assume the task of thinking at the end of metaphysics? Or would it seal—or, rather, threaten to seal—the exhaustion of thinking?

THREE

Twisting Free—
Being to an Extent Sensible

Suspending exorbitant tautology, holding it in suspense, deferring it, one could, then, open a space of return. Of the return from Being and its beyond, the return to beings, which at the same time would be the return *of* Being and its beyond, of their determination, to beings, to what metaphysics has always thought as the sensible. One might, then, look back to metaphysics, to its beginning, listening to a word with which the Greeks named a mixing of Being and beings, recalling what Heidegger himself says of τὸ καλόν:

> The beautiful is an element that is disparate in itself [*dieses in sich Gegenwendige*]; it grants entry into immediate sensible shining [*Sinnenschein*] and thereby at the same time soars toward Being; it is both captivating and liberating. Hence, it is the beautiful that snatches us from oblivion of Being and grants the view upon Being. (N I 227f.)

One might, then, set what is to be said within the orbit of one of the words with which Plato undertook to say the beautiful, one to which Heidegger has paid special attention, the word τὸ ἐκφανέστατον, in German, *das Hervorscheinendste*, in English, the most radiant, that which most shines forth.[1] The beautiful would be, then, the way in which Being shines forth in the midst of the sensible.[2]

(a)

Twisting free—a quotation, of course, from a text by Heidegger, indeed from that text on Nietzsche just cited, or rather, from David

---

1. *Phaedrus* 250 d. Heidegger, *Nietzsche* I 227f.
2. I have discussed this reading in its Platonic context in *Being and Logos: The Way of Platonic Dialogue* (Atlantic Highlands: Humanities Press, 1986), 153–159.

Krell's translation of that text. The translation, in this particular instance the translation of *Herausdrehung* as *twisting free,* is not straightforward. It twists Heidegger's text, resituating it within a metaphorics that in English is more seminal. It is thus a translation that is both multiparous and provocative, as I hope to be able to show. It is a translation that, in the most rigorous sense, does what it says, a translation that, to just the extent appropriate, twists free of its original.

The phrase quoted occurs near the end of Heidegger's course "The Will to Power as Art" (1936–37). The context is Heidegger's reading of Nietzsche's story of "How the 'True World' Finally Became a Fable."[3] Recall the story: it is a story of how truth drifts away to such an extent as finally to become itself just a story—indeed, in just over a page of *The Twilight of the Idols.* Recall, too, how Heidegger reads this very remarkable text, how he undertakes to determine just what is to be understood by Nietzsche's *Umdrehung (oder Überwindung) des Platonismus,* in Krell's translation, Nietzsche's overturning (or overcoming) of Platonism. Recall, then, further, what the reading establishes: that Nietzsche's overturning of Platonism proves to require not merely the inversion of the hierarchical opposition between the true and the apparent but a transformation of the very ordering structure (*das Ordnungsschema*) governing both the Platonic subordination and its inversion. It is to this requirement—that there be not merely inversion but also displacement—that Heidegger's conclusion is, then, linked. The conclusion, again in Krell's translation: "To that extent, overturning Platonism must become a twisting free of it."[4]

One direction in which Nietzsche would twist free of the Platonic opposition is marked by that new interpretation of the sensible to which Heidegger has pointed in Nietzsche's text (N I 243ff.). Releasing the sensible from its subordination to the supersensible,

3. Nietzsche, *Götzen-Dämmerung,* in vol. VI/3 of *Werke: Kritische Gesamtausgabe,* ed. Giorgio Colli and Mazzino Montinari (Berlin: Walter de Gruyter, 1967ff.), 74f. Heidegger, *Nietzsche* I 231–242. See also Jacques Derrida, *Éperons, Les styles de Nietzsche* (Paris: Flammarion, 1978). I have discussed the story in relation to Heidegger in *Delimitations,* 160–168.

4. "Insofern muss die Umdrehung eine Herausdrehung aus dem Platonismus werden" (N I 242).

foregoing also mere inversion, Nietzsche reinterprets the sensible as perspectival shining. By *shining* I am translating *Schein*, again following David Krell, who, most judiciously, twists this word free of its usual renderings, namely, as *semblance* or even *illusion*—most judiciously, for not to twist it free of those renderings would be still to enforce in the translation that very subordination of the sensible of which Nietzsche would twist free. It would be to devalue the sensible by reference beyond, by reference to that supersensible truth in subordination to which the sensible would be mere semblance. In short, it would be to violate in the translation the very twisting free that is at issue. Here one can see quite specifically one of the ways in which Krell's translation twists free of its original, splitting off from the German *Schein* just those of its senses that can remain intact in Nietzsche's overturning of Platonism. Let me speak, then, of *Schein* as *shining* or, to take also Krell's other suggestion, as *radiance*.

It is a matter, then, of Nietzsche's interpretation of the sensible as perspectival shining or radiance. One might well suppose that the most pressing problem with such an interpretation lies in its reliance upon the perspectival as somehow delimiting the shining. No doubt, one would need to consider whether the character marked by the word *perspectival* does not remain, all too decisively, within the orbit of the very opposition in question. No doubt, one would need to consider whether in the perspectival something more is thought than the simple negation of that kind of vision that would be correlative to the intelligible, the supersensible. When the sensible is interpreted as intrinsically perspectival, does it remain under the yoke of the Platonic opposition, at best just inverting that order? Or does it exceed that opposition, twist free of it?

I do not propose to attempt to answer this question, at least not directly; for the transformation at issue in it, the new interpretation of the sensible as perspectival shining is not in any case Heidegger's way of taking up that movement to which he points in Nietzsche's text. His is rather a twisting free into that domain that his text "On the Essence of Truth" calls *the open* (*das Offene*), or even *freedom* (GA 9: 185f.). In the language already in play in *Being and Time*, on which I want primarily to focus, it is a twisting free into ἀλήθεια, into disclosedness (*Erschlossenheit*). The question I want to raise has to do, then, not with the perspectival character of the sensible but with its shining: What happens to the shining of the sensible in the Heideggerian twisting free into disclosedness?

Twisting free—Being to an Extent Sensible. The coupling of *Being* and *sensible* bespeaks an orientation toward the question of the sensible within the project of fundamental ontology. The coupling echoes another word from *Being and Time,* echoes it across the space of translation, alluding thus to a certain problem of translation to which Derrida has called attention.[5] For the word *extent* would raise the problem of translating *Erstreckung,* the extending, the stretching, in and through which the space of disclosedness would be opened, the extending that is broached within the originary interpretation made possible in the Second Division of *Being and Time* by the transition to temporality, broached in the return from temporality to the question of the self. This extending between birth and death consists in a certain twisting together of future, beenness, and present, in short, Dasein's originary contortion.

The question that I shall attempt to raise bears on this coupling. Not that I want to take up again at this point the Heideggerian analysis of temporality. On the contrary, I would like to focus on certain analyses situated this side of the originary interpretation of Dasein as temporality, precisely in order to begin outlining a question that could eventually interrupt, or at least complicate still more, the transition to such an interpretation. It will be a matter of deferring this transition, of reading the First Division now in relative independence of the Second, especially of the originary interpretation in which the Second Division culminates. It will be a matter of attempting to ask in an effective way whether an analysis of temporality could ever suffice for developing the question of the meaning of Being. Is time the meaning of Being? Is it the sense (*Sinn*) of Being? Is it the sense, specifically, of the Being of the things of sense? Is it the coupling that joins Being and sense? Does it suffice for rendering Being to an extent sensible?

5. "... *Erstreckung,* a word whose translation remains dangerous" (*Psyché,* 407).

(b)

Let me, first of all, outline two broad configurations in relation to which the reading will be situated. Both have to do, though at different levels, with the metaphysical determination of Being as presence and with the way in which the project of *Being and Time* brings that determination into question, seeking to interrupt its smooth operation so as to twist free of it.

The first configuration, that of the very project of fundamental ontology, can be indicated perhaps most succinctly by recalling again the phrase that Heidegger himself recalls in the 1927 course *The Basic Problems of Phenomenology.* The project of inquiring into the meaning or sense of Being, of asking about that upon which Being is projected, that from which it is always already understood—such a project is, according to the 1927 course, a matter of inquiring *beyond Being,* of disclosing that *beyond* in such a way as then to exhibit precisely how it operates as the *beyond* of Being, as the horizon within which Being becomes understandable, within which Being has indeed always already been understood. The text of the course refers explicitly to the Platonic phrase ἐπέκεινα τῆς οὐσίας, openly marking a certain solidarity: "We, too, with this apparently quite abstract question about the condition of the possibility of the understanding of Being, want to do nothing but bring ourselves out of the cave into the light" (GA 24: 404).

A certain caution is needed here, lest one construe this expressed solidarity in such a way as to close off the project of *Being and Time* too definitively, too hastily, within the metaphysical determination of Being as presence. Not only because certain readings of the Platonic dialogues could perhaps succeed in exposing openings beyond the metaphysical determination, even precisely within the Platonic discourse on τὸ ἀγαθόν as ἐπέκεινα τῆς οὐσίας. But also—and with more direct bearing here—because the Heideggerian move beyond Being to its meaning or sense would not only make explicit how Being has always already been understood but also would expose the *limit* of that understanding, freeing the horizon so that it might operate in a more appropriate, extended, and differentiated determination of Being in its meaning.

And yet, from the very first page of *Being and Time*, the meaning or sense of Being is identified, is predetermined, as *time*. Yet, time is identical with Dasein; the identity is already established in the 1924 lecture,[6] and within the project of *Being and Time* it cannot but remain in force as long as the differentiation between the time of Being (*Temporalität*) and that of Dasein (*Zeitlichkeit*) does not become effective, as it was to have become in the never-published Third Division. To this extent, then, the thrust beyond Being also twists back to a being. Such a return will always risk simply reintegrating the *beyond* of Being into a being, thus sealing off the circulation between Being and beings, effacing all trace of excess, of transgression, or, rather, leaving open only the possibility of exposing excess within Dasein itself. It is not difficult to see how that anthropologistic reading of Heidegger, the inadequacy of which Derrida has so ably exposed,[7] could nonetheless have acquired a certain sham authorization. Nor is it difficult to see how Heidegger himself, detecting throughout the history of Western philosophy the operation of a regress from Being to the subject, could have taken the project of *Being and Time* as the fulfillment of the latent goal of the whole development of Western philosophy.[8]

This duplicity is even more pointedly outlined in Heidegger's text *On the Essence of Ground*, written in 1928. Here, too, Heidegger introduces the Platonic locution ἐπέκεινα τῆς οὐσίας, but now within a context in which the fundamental constitution of Dasein is determined as transcendence. He says: "Transcendence is properly expressed in Plato's ἐπέκεινα τῆς οὐσίας"—that is, to determine Dasein as the movement beyond beings to that horizon from which they are determined in their Being is to think ἐπέκεινα τῆς οὐσίας. Heidegger proposes even that one could, within certain limits, interpret that which for Plato is beyond Being, namely, τὸ ἀγαθόν, as a moment of the transcendence of Dasein; in this case, τὸ ἀγαθόν would be taken to have the character of *das Umwillen* (the for-the-sake-of) and thus would be "the source of possibility as such" (GA 9: 160f.).

---

6. "Der Begriff der Zeit," discussed above in chap. 2 (a).
7. See "Les Fins de l'homme," in *Marges de la philosophie*, 131ff.
8. GA 24: 106. See above, chap. 1 (a).

Everything depends, then, on demonstrating within transcendence a certain excess by which it is transcendence beyond Being, by which the return would, in turn, be limited. In this regard certain analyses in *Being and Time* are indispensable, analyses which undertake to expose something of an excess within the circuit of Dasein, that is, a certain exceeding of the determination of Being as presence. This transgression, as elaborated in the minute analyses of Being-in-the-world, broaches the second configuration to which I want to refer. Toward the end of section 31 of *Being and Time,* following the intricate analysis of understanding, Heidegger introduces a discussion of sight (*Sicht*). He cautions against taking sight to consist merely in "perceiving with the bodily eyes," but also against taking it to be "a pure non-sensory apprehension." Sight is not, in other words, to be delimited by correlation with either term of the Platonic opposition between sensible and intelligible, nor even with both terms. Sight is linked, rather, to understanding and to disclosedness as such: "Understanding goes to make up existentially what we call Dasein's *sight,*" which "corresponds to the clearedness which we took as characterizing the disclosedness of the 'there' " (SZ 146f.). In this determination of sight what is thus effective is the twisting into disclosedness; and this twisting is marked by this analysis as a twisting free of the Platonic opposition: sight corresponds neither simply to the sensible nor simply to the supersensible. Yet, what needs especially to be noted is the connection that Heidegger makes explicit between this determination of sight and a certain traditional priority, in fact, *the* traditional priority. Here is the most decisive passage: "By showing how all sight is grounded primarily in understanding . . . , we have deprived pure intuition [*dem puren Anschauen*] of its priority, which corresponds noetically to the priority accorded to the present-at-hand in traditional ontology" (SZ 147). Here I deliberately retain—for all its inadequacy—the English translation of *das Vorhandene* as *the present-at-hand* in order to stress what Heidegger's German here does not stress: that *Vorhandenheit* is nothing other than presence, even if perhaps still somewhat narrowly delimited.

How, then, have intuition and presence been deprived of their traditional priority by the analyses culminating in the grounding of sight in understanding? What these well-known analyses have shown to be prior to intuition of the present-at-hand is Dasein's circumspective concern with the ready-to-hand (*das Zuhandene*); in the latter case it is not a matter of beholding something sheerly and simply present—neither with the bodily eyes nor, as we say, with the mind's eye—but rather is primarily a matter of handling, in the sense that one handles tools and equipment. But such concerns must, in turn, be guided by circumspection (*Umsicht*), in which is sighted—that is, disclosed—the equipmental whole, the world, from out of which equipment can show itself to and in a handling. These analyses have, then, the effect of drawing Dasein, as it were, beyond what would be simply present, linking its comportment not only to that equipmental mode of Being for which a certain self-withholding, an unobtrusiveness, is constitutive, but also linking it, as sight, as understanding, to that complex of references that Heidegger takes to constitute the worldhood of the world, a complex for which presence, at least as delimited in *Being and Time,* is not at all constitutive. Hence, these analyses enact a certain thrust beyond Being as presence, a certain transgression. They twist free no less from the metaphysical determination of Being as presence than from the Platonic opposition between intelligible and sensible.

Such are, then, the two configurations, gathering at two different levels of analysis the same three figures: a twisting free of the Platonic opposition; a twisting into the sight of understanding, of disclosedness; a transgression toward the *beyond* of Being as presence.

Now it can be mentioned just how the word *Herausdrehung,* which David Krell has in Heidegger's *Nietzsche* translated as *twisting free,* is woven into the texture of *Being and Time.* In a passage in section 43, for example: "Therefore not only the analytic of Dasein but the working out of the question of the meaning of Being in general must be twisted free of the one-sided orientation to Being in the sense of reality" (SZ 201). The entire project of *Being and Time* thus requires a twisting free of the understanding of Being as reality, that is, as presence-at-hand. Another passage, introducing the fable of care told in section 42, recalls how in order to determine the Being of Dasein as care it was necessary from the outset to twist free of the traditional concept of that being that we ourselves are, the concept represented by the traditional definition of man as rational animal.[9] In this regard it is a matter of twisting free both of the determination of Being as presence-at-hand operative in this definition and also of the Platonic opposition on which it is based; it is a matter of twisting free into disclosedness in its rigorous determination as care. Thus in both passages *Herausdrehung, twisting free,* broaches those same three figures whose gathering appeared in the two configurations already outlined: twisting free of the Platonic opposition into a disclosedness beyond Being as presence.

(c)

Let me come now to the principal question that I want to address, the question of the sensible. The question is: What happens to the sensible in that complex of moves whose configuration has just been sketched? What happens to the sensible in that twisting free into a disclosedness beyond Being as presence?

In *Being and Time* the question of the sensible is taken up, though only briefly, in section 29 near the end of the analysis of disposition (*Befindlichkeit*). Heidegger addresses himself specifically to the question of the senses: "And only because the 'senses' belong ontologically to a being whose kind of being is dispositional Being-in-the-world, can they be affected [stirred, moved—*gerührt*] and 'have a sense for' something in such a way that what affects them shows itself in the affection" (SZ 137). It is not as though Dasein is first affected by things through the senses and then comes to have a certain disposition toward those things. Rather, conversely, it is only because Dasein is always already disposed, already attuned mood-wise to the world, that things from out of that world can affect the senses in some way or other, that things can show themselves so as

9. The passage reads: "To do this, it was necessary from the outset to twist the analysis free of directedness to the approach presented by the traditional definition of man, the traditional approach that is ontologically unclarified and fundamentally questionable" (SZ 197). In still another passage in which *herausdrehen* occurs, Heidegger indicates that a certain resistance is offered by language, that there must be a twisting free of a structure reinforced by language: "The ontological question of the Being of the self must be twisted free of the fore-having that is constantly suggested by the prevalent I-saying [*durch das vorherrschende Ich-sagen ständig nahegelegten Vorhabe*], the fore-having of a persistently present-at-hand self-thing" (SZ 323).

somehow to matter to Dasein. Thus, the operation of the sense would be founded, primarily upon disposition, more generally upon disclosedness as such. What happens to the senses in the Heideggerian twisting into disclosedness? They are subordinated to disclosedness as their a priori.[10]

This subordination of the senses is resituated and broadened by two passages in *Kant and the Problem of Metaphysics*. The first passage takes up the question of the senses within a context in which Heidegger is interpreting Kant's general conception of knowledge as primarily intuition and of finite, human intuition as receptive. Here is the passage in which he presents Kant's concept of sensibility:

> Human intuition is not thus "sensible" because its affection takes place through "sense" organs, but rather conversely: it is because our Dasein is finite—existing amidst beings that already are, delivered up to them—that it must of necessity receive [take upon itself, submit to— *hinnehmen*] the beings that already are, i.e., offer such beings the possibility of announcing themselves. In order for it to be reached by such announcement, these organs are necessary. The essence of sensibility [*Sinnlichkeit*] lies in the finitude of intuition. The organs which serve affection are thus sense organs because they belong to finite intuition, i.e., to sensibility. Thus, Kant was the first to arrive at an ontological, nonsensualist concept of sensibility. (KM 25)

This passage marks a certain shift in the concept of sensibility. The locus, the site, at which the essence of sensibility is determined is no longer that of the sense organs but rather that of the finitude of human intuition, of the need to offer beings an opening for announcing themselves, of the need of finite Dasein to be reached by those beings amidst which it is, as existing, thrown. The shift thus corresponds, within the context of Heidegger's interpretation of Kant, to the subordination of the senses announced in the existential analysis: within the Kant interpretation, the senses are subordinated to the finitude of intuition; in the existential analysis they are subordinated to disclosedness.

Toward the end of *Kant and the Problem of Metaphysics* the corre-

10. On this specifically phenomenological sense of a priori, see Heidegger's 1925 course, *History of the Concept of Time* (GA 20: 99–103).

spondence becomes much closer: not only by virtue of that series of displacements in which Heidegger moves from intuition to imagination to temporality, hence, to disclosive Dasein; but also, at a more specific level, in a passage in which, expanding the question of the senses into that of the body as such, he marks then a subordination of the body to transcendence. The passage begins with the concept of sensibility as shifted previously toward the finitude of intuition. Now it is a matter of inscribing such "pure sensibility" within pure reason or, in Heidegger's term, within transcendence: "This pure reason must be sensible in itself and not become so merely because it is connected with a body. Rather, conversely, man as a finite rational being can in a transcendental, i.e., metaphysical, sense 'have' his body only because transcendence as such is *a priori* sensible" (KM 166). Note here the curious conjunctions: *a priori* sensible, pure sensibility. Presumably, one is to understand by these locutions, not just pure intuition in that sense defined in the Transcendental Aesthetic, but, more radically, sensibility as such purified of the senses, its essential determination withdrawn from the domain of perception and sense. Sensibility withdrawn from sense. Withdrawn into what? Into transcendence. Yet, *transcendence*— whatever divergence the word may be taken to broach in the texts following *Being and Time*—serves to rename the site around which all the analyses of *Being and Time* were gathered. In the terms explicit in *Kant and the Problem of Metaphysics*, transcendence is the open horizon within which beings can come to show themselves; it is "primordial truth" (KM 119), i.e., ἀλήθεια, i.e., what in *Being and Time* is called *disclosedness*. It is also what *Being and Time* determines as the domain of meaning, or, rather, let me say now, of sense (*Sinn*). Sensibility moving within the space of this most gigantic ambiguity. Sensibility withdrawn from sense into sense. From sense into sense—though not, one would want to add, *in the same sense;* yet, the addition would broach an endless reduplication, distinguishing sense from sense only by appealing to the difference between different senses, presupposing to that extent the very distinction to be made. From sense into sense—that is, within the space opened within a single word, a gigantic space, the site of the first γιγαντομαχία περὶ τῆς οὐσίας, as of its *Wiederholung*.

What, then, of the sensible? What about those things that were believed accessible to the bodily eyes, those things whose shine Nietzsche would preserve even after truth itself had drifted out of sight? To what extent is the Heideggerian subordination of the senses carried over to their correlate? To what extent does the sensible too come to be withdrawn—in the same sense as the senses—from itself?

In *Being and Time* a certain subordination is indeed announced from the very outset of that chapter—the third of the First Division, entitled "The Worldhood of the World"—in which Heidegger addresses himself to the character of what ordinarily are called *things,* though his analysis in fact proceeds in such a way as to prohibit that word, this prohibition too serving to announce the relevant subordination. But what especially announces it is Heidegger's decisive focus on *das Zeug;* let me use, for convenience, the usual English translation, *equipment,* granting its inadequacy, granting too that in a sense the entire problem here is a problem of translation, of translating *das Ding* into *das Zeug.* Heidegger insists that equipment is what is encountered as *closest* to us. The sense of such proximity, the way in which it functions at various levels of Heidegger's discourse, is quite complex; but clearly one function that it has in the present context is to effect a decision regarding the kind of things on which the analysis will focus, a decision regarding the way in which things as such will be considered, not *as such* but rather as equipment; or, rather, what is decided is that the very sense of the *as such* is to be determined as equipmentality (*Zeughaftigkeit*). Not to begin with the analysis of equipment would be to submit at the outset to a certain divergence, a certain error, a certain encrusted concealment by which tradition has disguised things as such.

Heidegger's analysis, on the other hand, proceeds to recover the equipmentality of what would otherwise be called things. Equipmentality, that which would determine equipment in its character as equipment, is shown to consist in reference (*Verweisung*), or, rather, in the complex of references which are sustained by—and which, in turn, sustain—an item of equipment: the references of the Heideggerian hammer to the work to be done, to the other items of equipment to be used in the work, to the materials needed, to the eventual use of what is to be fabricated, to its range of possible users, etc. It is almost as though the hammer were only a point of intersection of a certain complex of references. It is almost as though in the translation of *das Ding* into *das Zeug* any surplus of the former over the latter had been made to vanish. It is almost as though the hammer had no shape, no color, no weight. It is almost as though all that would pertain to its sensible shining had been passed over or, if you will, concealed. It is almost as though the shining of the sensible had been extinguished. Almost—but not quite.

The fact that Heidegger's analysis includes no account of anything that might be taken to pertain to the specifically sensible character of things is prescribed, at least to an extent, by the very focus, the translation, adopted. It is a matter of drawing the focus away from anything that could be regarded as just sensibly present, as simply there to behold, whether as form or as content. It is a matter of leaving out of account everything about things that would pertain to them as present-at-hand, everything that could be apprehended by a gaze uninvolved in the complex of references. It is a matter of resisting at the outset being diverted into the present-at-hand, mistaking it to be primary and missing entirely the distinctive character of the ready-to-hand. It is a matter of bypassing the present-at-hand in order to be able subsequently to return to it as a *founded* mode, in order to be able to establish that it is derived from the ready-to-hand by a certain narrowing of interest, that what is primary is the ready-to-hand: "In order to expose what is merely present-at-hand, cognition must first push on beyond what is ready-to-hand in concern. *Readiness-to-hand is the ontological-categorical* determination of beings as they are 'in themselves' " (SZ 71).

The effect of Heidegger's analysis is thus to draw things away from what might otherwise be taken as their specifically sensible character, to withdraw them by drawing them into the complex of references, translating *das Ding* into *das Zeug*. This translation is not, of course, a matter of simple reduction: things are not simply reduced to functions of the referential complex (see GA 9: 162 n.). It is not quite as though whatever elements resist the translation could be simply excluded as sheer illusion. The shining of things is not itself so unproblematically translatable as to be simply transformed and carried over by the translation of *das Ding* into *das Zeug*. When things are drawn into the complex of references, a residue is indeed left behind, something untranslatable and yet, in the end, also insignificant, not bearing on the Being of things turned into equipment. For the very sense of the translation is to locate the determination of the Being of such things—hence, of things as such—within the complex of references: "The Being of the ready-to-hand has the structure of reference" (SZ 83). The effect of the translation is to assimilate things ontologically to the referential complex. As regards the determination of their Being, they are drawn into the referential complex and thereby withdrawn from what might otherwise be taken as their specifically sensible character. In short, the outcome is that Being—the Being of things—is to no extent whatsoever sensible.

The referential complex to which things are ontologically assimilated Heidegger finally identifies as world, its specifically referential structure constituting the worldhood of the world. Yet, world is only one moment within the whole that Heidegger designates as Being-in-the-world. In turn, Being-in-the-world is, from the outset, identified as a designation for the *Grundverfassung oder Seinsverfassung des Daseins* (SZ 52f.), as the fundamental constitution of Dasein, the constitution of its Being.

Here one would need to reexamine Heidegger's minute and intricate analyses of the connection of world to Dasein (SZ §18). In these analyses he shows how the worldhood of the world, the constitution of a referential complex, is inseparably bound up with Dasein's disclosedness. Specifically, he demonstrates that within such a complex there is a certain directionality leading to a toward-which (*Wozu*) that is primary, that is not itself toward or for (*zu*) something else. Such a primary toward-which he calls a for-the-sake-of-which (*Worum-willen*); it is something pertaining always to the Being of Dasein. Thus, in Heidegger's example, the hammer is for hammering, which is done in order to fasten down, for example, shingles, in order, in turn, to provide protection against bad weather, thus providing shelter for Dasein. Conversely, a for-the-sake-of-which marks out a certain series—or, rather, a complex—of references constitutive of the worldhood of the world. Yet, a for-the-sake-of-which is nothing other than a possibility, and, as such, it is precisely that to which Dasein, as existing, comports itself in that very comportment by which it is defined as existence. Heidegger can thus write: "To the extent that Dasein is, it always already lets beings be encountered as ready-to-hand" (SZ 86)—that is, in its very comportment to its own possibilities, in that comportment which Dasein essentially—that is, existentially—is, it has always already let a complex of references become effective, has let a world come into play, giving essential space to the determination of things as ready-to-hand. The very unfolding of world as such a space is thus inseparable from that projective understanding in which Dasein, projecting upon possibility, is preeminently disclosed to itself from such possibility. As Heidegger says explicitly in *On the Essence of Ground,* world belongs to selfhood; it is essentially Dasein-related (*wesenhaft daseinsbezogen*) (GA 9: 157).

Even without entering further into these analyses, the drift of things is clear, their drift toward Dasein. For things are, in the first place, assimilated ontologically to world in the sense that world is rigorously established as the locus of the determination of their Being. In *On the Essence of Ground* Heidegger, most remarkably, expresses this assimilation in exactly the same terms that he otherwise employs to express the way in which for Plato things are referred to an εἶδος: Dasein "lets world occur, and in and through world it provides itself with an originary aspect (image) [*Anblick (Bild)*], which is not explicitly grasped but which functions precisely as a pre-image (*Vor-bild*) for all manifest beings . . ." (GA 9: 158). But then, secondly, world is assimilated to Dasein, drawn into the orbit of existence, of Dasein's relatedness to its own Being—in such a way that things too are drawn along, everything, all things in their Being. Their way of showing themselves is assimilated to the circuit of Dasein's own self-showing. Now the drift of things is still clearer. One cannot but see, cast across Heidegger's text, the shadow of a very traditional schema: an *Aufhebung* of things, an assimilation of presence to self-presence. In short, modern metaphysics.

(d)

And yet, it is *only* a shadow, one in which the traditional schema is not only lengthened, stretched out, extended, but also broken, interrupted. For Dasein is not—at least, not yet—to be called spirit. Dasein is not simply spirit, not without the quotation marks that, for a few years still, will enforce a certain avoidance of spirit.[11] Furthermore, disclosedness is not simply self-presence; nor can it be assimilated to self-presence, except by a conflation that will always have to be undone, unsaid. From the outset of *Being and Time* Heidegger is intent on twisting disclosedness free of self-presence, on disentangling Dasein from subjectivity and consciousness, on setting it apart—if only, in the end, by quotation marks—from spirit.

Let me outline, very briefly, some of the strategies and analyses devoted to thus detaching disclosedness from the operation of presence. The first is found at the outset, in the very foresight (*Vorsicht*) that serves as directive in the existential interpretation, the sighting of Dasein in advance as *existence;* for to regard Dasein *existentially* means precisely to focus on Dasein's self-relation not as a relatedness of a being to itself but rather as its relatedness to its Being. Heidegger expresses this relatedness most succinctly, but also in its logic-defying contortedness, in the following statement—in German: "*Zu dieser Seinsverfassung des Daseins gehört aber dann, dass es in seinem Sein zu diesem Sein ein Seinsverhältnis hat*"; in English, roughly: "But then it belongs to the constitution of Dasein's Being that in its Being it has a relatedness-of-Being to this Being" (SZ 12).

A second strategy in this regard is to be found in the series of decenterings of Dasein's relatedness to its Being. Understanding, the sheer projection upon possibility, upon what one *can be,* upon one's *Seinkönnen,* comes to be joined to disposition (*Befindlichkeit*) and discourse (*Rede*), which bring into play in it elements foreign to the sheer circuit of self and possibility. In the elaboration of the structure of care, existence is still further decentered by being joined to two other constituents that are not simply moments of

11. See above, chap. 2 (c).

disclosedness, namely, falling (*Verfallen*), which designates Dasein's propensity to be disclosive in a certain worldly direction, and thrownness (*Geworfenheit*), which designates Dasein's peculiar relatedness to its disclosedness. In thrownness the decentering is especially marked, for example, in the following passage, which I take from the Second Division, lest it be thought that such negativity, such non-self-transparency, pertains only to inauthenticity or everydayness: "As existing it [Dasein] never comes back behind its thrownness in such a way that it could first properly [*eigens*—one could say: on its own] release this 'that-it-is-and-has-to-be' from out of *its Being*-its-self and lead it into the 'there' " (SZ 284). Dasein cannot detach itself from its *Da* so as to be able, on its own, to bring itself into its *Da;* it cannot assimilate its facticity to the circuit of its self-relation.

Yet, the most decisive break of all is the one exposed by Heidegger's analysis of death. Let me refer only to one of the decisive phases of that analysis.[12] Having established the character of death as possibility, Heidegger determines the character of authentic Being-toward-death—what he calls *Vorlaufen in die Möglichkeit*—as that mode in which Dasein, projecting upon this possibility, comports itself toward it in precisely such a way as to grant to death its character as utter possibility, as, in Heidegger's words, "the possibility of the impossibility of any existence at all." Heidegger continues: "Death, as possibility, gives Dasein nothing to be 'actualized' and nothing that Dasein could itself *be* as actual" (SZ 262). Thus, in distinction from all other possibilities, death is not something that Dasein can *be* but is rather such utter possibility that there is nothing to be actualized, nothing to be made present in an actualization. Nor is there even anything to be presented simply as possible: "By its very essence, this possibility offers no support for becoming intent on something, 'picturing' to oneself [*sich 'auszumalen'*] the possible actuality and so forgetting the possibility" (SZ 262). Whereas in every other instance Dasein is disclosed, imaged back to itself, from the possibilities on which it projects—in a kind of circling that, even if

---

12. Heidegger's analysis of death is discussed at length in chapter 5. Only in that context can the more radical import of the two passages here cited be developed.

decentered, is still not utterly alien to self-presence—in authentic projection upon death Dasein has *nothing* present before itself and understands itself only from this nothing.

This series of moves could of course be expanded, for example, by adding the analysis of guilt (as being the negative ground of a negativity), to say nothing of the negativities that come to light in the originary interpretation of Dasein as temporality. And yet, even without considering these further moments, one can discern a certain radicalizing: the various negativities that serve to decenter Dasein's Being itself are progressively more radically irreducible to the mere negation of presence, that is, to an absence that would remain wholly determined by its opposition to presence. It is because the Being of Dasein is invaded by these negativities, because Dasein is, as it were, turned inside out by them, extended outside itself, cast ecstatically, that Dasein is not simply spirit and disclosedness not simply the self-presence of consciousness. Even if—since negativity threatens to become determinate, since the *outside-*itself threatens to become an outside-*itself*—Dasein continues to be haunted by a phantom of presence, a spirit of spirit.

But what, then, about the sensible, which also gets projected in the Heideggerian shadow of the traditional schema? Most remarkably, the Heideggerian projection would seem only to reproduce the foreshortening to which the sensible has always been subjected. Though indeed disclosedness is extended beyond all hope of self-appropriation, it is just such extent that is denied to the sensible. What would be its extent beyond the circuit of disclosedness comes, in the end, to be projected into that circuit. More precisely, the sensible comes to be separated from itself, on the one side translated into *das Zeug*, on the other side reduced to a mere residue having no bearing on what such a thing—hence, the thing as such—is.

To twist free into disclosedness would not be, then, to broach a new interpretation of the sensible so much as it would be to reproduce within the new projection a familiar subordination—or, if you will, circumvention—of the sensible. One need, then, hardly be surprised at that all-too-familiar word, *meaning (bedeuten)*, that Heidegger finally introduces to designate the references by which world is structured (see SZ 87). However thoroughly meaning is set adrift in the turn away from Platonism, it still continues with no less sovereignty than ever to govern the interpretation of the sensible.

Yet, what is distinctive about the Heideggerian project in this regard is the way in which the subordination of the sensible to meaning serves to effect the transgressive move beyond Being as presence. Recall the configuration: the turn into disclosedness is a move beyond the mere apprehension of the sensibly present-at-hand to a concern with the unobtrusive ready-to-hand that is guided by a sighting of the referential context that is utterly irreducible to intuition of presence. This transgressive move, its very sense, requires that meaning govern the sensible.

There are two questions that I would like to raise about this move. The first is: Must the move beyond presence be also a move that displaces the sensible, bringing it under the yoke of meaning? Must the move be one that withdraws the sensible from its element, that effectively cancels what would otherwise be taken as the specifically sensible character of things? Must the move be one that abandons what Nietzsche called the *shining* of things? Or, rather, to make the question a bit more pointed: Under what presupposition would it be necessary to regard the move as being of such a character? Clearly one could answer: it is necessary that the move be one beyond shining only on the presupposition that *shining is reducible to presence.*

The second question concerns, then, the necessity and the source of this presupposition. How is it decided that the sensible can only portend presence-at-hand? Can such a decision be authorized outside the orbit of the opposition of sensible to intelligible? Or does it still reenact, even if from a certain distance, a familiar turn back from the intelligible, with which one would have the thing in its *full presence,* even if before the mind's eye, back to the sensible as perpetually incomplete presence? In other words, is it not precisely with respect to the intelligible, in view of the εἶδος, that the sensible shining of things is brought under the grid of presence? Is it not from the intelligible that one turns back to interpret the sensible as presence?

Need it be said that this question provokes at least a certain suspicion: that, for all its subtlety and despite all that it opens up, the Heideggerian move beyond presence, the turn into disclosedness, perhaps does not succeed in twisting utterly free of the Platonic opposition.

Let me attempt, then, in conclusion, to follow up just a bit this suspicion, to follow it up, ever so tentatively, in the direction of such a reinterpretation of the sensible as might be opened up by freeing the sensible from the grid of presence and from the yoke of meaning. A return to the sensible, a return that would not be merely a falling away from the originary, a return that would be originary in the very move of disrupting the simple directionality that would have defined the originary.

To free the sensible from the grid of presence would require demonstrating a certain undecidability; it would require showing that the shining of the sensible is undecidable with respect to the opposition between presence and absence. To put the matter in terms that allude to classical phenomenology but that would eventually have to be rigorously differentiated from what that position can permit, it would need to be shown how in the shining of the sensible a certain spacing operates so as to draw that shining out into a profiling and a horizonality that is irreducible to presence.

One would need also to insist on a certain originality of the sensible. This would not be to reinstate some allegedly pure perception correlative to a thing allegedly in the original. It would be, rather, to insist on the irreducibility of the shining of the sensible, to insist that it does not simply prefigure meaning, however necessary it may be for such shining to be drawn out into a figure of meaning, a schema, a certain spacing. To free the sensible from the yoke of meaning would be, then, to insist quite literally on the untranslatability of the shining. Shining and the sensible would be neither concepts nor words.

Thus freed from the yoke of presence and meaning, the sensible could, then, echo in that space opened up as disclosedness. Shining, if it were a word, would name the divergence and dispersion of the echo.

What, then, finally, about the question of Being? What about the predetermination of the sense of Being as time, the predetermination which the Second Division would both confirm and extend, even if not in the finally decisive way reserved for the withheld Third Division? If the sensible is freed from the yoke of meaning, if it is not to be assimilated to disclosedness, then *the simple unity of the Heideggerian question cannot but be disrupted,* in just the same way as the unity of Dasein's comportment to Being, the unity by which Dasein's comportment to the Being of things would be included in its comportment to its own Being. It will not be possible, then, to enclose the Heideggerian question within the compass of time, which, as temporality, extends no further than disclosedness. Furthermore, the Heideggerian question will no longer remain a question of meaning nor even, more broadly, of sense. Or, rather, it can be a question of sense only if that gigantic space within what would previously have been called the word *sense* is reopened. What, then, of the γιγαντομαχία to be waged there? If one could still speak of a horizon from which Being would be understood, if—granting all the slippage to which such a way of speaking would now be exposed—one could thus extend the Heideggerian question, it would be necessary to speak of that horizon as extended, as broken, interrupted, and yet as gathering—in a perhaps still unheard-of sense—existentially determined meaning and an irreducibly sensible shining, twisting them together while, with the other hand, untwisting them, contorting and distorting the senses of Being. Then it could be said that Being is to an extent sensible, in every sense of this word, which yet would no longer be either sense or word.

Again—and yet, not simply again—it would be a matter of the beautiful: Being shining forth in the midst of the sensible, Being shining in and from the shining of the sensible.

FOUR

Imagination—the Meaning of Being?

Is the meaning of Being not, then, a matter of imagination? Is it not imagination that in its flight opens to the shining of the beautiful? Is it not imagination that in its hovering spans the gigantic space of *sense*, thus gathering now what would previously have been called the horizon, the meaning, of Being? Is imagination not precisely this gathering? Is imagination not the meaning of Being?

Must imagination not prove to be the meaning of Being once phenomenology is thought through to its end, to an end that, in more than one way, exceeds the project of fundamental ontology?

Perhaps.

And yet, one will need to think phenomenology through toward its end, in more than one way, with Heidegger and also sometimes almost without Heidegger. One will need to come back to what Heidegger develops—even if largely in reference to the Greeks and to Kant—as the basic problems of phenomenology. As a first move toward reinscribing imagination.

One ought not pass too easily over the paradox that is made to appear as soon as imagination is introduced into phenomenology. Set upon returning to the things themselves, phenomenology would appear to require just the opposite direction from that which imagination is believed typically to take. Phenomenology, it appears, could have nothing to do with those flights of phantasy, those fictions, with which imagination—seemingly oblivious to the things themselves—would have to do. At most, phenomenology might engage in an analysis of imagination as a mode of comportment to be contrasted with other modes such as perception and memory; but in this case imagination would be regarded simply as another of those things themselves to which phenomenology would attend.

And yet, matters have never been that simple. First of all, because phenomenology has never been a simple turn to the things themselves, as though such things were somehow simply there, already deployed before a vision that would need only to be recalled from its distraction. Rather, the things themselves must be made accessible as they themselves show themselves, as they show themselves *from themselves.* The turn to them is thus one that must be rigorously carried out, so much so that it comes to determine the very sense of philosophic rigor. It is, then, in this connection that Husserl takes up the question of imagination in a more intrinsic way, declaring in that frequently cited passage in *Ideas I* that " *'fiction' constitutes the life-element of phenomenology.*"[1] Indeed, it can be shown that both the eidetic reduction and the transcendental reduction rely significantly upon certain operations of imagination. To this extent, imagination proves essential to the very opening up of the field of the things themselves, of beings as such. This is not yet by any means to establish imagination as the meaning of the Being of beings. But it is, at least, to broach a connection between imagination and the opening of a space in which beings can come to show themselves as they are, that is, in their Being.

What would be required, then, in order to establish imagination as the meaning of Being?

Let me recall, now more literally, the Heideggerian determination of meaning, or, rather, that characteristic circling that produces the determination of meaning: having set out to establish the meaning of Being, Heidegger comes around eventually to a more or less rigorous determination of meaning (*Sinn*), a determination of what meaning is, of what it shows itself to be within the disclosive opening of the fundamental-ontological project. The determination is carried out in reference to another determination already established at that point in the text, namely, of understanding as

---

1. Edmund Husserl, *Ideen zu einer reinen Phänomenologie und phänomenologischen Philosophie*, Erstes Buch, ed. Walter Biemel (The Hague: Martinus Nijhoff, 1950), 163.

projection (*Verstehen als Entwurf*). Heidegger writes: "Meaning is that in which the understandability of something maintains itself [*Sinn ist das, worin sich Verständlichkeit von etwas hält*]" (SZ 151). To inquire about the meaning of Being is, then, Heidegger adds, to inquire about Being itself insofar as it enters into *Verständlichkeit,* that is, into the domain of Dasein's understanding. One could say, then, that meaning is a medium or space (*Worin*) and that, consequently, to establish imagination as the meaning of Being would require demonstrating that imagination is the medium in which the understanding of Being is maintained, the space of ontological understanding.

But how is it that understanding needs something like a medium or space? How does understanding expand into that space and maintain itself there? What is the character of its operation within that space? And how might imagination be supposed to function as such a space, as a medium of understanding?

Heidegger proceeds, almost immediately, to offer what appears to be a more precise determination: "*Meaning is the upon-which of projection, from which something becomes understandable as something* [das Woraufhin des Entwurfs, aus dem her etwas als etwas verständlich wird]" (SA 151). This says: meaning is that upon which projective understanding projects, that horizon from which, then, something comes to be understood. Thus, to inquire about the meaning of Being is to inquire about that horizon upon which Being is projected and from which it is understood. It is to inquire about the horizon of ontological understanding.

But how, then, could imagination be supposed to function as such a horizon? Is it not proposed from the very beginning of *Being and Time*—as determining its interpretive fore-structure—that the meaning of Being is *time?* Is it not precisely the task of Heidegger's project to carry through, explicitly and at the level of conceptual understanding, that projection of Being upon time, that understanding of Being from time, that has always already been operative preontologically and that has secretly governed the entire history of ontology?

How, then, could *imagination* be supposed the meaning of Being? Only insofar as imagination proves to be essentially linked to the horizon of ontological understanding. Only insofar as it can be shown to bear on the very constitution, the opening, of that horizon. In short, only insofar as imagination turns out to be in some respect identical with time.

My concern is, then, to outline a series of sites at which such identity is at issue, sites at which imagination is—though in quite different ways and degrees—established as the meaning of Being. I shall consider four such sites. The first is that of ancient ontology, as interpreted by Heidegger during the Marburg period. The second site is that of the *Critique of Pure Reason,* specifically, of the transcendental schematism, again in the interpretation developed in the Marburg period. The third site is constituted by Heidegger's *Wiederholung* of the Kantian schematism within the project of fundamental ontology, specifically, as the problem of horizonal schema. The fourth site is one that Heidegger did not himself delimit, one that I shall attempt, in a very provisional manner, to expose by following through—perhaps a bit more radically—some of the upheavals that Heidegger's thought began to undergo shortly after the publication of *Being and Time.* On this site virtually all the previously operative identities of Heidegger's thought—one could indicate them by the following series: Dasein, time, imagination, truth—all these identities come to be unsettled, their terms forced apart, everything radicalized and in a very specific sense overturned. One of the questions that I shall want to address concerns a certain effacement to which imagination is submitted in the Heideggerian text. I shall want to ask whether the question of the meaning of Being—perhaps even in its very overturning—does not, over against that effacement, broach a certain reinscription of imagination.

(a)

The first of the sites is succinctly outlined in *The Basic Problems of Phenomenology.* In connection with his investigation of the thesis of medieval ontology concerning essence and existence, the thesis that essence and existence belong to the constitution of the Being of beings, Heidegger undertakes to show how these concepts and this thesis derive from a certain understanding of Being in ancient ontology. Central to this understanding of Being is a certain regress to the subject. Recall that in the texts of the Marburg period Heidegger maintains that throughout the history of ontology the understanding of Being proceeds by way of a certain regress to the subject, a regress that fundamental ontology would radicalize so as to bring the entire history of ontology to a decisive fulfillment.

In the case of what Heidegger calls, without further differentiation, Greek ontology, the relevant regress is to ποίησις (*Herstellen*, production), to the productive comportment of the τεχνίτης. Heidegger focuses on the way in which a certain kind of image functions within such comportment, an image sighted in advance, the anticipated look (*das vorweggenommene Aussehen*) of the thing to be produced. In production one has always already looked ahead to such an image so as then to be able to form the product according to the look thus anticipated. Such an anticipated look, Heidegger says, is precisely what the Greeks mean by εἶδος and ἰδέα. Thus, most remarkably, Heidegger can correlate εἶδος, as image, with imagination: "The anticipated look, the pre-image [*Vor-bild*] shows the thing as what it is before the production and as it is supposed to look as a product. The anticipated look has not yet been externalized as something formed, as actual, but rather is the image of imagination [*das Bild der Ein-bildung*], of φαντασία" (GA 24: 150). Heidegger stresses that such imaginal sighting is not ancillary to production but rather belongs positively to its structure, indeed, constitutes the very center of that structure. Imagination thoroughly governs production.

It is, then, in reference to production as thus centered in such imaginal sighting that Being comes to be understood in Greek thought. The effect of this reference is to privilege such sighting, that is, to prescribe that the meaning of Being is to be determined in reference to it, that Being is such as to show itself to precisely such sight. It is thus that in Greek ontology Being comes to be determined as εἶδος, as the look of things prior to their actualization, the look anticipated in imagination.

To this extent, then, imagination proves to be the meaning of Being. That is, as the anticipatory sighting of the εἶδος, imagination functions for the ancients as the horizon of ontological understanding, as that from which Being is understood, as that privileged operation in reference to which Being is determined as εἶδος. Being as εἶδος is precisely Being as anticipated in imagination prior to all actualization, prior to production in such a decisive sense that eventually such imaginal sighting can be regarded as quite separable from production and thus, as θεωρία, contrasted with ποίησις.

But what, then, about time as the meaning of Being? The way in which the imaginal character of the Greek determination of Being links up with the temporal character of that determination is indicated by the *anticipatory* character of the imaginal sighting, also by the *priority* that the anticipated look has with respect to all actualization, all production. In anticipatory imagination it is a matter of presenting the thing as it is prior to its being actually produced; as Heidegger notes, the anticipated look presents that which a being already was, τὸ τί ἦν εἶναι. It presents that which a being already was prior to *any* production, prior to *all* production—that is, as it *always* already was. Being as εἶδος is the absolutely prior, the absolute a priori, that which is earlier than every time.

Heidegger stresses repeatedly that the temporal character of the determination of Being remained largely unthought as such by the Greeks, the understanding of Being from time, by projection upon time, governing quite covertly the development of Greek ontology. They could not but have left still more unthought the connection of time to the other horizon that Heidegger shows to have been operative in the Greek determination of Being, the connection between time and imagination, their ontological identity.

Such is, then, the first of the sites, the site at which Being comes to be determined as εἶδος through regress to imagination as the central moment in production. Though the determination is equally temporal, the identity of the horizons, the identity of imagination and time, is left remote.

(b)

In that passage in *The Basic Problems of Phenomenology* in which Heidegger shows the Greek concept of production to be centered in imagination, he inserts a remark about Kant: "It is no accident that Kant . . . assigns to imagination a distinctive function in explaining the objectivity of knowledge" (GA 24: 150). The first site, that of the ancient determination of Being, is thus linked to what I shall regard as the second, the site circumscribed by the *Critique of Pure Reason* in that reading definitively expressed in *Kant and the Problem of Metaphysics.* At this site the identity of imagination and time will prove no longer to be left remote and unthought.

There are several respects in which Heidegger finds in Kant—as he was later to say in the 1973 Preface to the Fourth Edition of *Kant and the Problem of Metaphysics*—an *advocate* (*Fürsprecher*) of the question of Being. For instance, in Kant's thesis that Being is not a real predicate, Heidegger finds a differentiation from which a reopening of the ontological difference can be carried out. Or, again, in Kant's determination of the *personalitas moralis* in terms of respect (and as end in itself), along with his demonstration in the paralogisms that the categories of nature cannot legitimately be applied to the I of the "I think"—by these moves Kant in effect withdraws the subject from its traditional ontological determination as present-at-hand (*vorhanden*), thus drawing it toward the threshold at which, as in *Being and Time,* the question of the Being of the subject would be taken up anew beyond the limits of the ancient understanding of Being (GA 24: 177–209).

And yet, these moves stop short of that threshold—or, rather, all but one of the Kantian moves remain enclosed by the ancient determination of Being. The one exception, Kant's positive ontological contribution, is the move concentrated in the Kantian schematism. The entirety of *Kant and the Problem of Metaphysics* is organized around this move, the move in which Kant becomes, for Heidegger, an advocate of the question of Being, the move in which Kant comes to establish what Heidegger could interpret as—to cite again the 1973 Preface—"a connection between the problem of the categories, i.e., the traditional metaphysical problem of Being, and the phenomenon of time" (KM xiv). In the chapter on the schematism—"those eleven pages of the *Critique of Pure Reason,*" which, Heidegger says, "form *the heart* [das Kernstück] of the whole comprehensive work" (KM 86)—Kant broaches the question of the connection of Being and time. He broaches a transgression of the ancient determination of Being precisely by thinking that identity that the ancients left remote and unthought, the identity of time and imagination.

The transgression is presented as a *Grundlegung,* as a grounding of metaphysics that would proceed by regress to the subject, by regress to that understanding of Being that is prior to and makes possible all comportment to beings as such. Since Kant follows the tradition in regarding such ontological knowledge as a matter of a priori synthetic judgment and, hence, as a matter for pure reason, the Kantian *Grundlegung* takes the form of a critique of pure reason. The forcefulness of Heidegger's reading—I do not say, not yet, its violence—lies in the way in which it activates the eccentric dynamics of the Kantian project; that is, Heidegger shows that the project of grounding metaphysics is precisely such as to distort itself into a transgression of metaphysics and that, correlatively, pure reason is distorted into transcendental imagination.

Let me recall, in the very briefest form, the five stages that Heidegger outlines in the Kantian *Grundlegung.* The first stage identifies the essential elements, the two stems, of ontological or pure knowledge: on the one side, pure intuition, the synoptic form of all empirical intuition, time the universal pure intuition; on the other side, the pure concepts of the understanding, those directive unities in reference to which all empirical acts of reflection must be carried out, the pure unities, therefore, presupposed by all empirical concepts such as might be operative in experience of objects. At the second stage the problem is, then, how these two elements, themselves already in a sense synthetic, are brought together. Whence arises the synthesis by which their unification is achieved? Heidegger cites Kant: "Synthesis in general . . . is the mere result of *imagination,* a blind but indispensable function of the soul, without which we should have no knowledge whatsoever but of which we are scarcely ever conscious" (KM 59, citing A 73/B 105). It is a matter, then, at the third stage, of explicating the inner possibility of that pure, ontological synthesis by which would be constituted in advance of experience that horizon of objectivity, that understanding of the Being of objects, that would render experience possible. This explication becomes a matter of demonstrating the centrality of imagination in the pure synthesis, of tracing out in the two directions taken by the

Transcendental Deduction (from above and from below) the way between pure understanding and empirical intuition, explicating specifically how the two paths cross in imagination.

The aim of the entire *Grundlegung* comes to be accomplished at the fourth stage, the fifth stage then serving only to appropriate explicitly what has been gained. At the fourth stage the question is, accordingly, one of *ground*, of the ground of the inner possibility of ontological knowledge or, as Heidegger also terms it, of transcendence. That ground proves to be *transcendental schematism*. This proof, the demonstration of transcendental schematism as the ground of ontological knowledge, is what constitutes for Heidegger the heart of Kant's work.

The demonstration begins by explicating the character that must be had by that horizon of objectivity that presents in advance the Being of objects and that constitutes the condition of the possibility of their being experienced as objects. In order that it be possible for objects to offer themselves to experience, the horizon must have a certain offertory character (*Angebotcharakter*). In turn, this character involves a certain perceptibility (*Vernehmbarkeit*), a certain intuitive or sensible character, which, however, as prior to experience of objects, must be in the order of *pure* intuition. It follows, then, that in the constitution of the horizon of objectivity the pure concepts, in which objectivity would be thought as such, must be made intuitive, sensibilized; they require a pure sensibilization. This takes place as schematism: "Pure sensibilization takes place as a 'schematism.' In forming the schema [*Schema-bildend*] pure imagination provides in advance a view ('image') [*Anblick* ('*Bild*')] of the horizon of transcendence" (KM 88). Such is, then, the ground: the forming of the schema by imagination.

Rather than attempting to reconstitute Heidegger's intricate analysis of schematism, let me merely mention three main points that that analysis serves to establish. The first pertains to the general meaning of *sensibilization* or *schematism,* their meaning regardless of whether the operation is carried out at the empirical or the pure level. In every case it is an operation by which an image is procured for a concept. The point is that, since a concept can never be put into an image in the sense of a *representatio singularis,* since what is immediately intuitively viewed can never adequately present a general concept, the image of a concept must rather be such as to show how what is thought in the concept *looks in general.* Such an image Heidegger calls a *schema-image.* Sensibilization, schematism, procures for a concept a schema-image.

And yet, secondly, the schema-image is, strictly speaking, correlative not to a concept but to a schema. In this regard, Heidegger undertakes to expose in the Kantian analysis a fundamental reorientation with respect to the nature of conceptual representation. Essential to this reorientation is the recognition that in experience the concept is not intended in itself but only in its regulative function, only as regulating a certain unification, only as a rule. Yet, what is thus represented, a rule of unity in its way of ruling, is just the schema. Heidegger concludes: "This means at the same time that beyond the representation of this regulating unity of the rule the concept is nothing. What in logic is termed a concept is grounded on the schema. . . . All conceptual representation is essentially schematism" (KM 95, 97). That operation within experience that was initially, preliminarily, assigned to thought is thus shifted toward imagination: the element of empirical generality in experience has now come to be located in the schema and its correlate the schema-image. The eccentric dynamics are thus set in play, and the distortion of reason into imagination is under way.

But then—to come to the third point—what about *transcendental* schematism? Here it is a matter of procuring an image for the pure concepts of the understanding, for those rules by means of which the horizon of objectivity is formed. Such an image not only must be, as in every case, a schema-image but also must be pure, absolutely prior to all appearance of objects. Heidegger cites Kant: "The pure image of . . . all objects of the senses in general [is] time" (KM 100, citing A 142/B 182). Corresponding to the multiplicity of pure concepts, there is a multiplicity of ways in which the pure schema-image can be formed, a multiplicity of transcendental determinations of time. These forms are—again Heidegger citing Kant—a "transcendental product of the imagination" (KM 101, citing A 142/B 181).

Heidegger's conclusion is, then, that the ground of the inner possibility of ontological knowledge lies in transcendental schematism, that is, in the imagination's forming of time as multiplicity of pure schema-images. In this conclusion—and indeed throughout most of Heidegger's analysis—one can thus gauge the extent to which Heidegger's interpretation of the Kantian schematism is a *Wiederholung* of that interpretation of ancient ontology given in *The Basic Problems of Phenomenology*. In both cases it is a matter of imagination's providing, in advance, as a priori, certain images, certain pre-views, anticipated looks; indeed in the analysis of schematism Heidegger introduces precisely the same terms as in the analysis of ancient ontology, viz., *Aussehen*, εἶδος, ἰδέα. The difference is that in the Kantian schematism the a priori character of the image, its purity, is determined by reference to time as pure form of all appearances. As a result it not only becomes possible, in the Kantian instance, to think through in a more positive way the connection between imagination and the images that it procures; but also, since those images are precisely time itself as variously formed or determined, it becomes possible to think what the ancients left quite unthought, the *identity* of imagination and time. One could perhaps even venture to say that in the schematism Kant thinks the connection between Being and time precisely by thinking the identity of time and imagination.

Such is, then, the second of the sites, the site of transcendental schematism, the site at which the horizon of objectivity is formed as multiplicity of pure schema-images, the site at which Being is constituted in and through the imagination's determining of time—in short, the site at which Being is determined as time and as correlate of imagination.

(c)

Though the entirety of *Kant and the Problem of Metaphysics* is organized around the interpretation of transcendental schematism as the outcome of the Kantian *Grundlegung*, that interpretation is by no means the culmination of Heidegger's text but rather, within the structure of that text, serves as an opening onto a more originary dimension of the problematic. On the other hand, there can be little doubt but that in moving into this originary dimension

Heidegger approaches, if he does not indeed transgress, the limits of what can with some legitimacy still be called the Kantian problematic. In other words, he enters a dimension in which—as he was later to say in the 1973 Preface—"Kant's question comes to be subordinated to a *Fragestellung* that is foreign to it, even though conditioning it" (KM xiv). In the terms already used in 1929, it becomes much more decisively a matter of wresting from what Kant's words say that which, on the other hand, they want to say (*was sie sagen wollen*), a matter of such violence (*Gewalt*) as is necessary to expose the unsaid (KM 196/207).

Let me mention, ever so briefly, two of these moves at the limit that are especially pertinent here. The first moves, in effect, from time as a pure sequence of nows to that ecstatical-horizonal time that *Being and Time* determines as originary time, as temporality. Heidegger carries out the moves by way of an interpretation of Kant's account of the threefold character of synthesis, as synthesis of apprehension, of reproduction, and of recognition. The outcome of the interpretation is that the three phases of the imaginal synthesis correspond to the three ecstases of temporality, with which, therefore, imagination can be declared identical. Thus, transcendental imagination can carry out the forming of time as the now-sequence precisely because it is identical with originary time, with temporality. Hence, in this move the identity of time and imagination is not only thought but now thought precisely *as identity*.

The second of the moves carries through to the end the displacement of intuition and of thought that is already under way in Heidegger's interpretation of schematism, their displacement toward imagination. Now it becomes virtually a matter of reduction, in Heidegger's words, "nothing less than tracing pure intuition and pure thought back [*züruckführen*] to transcendental imagination" (KM 133). It is through this move that the Kantian *Grundlegung* distorts itself into a transgression, that the laying of ground turns out to be the exposing of an abyss, in the face of which Kant can only have retreated. Heidegger observes also that through this move what has been called transcendental imagination is transformed into something more originary, so that, in his words, "the designation 'imagination' becomes of itself inappropriate" (KM 135).

Later I shall want to raise some questions about this effacement that *imagination* undergoes in the Heideggerian text. In any case, it is clear that the effacement is for the sake of *Dasein* and that with these moves Heidegger is already engaged quite decisively in what he finally, in the last of the four Sections of *Kant and the Problem of Metaphysics,* comes to call a *Wiederholung* of the Kantian *Grundlegung.*

It is precisely at this point that I would like to diverge from *Kant and the Problem of Metaphysics* in order to take up, not the massive *Wiederholung* of that final Section, which opens onto the entire analytic of Dasein, but rather a much more minute and controlled analysis which, though not explicitly designated as such, is, in effect, a *Wiederholung* of the Kantian problem of schematism. This *Wiederholung* traces out the third of the sites on which I have proposed to focus.

I am referring to Heidegger's development of the concept of horizonal schema. This concept is first introduced in section 69c of *Being and Time.* At that point the ecstatic character of primordial temporality has already been established, and it is then a matter of limiting the centrifugal movement. The ecstases, Heidegger says, are not simply raptures in which one would be carried away, enraptured, not simply *Entrückungen zu:* "Rather, there belongs to each ecstasis a 'whither' toward which one is carried away [*ein 'Wohin' der Entrückung*]. This whither of the ecstases we call the horizonal schema" (SZ 365). A certain order of grounding is then outlined, though with only minimal development. The world, in its coherence with Dasein, is grounded on the horizonal character of temporality, and the unity of the world, its coherence as such, is grounded on the unity of the horizonal schemata. In turn, the unity of the horizonal schemata of the three ecstases is grounded in the ecstatic unity of temporality, in the unity of the ecstases.

In *The Basic Problems of Phenomenology* Heidegger returns to the problem of the horizonal schemata and develops the problem not only more thoroughly but also at a more fundamental level of his project, namely, as a first incursion into the field of the problem of

Temporalität, to which the missing Third Division of *Being and Time* (Part One) was to have been devoted. It is a matter, then, of developing an analysis sufficient to show how temporality (*Zeitlichkeit*) functions as that from which Being is understood, how time is the meaning of Being.

Here it must suffice merely to sketch the analysis in the very briefest terms.[2] The question of the understanding of Being is raised with reference to the equipmental context familiar from *Being and Time:* the question is that of how one has in advance an understanding of the Being of equipment, that is, of *Zuhandenheit,* or, more generally, of what Heidegger now terms *Praesenz.* He focuses on a specific connection within the structure of primordial temporality, a connection within the specific ecstasis of the present that belongs to the temporality of circumspective concern, viz., *Gegenwärtigung.* The question is, then, that of the connection between *Praesenz* and *Gegenwärtigung.* Heidegger states the connection thus: "Gegenwärtigung . . . *projects that which is* gegenwärtigt, that which can possibly confront us in and for a present, *upon* something like Praesenz" (GA 24: 435). *Gegenwärtigung* is thus characterized as a projection and *Praesenz* as the upon-which of the projection.

It is at this point in the analysis that Heidegger introduces the concept of horizonal schema as belonging to the structure of ecstatic temporality. He identifies *Praesenz* as the horizonal schema of that mode of the present that is under consideration. Thus, the structure of temporality is such as to include not only the ecstasis (in this case, *Gegenwärtigung*) but also the horizonal schema (in this case, *Praesenz*). In the temporalizing of the ecstasis, there is, then, a projecting upon the horizonal schema. In other words, within the temporalizing of temporality there is a primordial projecting, what one could call, recalling the determination of understanding as projection, a kind of protounderstanding. Heidegger says: "*Gegenwärtigung* is the ecstasis in the temporalizing of temporality that understands itself as such upon Praesenz" (GA 24: 435f.). Thus, it is by way of this protounderstanding that, in advance of the encoun-

---

2. I deal with this analysis in somewhat greater detail in *Delimitations*, chap. 10.

ter with beings, one understands their Being, in this case, *Praesenz* or, more specifically, *Zuhandenheit*. Heidegger says: "*Accordingly, we understand Being from the originary horizonal schema of the ecstases of temporality*" (GA 24: 436). Temporality (*Zeitlichkeit*) so regarded, that is, with regard to its inclusion of horizonal schemata in projection upon which a protounderstanding of Being arises—this is what Heidegger designates by the Latinate form *Temporalität*.

Now it is clear how Heidegger's analysis of *Temporalität* is a *Wiederholung* of the Kantian analysis of schematism. Just as Kant undertook, in the concept of transcendental schema, to think the connection between Being (in its traditional articulation according to the categories) and time; so too Heidegger, through the concept of horizonal schema and of the projection upon it in the temporalizing of temporality, undertakes to think the connection between Being and time—but now in reference to the more primordial, ecstatical-horizonal concept of time. Yet, it is—for Heidegger even less than for Kant—no longer a matter of some kind of reference of Being to time, of a kind of external projection of Being upon something other. Rather, it is a matter of an element within the structure of temporality, viz., the horizonal schema, that is identical with Being—or, rather, that is constituted as Being (in some more or less specific mode) in and through the projection, the protounderstanding, intrinsic to the temporalizing of temporality.

Such is, then, the third site, the site of protounderstanding, the site of the ecstatic projection upon the horizonal schema. In and through that projection the schema becomes, in the terms of Heidegger's reading of Kant, a pure *image* of Being, its schema-image. And indeed that projection is precisely what would have been, but no longer is, called *imagination*. Now the effacement is fully in force. Imagination will seldom again appear in the Heideggerian text, except in passages such as that in *The Origin of the Work of Art*, which serve in effect to enforce the effacement: ". . . it becomes questionable whether the essence of poetry, and this means at the same time the essence of projection, can be sufficiently thought from imagination [*von der Imagination und Einbildungskraft*]" (GA 5: 60).

(d)

When in *Being and Time* Heidegger first introduces the concept of horizonal schema, he outlines, though only minimally develops, a rigorous order of grounding: world grounded on the horizonal schemata in their unity; this unity, in turn, grounded on the unity of the ecstases of temporality. On the other hand, when in *The Basic Problems of Phenomenology* he returns to the problem of the horizonal schema, it appears that the order of grounding has become a bit less sure. Transcendence and world, as its correlate, are still emphatically referred to the ecstatic-horizonal unity of temporality as their ground. But the unity of the horizonal schemata is no longer referred to the unity of the ecstases as its ground; now Heidegger says only that to the unity of the ecstases there *corresponds* (*entspricht*) a unity of the schemata. It is as though there were both a centripetal unity, almost a center from which the ecstases would reach out and to which they would be regathered, *and* a centrifugal unity, the unity of the schemata that would form, as it were, a unitary horizon enclosing the field of the temporalizing of temporality. And it is as though both unities, that of the center and that of the limit, were equally essential to the temporalizing of temporality.

In *The Metaphysical Foundations of Logic* (1928) Heidegger again takes up the problem of the horizonal schema. Here too one notices the same indecision with respect to the connection between the unity of the horizonal schemata and that of the ecstases of temporality: again it is declared a matter of the horizonal unity corresponding (*entsprechend*) to the ecstatic unity. But now one can also discern another development alongside this apparent indecision:

> The whole of these ways of being-carried-away [*Entrückungen*] does not center in something which would of itself lack any being-carried-away, something unecstatically present-at-hand [*vorhanden*] and which would be the common center for the onset and outlet [*Ansatz und Ausgang*] of the ecstases. Rather, the unity of the ecstases is itself ecstatic. (GA 26: 268)

One cannot but read this passage as a further weakening of the centripetal unity, a further erosion of what in *Being and Time* was taken as the grounding unity, as the final term in the order of grounding proposed in that text. Temporality is being declared more radically ecstatic, which is to say more horizontal, more thoroughly governed, more limited, by the horizon than by any center from which the ecstases would proceed. Temporality is being submitted to a certain displacement. It is not, Heidegger now says, like "a living animal [that] can stretch out feelers in different directions and then retract them again" (GA 26: 268). Temporality, the outside-itself, displacement itself—now itself displaced.

This peculiar displacement could be regarded as linked to another problem, a problem that might be raised regarding the other connection proposed in the order of grounding. Not that Heidegger *raises* a problem about the connection between world and temporality. On the contrary, he affirms the connection most emphatically, not only in *Being and Time* but also in *The Basic Problems of Phenomenology*: "*The ecstatic character of time makes possible Dasein's specific overstepping character* [Überschrittscharakter], *transcendence,* and thus also world" (GA 24: 428). In *The Metaphysical Foundations of Logic* he remains equally emphatic: "Time is essentially a self-opening and expanding [*Ent-spannen*] into a world" (GA 26: 271). And yet, in the 1928 text, there is a shift, which serves perhaps to signal that, despite the emphatic affirmation, something is problematic here. The shift is toward the horizonal limit of temporality—that is, what is said to ground transcendence is not temporality in general but the horizonal schemata in their unity, what Heidegger now calls the ecstematic unity of the horizon of temporality: this, he says, is "the temporal condition of the possibility of *world* and of world's essential belonging to *transcendence* . . ." (GA 26: 269f.). Now there is no longer even any mention of another, corresponding unity that would be linked to a center. It is as though temporality had to be made more horizonal, shifted toward its horizonal limits, in order to secure its grounding connection with the horizon of Dasein, the horizon of horizons, world.

One could read this series of shifts toward the horizon, this eccentricity operating in Heidegger's text, as signalling something utterly problematic. One could read it as a series of compensatory moves that, in the end, only serve to render more obtrusive and more problematic a difference for which no such compensation could suffice. The question would then be: Can the ecstasis of temporality, the standing-out toward future, beenness, and present, ever suffice to ground that other ecstasis in which Dasein stands out toward, transcends to, the world? Or, is there not an irreducible difference between temporality and transcendence? Previously one might have undertaken to thematize such a difference by reference to the internality of temporality in distinction from the externality of world. Heidegger is intent, of course, on cancelling any such opposition between inner and outer—and yet is that not precisely the question? Does not temporality—precisely as *originary* time over against the time in which things come and go—does it not retain a trace of internality sufficient to constitute a gap separating it from world, a difference from transcendence?

It is a question, then, of two moments of ecstasy, of the difference between them that will prohibit that simple grounding of one on the other that was initially proposed. It is a question of the difference between temporality as an outside-itself and transcendence as Dasein's being outside-itself in a world. The difference is a matter of doubling: of the doubling of temporality in contrast to transcendence. For transcendence, Dasein's being outside-itself in a world, is precisely such that there is no *itself* that stands out into the world; or, equally, the *itself* is just the standing-out, the ecstasy. The same cannot hold, however, for temporality, because in the self-interpretation of temporality there is a doubling that sets apart originary time (in its identity with Dasein) and the time of concern, the time in which things come and go, a time that can, in turn, be redoubled as now-time, thus becoming still more removed from Dasein. The (re)doubling of temporality cannot but be, finally, a phantom of the doubling of inner and outer. One cannot but wonder whether temporality and its doubling, thus haunted, could ever be thought outside the opposition, outside an *itself,* outside itself. And if one insists that temporality nonetheless grounds transcendence, it must also be granted that temporality in its doubling presupposes transcendence toward a world in which time can be assigned, can be world-time.[3] To say nothing of the return of space to the determination of temporality and its doubling.

Indeed in this connection one could not but raise again the

3. See the discussion of the self-interpretation of temporality in chap. 2 (c).

question of spatiality, the question of the distinctive spatiality belonging to world and to transcendence, the question of a spatiality that will later be declared irreducible to temporality (see SD 24), that indeed would mark, not to say constitute, the very excess of transcendence over temporality. How could such a question be raised? Certainly not within the project of fundamental ontology.

One could perhaps understand in this connection why in *The Metaphysical Foundations of Logic* Heidegger says that to take up the problem of space in a radical way would require the transition to a metontology of spatiality. This says: the question could be taken up radically only through the overturning, the *Umschlag*, the μεταβολή, from Being to beings as a whole (*das Seiende im Ganzen*)—the overturning of fundamental ontology into metontology.

Of course, Heidegger does not develop the metontology of spatiality in the 1928 text, nor, under that title at least, in any other published text. And though indeed the entire problematic of metontology remains undeveloped and presumably provisional, there are, nonetheless, certain indications of how, within metontology, transcendence could be thought in its difference from temporality, indications of a way of interpreting Being-in-the-world outside that fore-structure that would direct everything in advance toward an eventual grounding in temporality.

Suppose, for instance, that one were to read, in reference to this question, the following passage from *The Metaphysical Foundations of Logic,* in which Heidegger anticipates the issue of metontology by discussing what in Aristotle corresponds to it, viz., theology (θεολογική):

> Τὸ θεῖον means: what simply is [*das Seiende schlechthin*]—the heavens: the encompassing and overpowering, that under which and at which [*worunter und woran*] we are thrown, by which we are benumbed and overtaken, the overwhelming [*das Übermächtige*]. θεολογεῖν is a contemplation of the κόσμος. . . . Let us keep in mind that philosophy, as first philosophy, has a twofold character: it is knowledge of Being and knowledge of the overwhelming. (This twofold character corresponds to the twofold of existence and thrownness.) (GA 26: 13)

Could one not, starting from such an indication, propose, then, a redetermination of thrownness—or, rather, an overturning of the ontological concept of thrownness into a metontological concept? It would be a matter of overturning thrownness, thought as ecstasis of *Gewesenheit,* as coming back to one's having-been, of overturning it into thrownness as coming back under *das Übermächtige.*

One could thus begin to outline a site—and now the sense of site is no longer just metaphorical—a site at which transcendence would exceed temporality. That very excess is what would be traced by the overturning into metontology.

The question is whether imagination, which fundamental ontology has thought in its identity with temporality, to the point of effacement—whether imagination might not also be overturned onto this site. One might then undertake to reinscribe *imagination* by determining it, for instance, in correlation with what Heidegger explicates in *Kant and the Problem of Metaphysics* as the primary sense of *image* prior to its assimilation to the problem of transcendental schematism—viz., image as the manifest look of something which at the same time shows how such things look in general (see KM 89f.). If the shining of that generality were sufficiently displaced from conceptuality, one could perhaps speak, as Heidegger does, of contemplation (*Betrachten*) of the κόσμος. One might also want to chart a certain course of imagination, following, for instance, certain moments of Kant's analysis of the sublime: a course such as that on which imagination, faced with sublime nature, strives to apprehend that magnitude or power that exceeds it; and, failing in its effort, is then thrown back upon itself in such a way as to make manifest that very excess of nature.[4]

But then—to conclude—what about imagination and the meaning of Being? Of course, it would still be necessary to say that time is the meaning of Being; for the very determination of meaning is governed by that of projection and thus by time as the originary projection. But now the very question would be overturned into something other than the question of the meaning of Being, into a question which, even if bound to that question and accessible only through it, would nonetheless exceed it. Overturned imagination—

4. Reference is made here to the interpretation of the sublime that I have proposed in *Spacings—of Reason and Imagination* (Chicago: University of Chicago Press, 1987), chap. 4.

its identity with time now disrupted—would be one way of thinking such excess.

Near the end of *The Metaphysical Foundations of Logic,* in the context of an explication of temporality as productive of world, Heidegger suddenly recalls the Kantian discovery of transcendental imagination:

> Kant, for the first time, came upon this originary productivity of the "subject" in his doctrine of the transcendental productive imagination. He did not succeed, of course, in evaluating this knowledge in its radical consequences, by which he would have had to bring about the collapse of his own building by means of this new insight. (GA 26: 272)

The Heideggerian case is of course different: the very plan for the demolition of the edifice of fundamental ontology is already sketched in this text. The question is only whether, in his case as in Kant's, imagination does not chart the way from ground to abyss.

Mortality and Imagination

The Proper Name of Man

Abyss and excess—in a word: death.

Let me begin with the end. With death and with what is said of it, from it. With the end of man. Also with the end of his name.

I shall have to elaborate this beginning before I can specify the questions with which I shall then attempt to deal.

One hears, of course, that a man's name lives on after his death. In a certain sense this is true not only of proper names but also of the common name *man*. And yet, in the most decisive sense the common name does not live on: the end of man is also the end of his name, of the name *man*. Let me refer here to the transition in Hegel's *Encyclopedia* from anthropology to phenomenology, the transition in which the end of man, thought dialectically, is also thereby recovered as the very opening of *Wissenschaft*. Man would be superseded by consciousness and, finally, by spirit. His name too would be superseded, a new inscription effacing and yet preserving the name *man*. Much the same could be said in reference to Nietzsche and Heidegger, even if one insists on not enclosing these transitions within the Hegelian *Aufhebung* and on differentiating these openings from that of *Wissenschaft*: *Mensch* is replaced by *Übermensch*, and ἄνθρωπος gives way to the Dasein in man.

Today it goes almost without saying that the name of man can no longer be thought of as a purely exchangeable signifier, that is, as a signifier that could be freely exchanged for others while leaving the signified fully intact, unaffected by the exchange. With the name of man the situation would not be like—to recall an example from the *Cratylus*[1]—that in which a master could freely change the name of a slave without affecting the latter. Or, rather, it would be like that situation if the issue were that of exchanging the name *slave* for another; for the name *slave,* functioning performatively in certain social networks, can enforce, if not constitute, the very condition that it would seem only to name, making the slave no less enslaved to the name than to the master who bestows it.

The end of man is even less a free exchange. For, at least beginning with Nietzsche, it is bound up with a destabilizing of that very system of oppositions that hitherto guaranteed a *beyond* of language, a *beyond* in which man as such would remain untouched by all changes of his name. With the total trembling of the system of classical oppositions, every such retreat of meaning is reclaimed and set again adrift in language. Once the question of the end of man breaks through the final metaphysical security, man can no longer isolate himself from the question and from the exchange of names in which it issues. Today one cannot interrogate the name of man without also interrogating what would formerly have been distinguished—but can no longer be simply distinguished—as man himself, the essence of man. The question of the name of man would be a question of man himself, were it not that this very connection serves to undermine the very possibility of a *thing itself.* This is why one can ask about the *proper* name of man without simply reasserting the classical opposition and the system of antinomies generated by it, the system through which the *Cratylus* subtly and comically circulates. One can ask about the proper name without first separating signifier from signified so as, then, to require some supervenient connection in order to legitimate the question of the proper name. If the separation is foregone from the outset, then the question of the name of man cannot but be a question of the name proper to man. Not because man would precede speech in such a way that proper naming would have to follow some pure foresight; but, rather, because man, always already speaking, naming himself, for example, ζῷον λόγον ἔχον, is *always already spoken,* always already woven into the fabric of language. To ask about the

1. *Cratylus* 384 d.

proper name of man is to ask about the name proper to what has already been named ἄνθρωπος, *Mensch, man.* It is to ask about the name proper to a being that is inextricable from its already operative self-naming, inextricable from the name that it has always already given itself. It is not a matter of bridging a gulf between two incomparable terms, man and his name, if for no other reason than that language is always already on both sides—which is to say that there is no gulf.

And yet, there could be no question if a certain separation were not possible, a certain gap that would be the space of the question of the proper name of man. The possibility of such a gap requires only that the analysis of that being that has been called man—a phenomenological analysis, for example, as in *Being and Time*—not be utterly controlled by what has been the name of man. It requires that such an analysis be capable of eliciting a manifestation that diverges from what is already said in the name. The question of the proper name of man would be installed in the space of that divergence.

It would be a question, then, of the name proper to that being already named man, proper to it as it comes to be manifest in and through, for example, the existential analysis of Heidegger's *Being and Time.* To be proper to that being means to declare the proper *of* it, to say what is in the most rigorous sense *its own.*

Being and Time begins with the proper of that being that has been called man but is now to be named Dasein. It begins by differentiating the ownness of Dasein from the essence of *das Vorhandene,* linking the former, as *Jemeinigkeit,* to comportment to possibility: Dasein is that being that "comports itself to its Being as its ownmost possibility" (SZ 42). This determination of Dasein's essence as existence is the hermeneutical foresight (*Vorsicht*) that governs the entire existential analysis and that, in turn, is confirmed, articulated, and deepened by that analysis. It is primarily this determination that, opening a gap within what is called essence, makes the Heideggerian analysis diverge from man to Dasein. In that divergence something else also happens that is utterly decisive: what is man's—or, now, Dasein's—own comes to be manifest as including a peculiar disowning. This disowning is not simply assimilable to the classical schema by which whatever is unessential would be separated from the essence, set aside in order to display the essence in its purity. Rather, the disowning is such as to belong to man's ownness. It is a disowning that—one would have to say, at the risk of compounding the problem—belongs essentially, properly, to ownness, as constitutive of that very ownness. Dialectic makes it manifest that it is proper to man to be disowned into spirit, to come into his own only in being disowned—even if also preserved—as man. To say almost nothing yet of Heidegger, of the way in which Dasein bespeaks man's being disowned into the *Da,* turned out into the clearing.

What, then, about the proper name of man? It would be necessary not only that it say this disowning but that it say the disowning precisely in saying the ownness of man. It must say both at the same time, without any interval. In other words, the proper name must say what constitutes man in his ownness while, in that same appellation, saying also the disownedness operative in that very constitution. The name must say the utter separation from self that belongs to oneself, the submission of oneself to a radical alterity.

Heidegger proposes such a name.

He proposes it repeatedly in various texts from the early 1950s. Let me cite the proposal in the formulation given in the text "The Thing" and repeated verbatim in "Building, Dwelling, Thinking": "Mortals are men. They are called mortals because they can die. To die means to be capable of death as death. Only man dies."[2] Not only does Heidegger thus propose the name but also, as the passage continues in "The Thing," he comes to convert the proposal into a performative: "Mortals *we now call* mortals—not because their earthly life comes to an end, but because they are capable of death as death [emphasis added]." Through the appellation thus performed in the text, *mortal* becomes, in this text and beyond, the name of man, displacing, if not entirely replacing, *Dasein.*

It is on this appellation that I would like to focus, this

---

2. VA 177. The lecture "Das Ding" was first presented to the Bavarian Academy of Fine Arts on 6 June 1950. The passage is repeated in "Bauen, Wohnen, Denken" (VA 150), which was first presented on 5 August 1951; and in a slightly different formulation in "Dichterisch Wohnet der Mensch" (VA 196), which was first presented on 6 October 1951.

nomination—or, rather, renomination—of Dasein as mortal. For this purpose it will be necessary to retrace certain moments of the analysis of death in *Being and Time* as well as the reinscriptions of that analysis in several later texts, including the one just cited. I shall want especially to mark the way in which what I shall call, provisionally, a certain coincidence of ownness and alterity comes repeatedly into play.

In focusing on Heidegger's move from Dasein to mortal, I shall also want to raise the question of a certain move back from Dasein. Specifically, I shall want to ask about a certain reversal of that move that Heidegger traces in presenting the project of fundamental ontology as a *Wiederholung* of the *Critique of Pure Reason*. Could the renomination of Dasein as mortal be made to broach a certain reversion from Dasein to imagination?

Throughout, then, it will be a question of mortality, of the way in which death, proper to man, is yet other, set apart so as to be alien and alienating, an operation of disownment. And it will be a matter of asking whether death in its proper alterity remains open to imagination. Can one imagine one's own death?

(a)

From the outset the analysis of death in *Being and Time* is oriented to the question of delimiting Dasein as a whole. The question is: How can a being that has death as its end be delimited as a whole and, hence, be accessible as such to ontological analysis?

The argumentation by which Heidegger poses the question is direct, seemingly—as he will remark—too formal. In effect, it simply outlines the way in which care, which forms the structural whole of Dasein, manifestly contradicts (*widerspricht offenbar*) the possibility of Dasein's being a whole—that is, the way in which the structural whole of Dasein contradicts and thus would preclude Dasein's being a whole. Specifically, the argumentation is that living Dasein cannot be a whole because, as being-ahead-of-itself (*über sich hinaus*) (cf. SZ 192), it always has possibilities still to be settled, has something still outstanding right up to the moment of death. In becoming whole, in coming finally *to be* wholly itself, it would, at the same time, within the unity of that final moment, cease to be, would *not be*. Death would be that moment in which being and nonbeing would coincide in what Heidegger calls here merely their *contradiction*. And yet, is it certain that being and nonbeing can be thought, without residue, by way of the classical concept of contradiction, least of all when it is a matter of their coincidence? What is broached here is more complex, perhaps immeasurably so: this coincidence of being and nonbeing in what I shall call their *opposition,* using this word not even provisionally but only as a way of marking the place of something that, exceeding the system of classical concepts, still remains to be thought and to be named.

To the extent that the argumentation reverts to the classical concept of contradiction, it is indeed too formal; it remains also, as Heidegger suggests, enclosed in the ontology of *Vorhandenheit*. And yet, what it poses merely as a contradiction is precisely *die Sache* that the entire analysis of death in *Being and Time* and beyond will attempt to think: the coincidence of being and nonbeing in their opposition.

In *Being and Time* virtually the entire analysis of death is concentrated in a single short paragraph, which, of course, it will be necessary to read with utmost care. Everything preceding this crucial passage serves to prepare its context; what follows only extends, even if sometimes decisively, the rigorous analysis provided by that paragraph.

Let me reconstitute, as briefly as possible, the series of preparations, especially marking in them the recurrent broaching of *die Sache* that the initial argumentation has outlined as a coincidence of being and nonbeing in their opposition.

First of all, Heidegger establishes for the analysis a context in which death will not be inscribable simply as an occurrence (*Begebenheit*). Death is not simply repeatable from one instance to another; it is not something capable of occurring in various instances with an identity determined independently of every instance, so that one might investigate it by observing the death of others. What precludes any such substitution is the mineness (*Jemeinigkeit*) of death, its ownness. The nonbeing that in death would come to coincide with one's own being, the alterity of death, is not to be compensated for, theoretically, by the shift to the other Dasein.

In every instance death belongs to Dasein as Dasein's own, not as an independent universal that comes to be instantiated. In his 1925 lecture course *History of the Concept of Time* (the penultimate draft of *Being and Time*) Heidegger says simply: "There is no such thing as death in general" (GA 20: 433)—that is, *death* is not a common name but a proper name. On the other hand, Heidegger could not have said, without violating the very possibility of such ontological analysis, that death is therefore something unspeakably individual. Clearly the foresight that construes Dasein as existence sets in question and in motion the classical opposition, associating it decisively with *Vorhandenheit.*

The ownness of death lies, then, in the way that death belongs to existence. The analysis of death thus requires an existential context, that is, it must proceed by marking and determining the connection by which death belongs to existence. According to the determination of the being of Dasein as care, Dasein's existence consists in its being always "ahead of itself," "beyond itself" (*über sich hinaus*), in its projecting out beyond what it has become, out upon what it still has to actualize. Perpetually incomplete, Dasein always projects ahead to what it *not yet* is. Death would be the final "not-yet," the one by which Dasein would be delimited as a whole if it could be so delimited without being itself annihilated in that very delimiting.

Let me move quickly over the series of examples by which Heidegger seeks to determine the character of the not-yet. The fruit that is not yet ripe most resembles Dasein. For its not-yet, that which it not yet is, is neither something outstanding that comes to be added on like the unpaid balance of a debt nor something merely not yet perceived, as when the moon is not yet full. Not only does the fruit itself become what it not yet is, become ripe; but also that very becoming, the ripening, belongs to its very Being. Heidegger writes: "Correspondingly, as long as Dasein is, it too *is always already its not-yet*"(SZ 244)—that is, in becoming what it not yet is, Dasein is always already related to its not-yet, out beyond itself. But what has especially to be marked is the difference. When the fruit has become ripe, it has reached a certain fulfillment (*Vollendung*) in the sense that its possibilities have all been actualized. It is utterly different for Dasein when it arrives at its end: death is not fulfillment, for it is the moment in which Dasein's possibilities are taken away, withdrawn, rather than being actualized. For Dasein the end is never simply full but is, rather, a completion to which belongs withdrawal, annihilation, of possibilities. For Dasein the end annihilates what otherwise still could be rather than simply consigning to the past what has been. The ripe fruit drops finally to the ground; but Dasein dies always in the midst of life.

There is still another difference, or, rather, again the same difference already marked in withholding the analysis of death from the field of *Mitsein*. For Dasein death is not an occurrence; it is neither something that simply happens at the end nor something that, as with the ripening fruit, happens all along right up to the end. For death is Dasein's *own*—that is, something to which Dasein is always already related *as its own*, a possibility in which Dasein's very being is at issue and to which Dasein always already comports itself. It is not a matter of being *at* an end in any sense but of being *toward* the end (*Sein zum Ende*). And it is not a matter of simply being intrinsically directed toward the end but of comporting oneself toward the end as one's own possibility. The fruit merely progresses to its end, but Dasein, comporting itself to that end, is cast back from it in such a way that a certain space is opened, a reserve of freedom. In the end the fruit is consumed, but Dasein is given back to itself.

Hence, too, the difference that Heidegger will never cease to remark between perishing (*Verenden*) and dying (*Sterben*). Again and again he will say: only man dies.

At the threshold of the paragraph in which the existential analysis of death is concentrated, Heidegger poses two additional sets of examples. The examples serve to delimit the sense in which death, no longer inscribable as something outstanding, as *Ausstand*, is, rather, something impending, *Bevorstand*, to which Dasein comports itself. The first set of examples enumerates some of the kinds of things that can impend for Dasein: a storm, the remodelling of the house, the arrival of a friend. In these instances what is impending is simply a being, and one could perhaps even correlate the three examples with the three modes rigorously distinguished in *Being and Time: Vorhandenheit, Zuhandenheit, Mitdasein.* In any case, what utterly distinguishes death from these examples is that it is not simply a being but also nonbeing, or, rather, both, coinciding in their opposition.

The second set of examples is different. Now it is a matter of certain ways of being that Dasein can take up: a journey, a disputation with others, foregoing something that one could be. Such possibilities, such possible ways in which Dasein can be, impend in ways less incomparable to the impending of death. Indeed, the existential analysis of death, now ready to commence, could be read as a differentiation of death from such possibilities.

(b)

Let me turn now to that paragraph in which Heidegger concentrates virtually the entire existential analysis of death. The paragraph is not as explicitly marked as one might expect; it is inscribed in the midst of seemingly coordinate developments within a section (§ 50) entitled "Pre-sketch [*Vorzeichnung*] of the existential-ontological structure of death." It is essential to note that the "pre" ("*vor*") does not signify that the sketch given in this section is simply preliminary, something to be replaced eventually by a more adequate account. Rather, it is a pre-sketch only in the sense that it is situated prior to any differentiation between authentic and inauthentic modifications. It provides an analysis of the formal, undifferentiated structure of Being-toward-death. That analysis is, for essential reasons, centered in the analysis of Being-toward-death as a mode of existence. For this central analysis, which everything up to this point has served only to prepare, Heidegger requires only a few sentences. They must be read with care.

To begin:

> Death is a possibility-of-being [*Seinsmöglichkeit*] which Dasein itself has always to take over. With death, Dasein stands before itself in its *ownmost* can-be [*in seinem* eigensten *Seinkönnen*]. In this possibility what

is at issue for Dasein is its being-in-the-world as such. Its death is the possibility of no-longer-being-able-to-be-there [*die Möglichkeit des Nicht-mehr-dasein--könnens*]. (SZ 250)

Let me try to mark some major connections in these opening sentences.

Everything turns here around the character of death as possibility, death as having the character of possibility. Death is a possibility that Dasein has always to take over—that is, it is a possibility to which Dasein must comport itself, indeed—one might suppose—the only possibility to which Dasein has no choice but to comport itself. Comporting itself to this possibility, Dasein stands before itself in its can-be—that is, Dasein is given back to itself, disclosed to itself, from that possibility.

That possibility is Dasein's own and yet in a way that distinguishes it from all other possibilities that Dasein may take up: death is the possibility that is most Dasein's own, Dasein's *ownmost* possibility. Eventually Heidegger's more extended analysis will demonstrate that death is Dasein's ownmost in that it is that possibility by projection upon which the very space of ownness would first be opened up.

Taking over death as possibility, Dasein stands before itself in its ownmost can-be. What is it that Dasein can be in dying? Presumably, one would have to answer: nothing—even though it is impossible for Dasein simply to *be nothing*. In any case, one could say that in this possibility nothing in particular, nothing definite, is at issue for Dasein but, rather, its Being-in-the-world as such (*schlechthin*). At issue is Dasein's no-longer-being-able-to-be-there—that is, its no longer being Dasein, which can only mean—and yet cannot simply mean—its *being nothing*.

Reading further: "If Dasein stands before itself [*seiner selbst sich bevorsteht*] as this possibility, it has been *fully* referred [*verwiesen*] to its ownmost can-be. Thus standing before itself, all relations in it to another Dasein are undone."

Here again the text traces the same circuit of impending (*Bevorstehen*): Dasein standing before itself—that is, projecting upon impending death and, in turn, being disclosed to itself from this possibility. Now the circuit is also described as Dasein's being fully referred to its ownmost can-be. To be referred (*verwiesen*) is also to be exiled; *ein Verwiesene* is an exile or outlaw. Hence, the self-disclosure is one that effectively exiles Dasein, that is, banishes it from its familiar, everyday surroundings, banishes it *fully*, hence undoing all relations to another Dasein. To stand thus before itself is to have gone fully into exile. Only in exile does Dasein come back to what is most its own.

But why exile? Why so fully exiled from the familiar that even all relations to others are undone? It can only be because death, Dasein's ownmost, is the possibility of being fully banished from the familiar, because death is the very possibility of utter exile. Death detaches Dasein from its everyday involvements, undoes its ties to the familiar, because death is the possibility of losing all possibilities, the possibility that would suspend all others. Death, annihilating all possibilities, has no common measure with other possibilities nor, therefore, with the connections which they govern and which, in turn, structure a world so as to govern all relations with things and with others. Death is nonrelational (*unbezüglich*).

As the possibility of utter exile, death is the extreme possibility. Let me read on: "This ownmost nonrelational possibility is at the same time the extreme one [*die äusserste*]. As can-be, Dasein is not able to surpass [*überholen*] the possibility of death. Death is the possibility of the utter impossibility of Dasein."

The transition traced here is almost direct: since death is nonrelational, detaching Dasein from all other possibilities and involvements, it is *die äusserste Möglichkeit*, the extreme, uttermost, outermost possibility. One could say that death, suspending all other possibilities, also in a sense delimits them: it cannot be outstripped, surpassed, circumvented, in favor of some further possibility. Death is unsurpassable (*unüberholbar*).

One could also say—though Heidegger does not—that death is the *seal* of Dasein's possibilities: it settles them once and for all, decides them irrevocably; it closes them off, seals their lips, as it were; it silences them. Death marks and enforces this closure like the wax seal with which one seals a letter: living possibilities closed off, their silent traces now enclosed in the letter sealed by death. Later it will be necessary to ask: What image or design is imprinted on the wax seal? What is inscribed on the seal of death?

The analysis is now virtually complete. The text continues by gathering up the determinations of death that have emerged: "Thus *death* reveals itself as the *ownmost, nonrelational, unsurpassable possibility.* As such, death is something *distinctively* impending."

One should note how the three determinations of death as possibility distinguish death from all other impending possibilities, for example, from such possibilities as those enumerated at the threshold of the analysis: a journey, a disputation with others, foregoing something that one could be. The distinction is especially notable with respect to these examples because, in effect, they allude to certain limited forms of separation that in the case of death are posed without limit: a journey, that is, separating oneself from the familiar surroundings, from the everyday; a disputation with others, that is, separating oneself from the opinions of others; foregoing something that one could be, that is, separating oneself from some further possibility. Death, on the other hand, separates to the uttermost. Death is utter exile.

The passage concludes by making it explicit that Being-toward-death is a mode of disclosedness, indeed a mode that enjoys a certain privilege: "Its existential possibility is grounded on the following: that Dasein is essentially disclosed [*erschlossen*] to itself, specifically in the manner of the ahead-of-itself [*Sich-vorweg*]. This moment in the structure of care has its most originary concretion in being-toward-death."

Why the privilege? Why is Being-toward-death the most originary among those forms of disclosedness structured by projection? In what sense is it most originary? What can originary and origin (*ursprünglich, Ursprung*) mean here? One direction is clearly marked: because death is the possibility that suspends all others, thus suspending also Dasein's relations with others in the everyday world, disclosure from this possibility serves to draw Dasein back before itself alone, to recall it from dispersion in the world back to a certain unity with itself. A certain wholeness. One should recall here the discourse that generated the very need for the analysis of death, the discourse, just preceding that analysis, in which Heidegger formulated the problem of securing an originary interpretation (*eine ursprüngliche Interpretation*) of Dasein; specifically one should recall that that discourse determined the very sense of *originary* in terms of unity and wholeness (SZ 232). One may say, then, that to be disclosed originarily is to be disclosed at that origin where Dasein is one with itself; it is for Dasein to be disclosed in its ownmost.

And yet, this is not the only direction. For that possibility from which Dasein would be disclosed at the origin is nothing but the very annulment of origin. One cannot but wonder that Dasein's ownmost is precisely that possibility that separates to the uttermost, that separates Dasein not only from others and from its world but also *from itself*, from all else that it could be, or, rather, from *all* that it could be, since it cannot simply *be dead*. One sees, then, that the coincidence of being and nonbeing, inscribed in the analysis of death from the outset, even, in a sense, producing that analysis, comes to be reinscribed at the end of the analysis as the coincidence of ownmost and othermost.

Dasein would *be nothing,* would be *itself* in being *other,* ownmost and othermost, homecoming in exile.

(c)

What follows the analysis that I have just retraced only serves to extend that analysis, though at some points quite decisively. Let me outline three such extensions, moving quickly through them so as to reach by the most economical route the point at which they serve to extend the question of the coincidence of owness and alterity, the question that has essentially governed the analysis.

Whereas the analysis has determined Being-toward-death as a mode of existence, the first of the extensions to which I want to call attention relates this phenomenon to the other two moments of the care-structure, thrownness (*Geworfenheit*) and falling (*Verfallen*). The question is, first of all, how Dasein initially comes into relation to that possibility upon which it projects in Being-toward-death. How does Dasein come upon this possibility? Heidegger's answer: always already. He writes: "The ownmost, nonrelational, unsurpassable possibility is not one that Dasein procures for itself subsequently and occasionally [*nachträglich und gelegentlich*] in the course of its being. But rather, whenever Dasein exists, it is also already *thrown* into this possibility" (SZ 251). Thrown into this possibility, thrown into disclosive projection upon it, Dasein can, nonetheless, occupy the space of disclosure in such a way that what comes to be disclosed from that possibility gets evaded or covered up. Hence, the other moment: not only *can* Dasein fall away from such disclosure but for the most part it *does* so: ". . . proximally and for the most part Dasein covers up its ownmost Being-toward-death, fleeing *before* it" (SZ 251). Being-toward-death is thus also determined by thrownness and falling, even though it is of existence that it is the most originary concretion.

The second of the extensions is prepared by the relating of Being-toward-death to falling. It involves the transition to the inauthentic modification, to that everyday Being-toward-death that is shaped by Dasein's falling away from itself toward the world of its everyday concerns. Falling would bring Dasein back from exile, making it at home even with death, which, correspondingly would be levelled down into an occurrence, something actual taking place within the world, belonging there. Death as ownmost possibility becomes death in general, instantiated here and there among others. Death becomes a common name.

The third of the extensions is the most decisive. It is the extension of the analysis of death into the field of authenticity (*Eigentlichkeit*). Authentic Being-toward-death would require comportment to death *as ownmost possibility*. That is, instead of a comportment to death that would transform it into something actual, there would be required a comportment that would let death be as possibility: "In such Being-toward-death this possibility must not be weakened; it must be understood *as possibility*, it must be cultivated *as possibility*, and *sustained as possibility* in the comportment to it" (SZ 261). Thus, authentic Being-toward-death can be a matter neither of dwelling (*sich aufhalten*) on death, brooding and pondering over when and how it will come, nor of awaiting it (*Erwarten*), since in both cases the possibility character of death would be weakened in favor of actuality. What is required, instead, is that death be granted its full character *as possibility*. For such a mode of Being-toward-death Heidegger proposes the name: *Vorlaufen*. It would be a matter of casting ahead toward this possibility, but in a way that would forego diverting it into some actuality. Instead of transforming death into an actuality, *Vorlaufen* would adhere to its character as *sheer possibility*, would sustain it as possibility.

But what is the character of death as sheer possibility? It is its character as the possibility "of the impossibility of existence as such" (SZ 262). More explicitly, Heidegger continues: "Death, as possibility, gives Dasein nothing to be 'actualized' and nothing that Dasein could itself *be* as actual." Thus, in distinction from all other possibilities, death is not something that Dasein can *be* but is, rather, such sheer possibility that there is nothing to be actualized. Dasein cannot *be dead*.

Furthermore, Heidegger writes that death is not even something to be pictured, to be represented as possible:

> By its very essence, this possibility offers no support for becoming intent on something, "picturing" to oneself [*sich "auszumalen"*] the possible actuality and so forgetting the possibility. (SZ 262)

Let me underline the point: in death as possibility there is *nothing* to present or represent. In its authentic projection upon death, Dasein has nothing present before itself, and its disclosure back to itself from this possibility can only be a disclosure from this nothing, not from any image, from anything that Dasein can imagine. One cannot imagine one's own death. Death marks the limit of imagination. Death is a seal on which no image, no design, is imprinted. Nothing is inscribed on it.

Precisely as Dasein's *ownmost* possibility, death has such utter alterity that it is decisively withdrawn from presence and representation. If, nonetheless, one were to insist on representing it, for instance, picturing it as an event that befalls a certain Dasein, one could do so only at the cost of covering over, concealing, its very character as withdrawn from presence. One could insist on imagining one's own death only at the cost of turning into what in the 1930's Heidegger will come to call errancy (*die Irre*).[3] To turn thus

---

3. See *Vom Wesen der Wahrheit* §7 (GA 9: 196–198). The First Edition of this text appeared in 1943. As a lecture it goes back to 1930.

to imagining one's own death could not but turn death into a common name.

As *ownmost,* death is also *othermost.* And yet, such coincidence could never be flattened out into mere conjunction. Or, rather, it could be so neutralized only at the cost of errancy—neutralized, for example, through the common schema that pairs the negativity of death with the prospect of an afterlife such that Dasein's being dead is displaced into a being again alive. In its most rigorous form, the schema is that of *Aufhebung,* and the negativity of death would be always thinkable as determinate negation. But death would have become a common name; and—to activate all too immediately a much later Heideggerian context, that of *Was Heisst Denken?*—one would have ceased, or, rather not yet have begun, to think, that is, to be drawn along in openness to what withdraws. To think death would require, then, that instead of neutralizing the operation of alterity, one grant the alterity its uttermost character. One would want, then, to say that death, precisely in being ownmost, is the absolutely other—even though one could not but then withdraw the saying, leaving only its trace. At least insofar as absolute must be thought as absolution *of otherness.* Death would be still more absolute: absolution *from presence.*

If death is coincidence of being and nonbeing in their opposition, if death is both ownmost and othermost, then being-toward-death cannot, except in errancy, be neutralized into a persistent state or condition, not even if precautions are taken to distinguish such a state from *das Vorhandene.* Even the projection structure, existence as such, which bears the entire weight of Heidegger's analysis, begins now to slide under the weight of the analysis of death as both ownmost and othermost, as a possibility that is utterly *nonpresentable,* and as a possibility upon which Dasein would *always already* have projected. Not only does the projection structure, as outlined in the preparatory analysis in the First Division of *Being and Time,* lack any reference to any such peculiar configuration as has emerged, that of coincidence in opposition; but also it cannot but appear inappropriate to describe as projection the relation to a possibility that is utterly nonpresentable and that is such that, if the relation to it were a matter of projection, Dasein would have always already to have projected upon it. Sliding thus under the weight of these results, the projection structure needs to be reinforced, supplemented, and eventually reconstituted by a certain energy that would hold being and nonbeing together precisely by holding them apart, that would let them be coincident in their opposition, spacing them in a way that lets them be together in their very opposition, without reduction and without synthesis. Such energy of holding together by holding apart, such hovering (*Schweben*) between what one would, if it were possible, call absolute opposites—such is what in a decisive phase of German Idealism was called imagination (*Einbildungskraft*).[4] Imagination, thus determined, would of course exceed the mere power of imagining in the sense of presenting images to oneself. And, as thus determined, imagination would be not merely something limited by death but rather the very power by which one would be able to comport oneself to death, to the limit. Imagination would be the power of hovering between death as ownmost and death as othermost. Imagination would sustain death in its more than absolute alterity.

In the analysis of death as coincidence of being and nonbeing in their opposition, as both ownmost and othermost, doubling is thought in the most concentrated configuration. Indeed, the very structure of doubling is said directly in the conjunction: *coincidence* and *opposition*. It is said, too, in *imagination*.

(d)

There is, of course, no such turn back to imagination in Heidegger's work. Indeed, by 1936 Heidegger is prepared, no doubt for certain strategic reasons, to declare it "questionable whether the essence of poetry, and this means at the same time the essence of projection, can be sufficiently thought from imagination" (GA 5:60). Heidegger uses both the Latinate and the Germanic form, *Imagination* and *Einbildungskraft,* as if to emphasize the break. These words seldom again appear in Heidegger's texts.

4. See especially J. G. Fichte, *Werke*, ed. I. H. Fichte (Berlin: Walter de Gruyter, 1971), 1:215–16. Cf. my *Spacings—of Reason and Imagination,* chap. 2.

On the other hand, the words *death* and *mortal* never cease to reappear. Not that the later discourses on death replace, revise, or even reopen the analysis of death completed in *Being and Time*. On the contrary, all the later discourses serve constantly to confirm the earlier analysis by reinscribing it within contexts that otherwise decisively exceed that of *Being and Time*.

There can be no question here of reconstituting the entire itinerary. Let me, rather, simply refer—very schematically—to four of the texts along that itinerary.

First of all, from the recently published manuscript that Heidegger composed in the years 1936–1938 under the title *Beiträge zur Philosophie*. Here he writes directly of what I have tried more circuitously to outline in *Being and Time* as the coincidence of being and nonbeing in their opposition. Heidegger calls it belongingness (*Zugehörigkeit*) and writes that in Being-toward death, "the essential belongingness of the nothing to Being is hidden [or harbored—*verbirgt sich*]" (GA 65: 282). Thus, as he continues, now reinscribing the analysis, death is "the highest and extreme attestation [*Zeugnis*] of Being" (GA 65: 284). Testifying to Being by attesting to the nothing that belongs to it, death opens man to what is uncommon: "In the strangeness and uniqueness of death there opens up what is strangest amidst all beings—Being itself—which essentially unfolds as something strange [*das als Befremdung west*] (GA 65: 283).

The second text is the essay "The Thing" dated 1950. This is one of the texts in which man is named mortal, and I have already cited from it most of the following sentences, which, in announcing the proper name of man, recall the analysis of death in *Being and Time:* "Mortals are men. They are called mortals because they can die. To die means to be capable of death as death. Only man dies. The animal perishes. It has death neither ahead of itself nor behind it" (VA 177).

Now Heidegger introduces suddenly a strange inversion, beginning the next sentence thus: "Death is the shrine of the nothing, that is, of that which in every respect is never something that merely is [*nicht etwas bloss Seiendes*] but which nevertheless essentially unfolds [*west*], even as the mystery of Being itself." A shrine is a tomb or a hallowed place or thing that commemorates one no longer among us, one who is not—and nevermore can be—present, one who is dead. The shrine lets those who remain somehow call to mind that one who will nevermore be present; it calls forth one who, henceforth, is not, is nothing. A shrine is also, especially as the German *Schrein,* a case or casket in which, most notably, the dead one would be enclosed, sealed off, and in a sense preserved as one who would *be dead,* who would—if it were only possible—both be and not be, producing a coincidence of being and nothing. As the shrine of the nothing, death attests to what the *Beiträge* has named the belongingness of the nothing to Being.

The text continues by outlining precisely this belongingness: "As the shrine of the nothing, death shelters in itself the essential unfolding of Being [*birgt . . . das Wesende des Seins in sich*]. As the shrine of the nothing, death is the shelter [*das Gebirg*] of Being."

Again there is an unmarked break in the text: the analysis from *Being and Time* is suddenly recalled again, this time performatively: "Mortals we now call mortals—not because their earthly life comes to an end but rather because they are capable of death as death." Thus recalled, the analysis is, finally, reinscribed in the context that has been prepared: "Mortals are who they are as mortals, essentially unfolding within the shelter of Being [*wesend im Gebirg des Seins*]. They are the essentially unfolding relation to Being as Being."

The third text is *The Principle of Ground,* dated 1955–56. The relevant passage has as its context—which I cannot here even begin to reconstitute—a discussion of Being as abyss (*Abgrund*), a discussion in which Heidegger proposes to have recourse to the essence of play (*Spiel*) in order to think Being as abyss. He specifies that it is a matter of the play into which we mortals are drawn insofar as we dwell in proximity to death. An abrupt reference to death as Dasein's extreme possibility recalls the analysis from *Being and Time* and leads up to the passage that I would like to cite: "Death is the still unthought measure [*Massgabe*] of the immeasurable, that is, of the highest play into which man is in an earthly way brought. . ." (SG 187). To say the least: the character of death as extreme (*äusserst*), as outermost, that was determined in the earlier analysis is now reinscribed in the determination of death as the measure of the immeasurable. At the same time, one might also read the immeasurable as reinscribing the opposition that the analysis in *Being and Time* determined, first, between being and nonbeing and, finally, between ownmost and othermost. The coincidence of these in their opposition—that is, death—would enshrine and thus measure the most extreme extremes, those so extreme that the space between them would be immeasurable, a space of abysmal play, or— let me now say—a space spaced in the play of imagination.

The final text is "The Essence of Language," dated 1957–58. Again the analysis from *Being and Time* is recalled; again it is reinscribed: "Mortals are those who can experience death as death. Animals are not capable of this. But animals also cannot speak. The essential connection between death and language flashes up, but is still unthought" (US 215). Now the analysis of death is reinscribed in a context where the very question is that of inscription, language, names.

And so I return, finally, to the question of the proper name of man. All that I have said would, of course, only serve to confirm the name that Heidegger proposes: *mortal* is the proper name of man. It is proper even to the extreme that is today required, for, once death has been determined as coincidence of ownmost and othermost, the name *mortal* would say the disowning of man precisely in saying his ownness.

But, especially if one were to take up that connection that Heidegger lets flash up in the last passage that I cited, one would need to pursue in still another direction the question of the proper name of man. One would need to ask—and *Being and Time*, without enunciating it, already provokes the question—whether mortality is not only the proper name of man but also the very condition of possibility of names as such, that is, whether the relation to death is not always already in play in the very opening of language. In this case mortality would prove to be a proper name in a twofold sense: both the name most extremely proper to man and the name that would be most properly a name by saying what is proper to itself and to every name, what opens all naming and language.

And so, all that I might say, if I were to pursue this further question, would only serve to confirm in a further sense that name

that Heidegger has proposed. And yet, confirming that name, perhaps even extending ever so slightly what would be said with it, I
would also want, on the other hand, to reinscribe the entire
Heideggerian analysis in the context of another name; for *imagination* would say differently that coincidence of ownness and otherness that is mortality.

Sacrifice of Understanding

At the limit, the extreme limit, the projection structure that would constitute understanding begins to slide. Unable to bear that limit, it will eventually have to be abandoned for the sake of the limit and of the disclosure that takes place at the limit. With the analysis of death there will prove to have commenced a sacrifice of understanding, a sacrifice in the face of death, a sacrifice for the sake of nothing, understanding being given up to the essential unfolding of Being.

Yet, the connections established in *Being and Time* are such that understanding could not be sacrificed without a profound disturbance being introduced into the delimitation of truth. Truth, determined originarily as disclosedness (*Erschlossenheit*), will likewise begin to slide. It will slide away from Dasein to such an extent that, in the self-interpretations that commence in the late 1940s and, in effect, mark the redeterminations produced by this and other shifts, Heidegger will say openly that the truth of Being is not exhausted in Dasein.[1] But only in much later texts (most notably, in "The End of Philosophy and the Task of Thinking" [1964]) will he

1. Because of the strategy that the self-interpretations put into play as well as the complexity of the analyses and the shifts, Heidegger's formulation, though open, involves a complexity of reference and counter-reference. Let me extract from its very developed context in the "Introduction to 'What Is Metaphysics?'" (1949) only the following statement: "From 'existence', rightly thought, it is possible to think the 'essence' of Dasein, in whose openness Being manifests and conceals itself, grants and withdraws itself, without this truth of Being exhausting itself in Dasein and without its being at all possible to equate this truth with Dasein in the manner of the metaphysical proposition: all objectivity is, as such, subjectivity" (GA 9: 373f.).

abandon *truth* for ἀλήθεια.² Yet, in contrast to the case of under-standing, all these moves will only serve to preserve and secure what from the beginning Heidegger attempted to think in the space between ἀλήθεια and truth, in the space of this translation.

Understanding, on the other hand, comes to be sacrificed. In-deed, the sacrifice will already have been prepared, unobtrusively, in the very inscription of understanding.

It will be a matter, then, of attending to these preparations and of witnessing then the performance of the rite.

(a)

Understanding—an open inscription.

Even where it might seem least so, in the texts of the Marburg period, centered in *Being and Time.*

Is this perhaps also where there is least understanding of open inscription, of its complications, where these are even least under-standable? At least in comparison with Heidegger's later texts.

The inscription of *understanding* (*Verstehen*) will never have been quite rounded out and closed off within the text. Neither will the project announceable under the title: understanding of Being

---

2. "In any case, one thing becomes clear: the question of ἀλήθεια, of unconceal-ment as such, is not the question of truth. For this reason, it was inadequate [*nicht sachgemäss*] and thus misleading to call ἀλήθεια, in the sense of clearing, truth" (SD 77). This abandoning of *truth* is related to the discussion between Heidegger and Friedländer concerning the meaning of ἀλήθεια among the Greeks and concerning the transition, which Heidegger had sought to mark in his interpretation of Plato, from ἀλήθεια (as unconcealment) to ὀρθότης (correctness). Regarding this discus-sion see Bernasconi, *The Question of Language in Heidegger's History of Being*, chap. 2. I have outlined the discussion, more briefly, in *Delimitations,* chap. 14.

To the above statement Heidegger adds the following note: "How the attempt to think a matter can for a time stray from what a decisive insight has already shown is demonstrated by a passage from *Being and Time,* 1927 (p. 219): 'The translation [of the word ἀλήθεια (Heidegger's addition)] by means of the word "truth" and even the theoretical-conceptual determinations of this expression [truth (Heidegger's addition)] cover up the meaning of what the Greeks established as basically "self-evident" in the prephilosophical understanding of their terminological employment of ἀλήθεια.'" The final differentiation thus secures what Heidegger attempted to think from the beginning.

(*Seinsverständnis*). Which is to say that the text too remains open. Which is not simply to say incomplete, as one says—all too carelessly, no doubt—of *Being and Time*.

The drafts of the inscription turn on displacement, on inversion, on destabilizing determinations and concentrations.

A displacement introduces the most systematic inscription, the one written in *Being and Time* under the title "Da-sein as Understanding" (SZ §31). Instead of its ordinary sense, *understanding* is now to designate one of the constituents of the Being of the *Da*, a constituent whose place has already been outlined by a previous analysis: it is that disclosedness (*Erschlossenheit*) that takes place in connection with what the analysis of world has determined as the for-the-sake-of-which (*Worumwillen*), as the focal point in which a totality of equipmental references constitutive of a world is gathered and in a sense determined. Inscribed at this site of the existential analysis, understanding is withdrawn from the ordinary sense, from understanding "in the sense of *one* possible kind of knowing among others, as distinguished, for instance, from 'explaining' ['*Erklären*']"; or, rather, the ordinary sense is retained, but only "as an existential derivative" of the primary understanding. The displacement is thus also a doubling of sense and a subordination of the ordinary sense to its originary double.

This displacement, placing understanding at its primary site, is, in turn, linked to an inversion. The inversion is one that deprives intuition of its traditional priority, most notably, of that priority over understanding that Heidegger shows it to have, for instance, at a certain level of the Kantian problematic (KM 20ff.). Now inscribed as the site of a certain disclosedness of world, understanding would always already have outreached any intuition; and intuition, insofar as its alleged priority "corresponds noetically to the priority of the present-at-hand [*des Vorhandenen*] in traditional ontology" (SZ 147), will always merely have narrowed and reduced the expanse opened by understanding, while, precisely as the condition of its operation, remaining grounded on understanding. In other words, understanding would serve not to stabilize intuition—referring to the most radical formulation of the Kantian problematic, that of Fichte's

Wissenschaftslehre[3]—but quite to the contrary: understanding would always already have destabilized any presence that intuition would sustain, exposing Dasein ecstatically to a world.

The inscription of understanding in *Being and Time* is not only the most systematic but also the most rigorous in the sense that it effects a structural determination of the phenomenon. This rigorous determination is most conspicuous against the background of the inscription in the 1925 lecture course *History of the Concept of Time*, which, delivered just months before *Being and Time* was actually written (and used extensively in that final writing), covers in the same systematic order more than half of the book published in 1927. In the lecture course understanding is characterized as a mode of discoveredness (*Entdecktheit*) (GA 20 §28b). What is lacking, what does not appear until *Being and Time*, is the determination of understanding as projection (*Entwurf*). It is only with the development of this determination—and, no doubt, by virtue of a certain structural complicity with it—that the distinction between discoveredness (*Entdecktheit*) and disclosedness (*Erschlossenheit*) is finally displaced from the space between Dasein and world (which it still serves to divide in *History of the Concept of Time*) and brought, instead, to mark the differentiation between beings within-the-world and world itself.[4]

3. "It is clear that in this inquiry we have no fixed point but rather revolve in an eternal circle unless intuition, in itself and as such, is first stabilized [*fixirt*] . . . ; and everything that is stabilized is stabilized purely in the understanding [*Verstand*]." The circling that is to be limited through the stabilization is that of imagination, which, in the order that the Deduction of Representation would follow, has priority over intuition; this priority marks the limit of the solidarity of Fichte's early *Wissenschaftslehre* with the traditional priority of intuition and presence. (Cf. my discussion in *Spacings—of Reason and Imagination,* chap. 2.) Understanding, though essential for stabilization, would seem even more derivative: "Understanding is a dormant, inactive power of the mind, the mere receptacle of what imagination brings forth and what reason determines or has yet to determine; whatever may have been told of its doings at one time or another" (*Grundlage der gesammten Wissenschaftslehre* [1794], vol. 1 of *Werke,* ed. I. H. Fichte, 232f.).

4. In *History of the Concept of Time,* Heidegger refers to "the specific discoveredness [*Entdecktheit*] of the world, which we have called disclosedness [*Erschlossenheit*] to distinguish it from that of Being-in"; but he insists, nonetheless, on the unity of the "phenomenon which we call discoveredness" (GA 20 §28a). The realignment of the distinction in *Being and Time* becomes most emphatic in the analysis of truth: "The earlier analysis of the worldhood of the world and of beings within-the-world [*des innerweltlichen Seienden*] has shown, however, that the discoveredness [*Entdeckt-*

And yet, the determination of understanding as projection brings more fully into relief a certain decentered or disoriented character that, all along, differentiates it from positing (*Setzen*) in the transcendental sense. In understanding, Dasein projects upon possibilities, and yet without grasping them thematically, since any such grasp would have the effect of depriving them of their very character of possibility. Dasein's projection upon possibilities is, rather, such as to let them be *as* possibilities. Projective understanding neither simply gives rise to possibilities nor does it appropriate them as possibilities, though Dasein may, of course, seize upon them so as to actualize them. But, as the structure of understanding, projection lies between origination and appropriation. In the direction of origin it is *thrown* projection, (dis)oriented toward what will always already have arisen: "As essentially dispositional [*befindliches*], Dasein has always already gotten itself into definite possibilities" (SZ 144). To say nothing of the disorientation that projective understanding bears—or, rather, is made to bear—within itself: Dasein cannot but project upon a possibility that both is most proper to itself and yet absolutely cannot be appropriated. Fundamental ontology cannot but regard Being-toward-death as a mode of projective understanding, even at the cost of disorienting the projection structure and starting its slide toward the abyss.

Temporality, too, proves to be something like a mode of projective understanding, at least according to the analysis in the 1927 course *The Basic Problems of Phenomenology*. That analysis, reversing the founding order laid out in *Being and Time*, would uncover within each ecstasis of primordial temporality, within the very temporalizing of the ecstases, a projection upon a horizonal schema—that is, a kind of protounderstanding, a projective understanding concentrated, as it were, within the structure of ecstatic temporality.[5] The demonstration that and how temporality is the horizon of the understanding of Being would terminate in the uncovering of

heit] is *grounded* in the disclosedness [*Erschlossenheit*] of the world. But disclosedness is that basic character of Dasein according to which it *is* its there [*Da*]. Disclosedness is constituted by disposition, understanding, and discourse and pertains equioriginarily [*gleichursprünglich*] to world, to Being-in, and to the self" (SZ 220).

5. See above, chap. 4 (c). I have discussed this analysis in somewhat greater detail in *Delimitations*, chap. 10.

a protounderstanding operative within the very temporalizing of temporality as such. Temporality would prove to be not a horizon beyond understanding that would make understanding possible but rather a harboring of understanding, an unfolding of understanding within itself. In the end, there would be not only a temporality of understanding but also an understanding of temporality. There would be nothing, not even temporality, beyond understanding.

Not even the project itself that was to have been carried out by *Being and Time:* it, too, moves entirely within the structure of projective understanding. With all its analyses, fundamental ontology would do no more than effect a transition from the preontological understanding of Being to a properly ontological, i.e., thematic, understanding of Being. Thus, *Being and Time* moves within the space of a projection; and this is why there can arise the demand that is finally broached in the 1928 lecture course *The Metaphysical Foundations of Logic,* the demand that fundamental ontology undergo a certain turn, that it be overturned. Corresponding to the intrinsic reference—the (dis)orientation—of understanding back to thrownness, there is an inner necessity that ontology turn back to the place of its beginning. For the understanding of Being, which it is the sole task of fundamental ontology to develop, occurs only in Dasein and thus presupposes the factical existence of Dasein. But the latter, in turn, presupposes the factical extantness (*Vorhandensein*) of nature, of the totality of beings, of beings as a whole (*das Seiende im Ganzen*). Heidegger concludes: "Thus there arises the necessity of a special problematic that has for its theme beings as a whole [*das Seiende im Ganzen*]. This new interrogation [*Fragestellung*] lies in the essence of ontology itself and results from its overturning [*Umschlag*], its μεταβολή. This problematic I designate *metontology*" (GA 26: 199). Here, then, thrownness cannot but overtake (finite) understanding, requiring its overturning, turning fundamental ontology back to beings as a whole, turning it into metontology, releasing a doubling return, from the meaning of Being to beings (as a whole). Thus, referring to the analysis of time as the meaning of Being, Heidegger goes on to trace explicitly the return and the doubling:

But this temporal analysis is, at the same time, the *turn* [*Kehre* (Heidegger's italics)], in which ontology itself expressly runs back into the metaphysical ontic in which it implicitly always stands. Through the movement of radicalizing and universalizing, it is a matter of bringing ontology to the overturning [*Umschlag*] latent in it. Here the turning [*das Kehren*] is carried out, and it occurs as the overturning into metontology. In their unity, fundamental ontology and metontology form the concept of metaphysics. (GA 26: 201f.)

The doubling of metaphysics occurs as a turning, as an overturning; if one brings also into play the designation of the move to *Temporalität* (to time and Being) as a turning,[6] then it may be said, too, that the turning is itself doubled: a turning to the beyond of Being (fundamental ontology) and a turning back from the beyond, back to beings (metontology).

The latter turn is also a return from understanding to the field of beings as a whole within which understanding will always have erupted.

Such is, then, in the broadest strokes, the inscription of understanding, its *open* inscription in and around *Being and Time*. To say that the inscription is open is to say, too, that understanding is threatened, threatened by the prospect of overturning, as in the draft of metontology, threatened by the prospect of effacement, of sacrifice.

(b)

The first phase of the sacrifice of understanding occurs in Heidegger's inaugural lecture of 1929, "What Is Metaphysics?" In the text of this lecture the doubling is very near the surface: it is a discussion about metaphysics, one that comes to identify metaphysics as the basic happening (*Grundgeschehen*) of Dasein, but which, on the other hand, proceeds by addressing a particular metaphysical ques-

---

6. This designation is found, for example, in the "Letter on Humanism": "Here the whole is turned around [*Hier kehrt sich das Ganze um*]" (GA 9: 328). In the same context he refers, even more explicitly, to "the thinking of the turning [*Kehre* from 'Being and time' to 'time and Being'." The designation is, of course, implicit in the title originally proposed for the never published Third Division of Part One of *Being and Time*, namely, "Time and Being."

tion (GA 9: 103, 122). A later text, reflecting back upon it, marks its double character even more explicitly: its thinking is both metaphysical and no longer metaphysical (GA 9: 304).

In "What Is Metaphysics?" there occurs a sacrifice of understanding, not yet of the *Verstehen* openly inscribed in the Marburg texts, but of what Heidegger calls *Verstand*, echoing a tradition that reaches back to Kant, especially by way of Hegel. Heidegger identifies *Verstand* as the thinking that would be determined by the rules of traditional logic (GA 9: 107); he identifies it also as what provides the standard for all calculating and regulating (GA 9: 305). On the other hand, *Verstehen* is silently left in place; the Introduction that Heidegger later provided for "What Is Metaphysics?" indicates that it is a matter of retaining *Verstehen* precisely by doubling it along the same lines as those that serve to double the text itself.[7]

Verstand is forsaken in the course of an overturning in which the entire text "What Is Metaphysics?"is engaged. The overturning is structurally akin to the turn broached in *The Metaphysical Foundations of Logic* as an overturning into metontology. It is also akin to a decisive turn that occurs within *Being and Time:* following the demonstration, by way of the analysis of death, that Dasein's Being-a-whole is ontologically possible, there is a turn back to the *ontic*. The turn is presented as fulfilling a methodological requirement: it is a turn to conscience as Dasein's ontic attestation to its authenticity, a turn through which Heidegger undertakes to show, more precisely, that conscience is an ontic attestation in which Dasein attests to itself its possible authenticity (SZ §54). And yet, though indeed anticipating the radical overturning broached in the draft of metontology, the turn back to beings, clearly the turn to conscience is, in the end, governed largely by the project and the directionality

---

7. Heidegger refers to the bind in which a thinking is involved that would proceed from the representing [*Vorstellen*] of beings to the thinking of the truth of Being: in a certain way it would still represent the truth of Being, and yet, as representational, it would be inappropriate to what would be thought. He continues: "This relation [*Verhältnis*], stemming from metaphysics, entering into the referral [*Bezug*] of the truth of Being to the essence of man, is conceived as 'understanding' ['*Verstehen*']. But here understanding is, at the same time, thought from out of the unconcealment of Being." Thus doubling *Verstehen*, he then proceeds to develop its no-longer-metaphysical double by reference to projection, thus also doubling the latter (GA 9: 377).

of fundamental ontology; it is a turn back that is, quite decisively, for the sake of the advance toward the beyond of Being.

But now, in "What Is Metaphysics?", it is a matter of an overturning required neither by the radicalizing of the duality within metaphysics (πρώτη φιλοσοφία/θεολογία) (GA 26: 202) nor by the methodological structure of phenomenological analysis. Now the overturning is required by the very occasion of the lecture, by the character of the deed that the discourse would, as such, carry out. For as an inaugural lecture, it is addressed to those within the university, addressed to the problem of the university:

> The fields of the sciences lie far apart. The ways they treat their objects differ fundamentally. Today this disintegrating multiplicity of disciplines is held together still only by the technical organization of the universities and faculties; and it is kept significant only by the practical establishment of goals in each field. On the other hand, the rootedness of the sciences in their essential ground has atrophied. (GA 9: 104)

It is to this problem, above all—the uprootedness of the sciences and the corresponding disunity and disorientation of the university—that the lecture is addressed. It addresses this problem precisely by recourse to that from which the rootedness and the unity of the diverse sciences must be thought: in all the sciences, Heidegger says, we relate ourselves to beings themselves and do so in such a way as to grant to those beings the first and last word (GA 9: 104). It is not, then, a matter of an ontology that would address the sciences from above, delivering a ground to them; rather, it is a matter of an overturning that would turn back to beings themselves, a matter of a return that would submit the discourse to precisely that to which all the sciences are essentially submitted. Through the return to such submission, the lecture is addressed also, more indirectly, to the question of leadership (*Führerschaft*): "This position of service in research and theory unfolds in such a way as to become the ground of the possibility of a proper though limited leadership in the whole of human existence" (GA 9: 104f.). In short, the problem of the university cannot but broach also the problem of politics.

Thus, the turn in which "What Is Metaphysics?" engages is a return to beings themselves, not to those corresponding to any particular science but to beings as a whole (*das Seiende im Ganzen*), into which the being called *man* erupts in the pursuit called *science*. And yet, the lecture would pursue the return still further, in the direction indicated by the necessity, in order to delimit beings as a whole, of referring beyond beings to nothing. The lecture would press on, following the downward way, on into the nothing. This way is the altar on which *Verstand* is to be sacrificed, on which it is to be sacrificed for nothing, in an expenditure without return. For *Verstand* could not but declare all discourse on the nothing absurd: such discourse, even in an interrogative mode, cannot avoid saying of the nothing that it *is*. Such discourse cancels, on the one hand, what it would say, on the other; and so, in the end, when the results are calculated, it is a discourse that accomplishes nothing, a discursive expenditure without return, a discourse that *says nothing*. But that is precisely the way that the lecture would pursue, the way of a discourse that would *say nothing;* and what is required to open that way is only that *Verstand* be sacrificed, that its power be shattered by an originary questioning that presses on into the nothing.

And yet, in order to be able to press on on that way toward the nothing, it must be possible to encounter the nothing. Thus, the lecture focuses on that disposition, that mood or attunement (*Stimmung*), in which man is brought before the nothing. It is a matter of reinscribing what *Being and Time* called anxiety (*Angst*) and of saying how it is that anxiety carries man on beyond beings as a whole so as to bring him before the nothing.

Here is what the lecture says, first of all. In anxiety "all things and we ourselves sink into indifference" and in this sense slip away into a non-sense; we can get no hold on things or on ourselves, and we are overcome by this non-hold. It is thus that anxiety reveals the nothing. Or, rather, in inducing the slipping away of beings, anxiety leaves us hovering (*schweben*): we ourselves, beings in the midst of beings, slip away from ourselves, so that in this regard the hovering is, as in the case of Being-toward-death,[8] a hovering between ownness and otherness (GA 9: 111f.).

Thus, the lecture also says still more. In this slipping away of beings, the nothing, which is thus revealed, is encountered at one

---

8. See above, chap. 5 (c).

with beings as a whole, in and as the slipping away of beings as a whole. It serves, then, to reveal "these beings in their full but heretofore concealed strangeness as utterly other—over against the nothing." Then: "In the clear night of the nothing of anxiety the originary openness of beings as such arises: that they are beings—and not nothing" (GA 9: 114). Anxiety, bringing man before the nothing, brings him also before beings *as such,* thus extending him "beyond beings as a whole" (GA 9: 115), turning him back again toward Being. Thus, finally: "The nothing does not remain the indeterminate opposite of beings but reveals itself as belonging to the Being of beings" (GA 9: 120).

It is a matter not only of hovering between beings as a whole and the nothing of their slipping away; but also of a hovering between beings as a whole and Being, a hovering, in anxiety, around the nothing, a hovering that holds together, that holds itself simultaneously upon, the upward and the downward way.

Thus, by sacrificing *Verstand* and pressing on into the nothing, the lecture extends the downward way, on beyond beings; it breaks with the claim that *Verstand* would make to control, even to originate, all negation; and it presses on into a discourse on modes of negation whose power shatters any such claim: unyielding antagonism, stinging rebuke, galling failure, merciless prohibition, bitter privation (GA 9: 117). And yet, precisely, by pressing on on the downward way, the lecture *also* circles back onto the way upward, toward Being—hovering, thus, on the way.

The lecture concludes with a question that would be the interrogative double of what arises in the clear night of the nothing of anxiety. Granted that the outreach into the nothing, going beyond beings, is metaphysics itself, this question would be, then, the basic question (*Grundfrage*) of metaphysics: Why are there beings at all and not, rather, nothing?

It is in the Afterword added to "What Is Metaphysics?" in 1943 that Heidegger explicitly marks the double character of the text of the 1929 lecture: in asking the question "What is metaphysics?" this text questions beyond metaphysics and is linked to a thinking that has entered already into the overcoming of metaphysics; and yet, it cannot but bring into play the very language of that which it would be engaged in overcoming. Thus: "This questioning must think metaphysically and, at the same time, must think from out of the ground of metaphysics, i.e., no longer metaphysically" (GA 9: 303f.).

It is also in this Afterword that there occurs a notorious passage that Heidegger drastically altered between the 1943 edition and the 1949 edition. The passage occurs in the course of a discussion whose parameters are expressed in this way: "The utterly other of all beings is not-being [*das Nicht-Seiende*]. But this nothing [of beings—Heidegger adds in a marginal note] essentially unfolds [*west*] as Being" (GA 9: 306). Here it is again the clear night of the nothing that is invoked, the outreach beyond beings to nothing, which, in its utter otherness with respect to beings, brings man before beings *as such*, turning him back toward Being. What is in question, then, in the discussion is the movement between beings and Being, the coherence between their revelations. Or, rather, what is in question is the doubling return from Being to beings.

The two editions of the Afterword agree "that a being never is without Being [*dass niemals ein Seiendes ist ohne das Sein*] (GA 9: 306); the only difference in this regard is that the 1943 edition includes an *aber* (*dass niemals aber . . .*)—later deleted—to mark the contrast with the complementary statement. In the 1943 edition that statement says: "that Being indeed essentially unfolds without beings [*dass das Sein wohl west ohne das Seiende*]." But then, in the 1949 edition it says: "that Being never essentially unfolds without beings [*dass das Sein nie west ohne das Seiende*]." The difference could hardly be more sharply focused: what the later edition adds, by the alteration of a single word, is the doubling return from Being to beings. And yet, the difference is blurred and the bearing of the passage and of the alteration is rendered much more complicated by the series of marginal notes keyed to it and published in the *Gesamtausgabe*. One note, in particular, in the 1949 edition explicates *das Sein . . . west* by explicating *Wesen von Sein*, declaring the latter phrase ambiguous and drawing then a distinction between "*Ereignis*, not effected by beings" and "*Seiendheit-Washeit*."[9] One can only

9. The note in its entirety reads: "Wesen von Sein: Seyn, Unterschied; 'Wesen' von Sein mehrdeutig: 1. Ereignis, nicht durch Seiendes bewirkt, Ereignis—Gewähr-

wonder at this divorce between two ways in which Being can essentially unfold (*west*): as *Ereignis,* hence without beings; or as *Seiendheit,* into which Being would dissolve (indeed has dissolved, namely in—i.e., as—the history of metaphysics), giving full sway to beings.[10] Is it a matter of deciding between a thinking beyond Being, a thinking that could not but run the risk of tautology, *and* a thinking that would remain this side of Being, a thinking that could not but remain uniformly metaphysical? Can the doubling return from Being to beings only reproduce metaphysics? Or does it open upon and belong to the thinking beyond Being, as "What Is Metaphysics?" would seem to have shown.

Toward the end of the Afterword Heidegger refers again to what in "What Is Metaphysics?" was called *Verstand,* now linking such "logical" understanding still more directly with calculation (*Rechnung*), with calculative thinking. Then, drawing the decisive contrast, Heidegger launches upon one of his most astonishing passages. What he contrasts with calculative thinking is a thinking that is determined from the other of beings (*aus dem Anderen des Seienden*). He calls it essential thinking (*das wesentliche Denken*) and describes it as a thinking that squanders, lavishes, expends itself (*verschwendet . . . sich*) upon Being for the truth of Being. Because it answers to the need (*Not*) to preserve the truth of Being, because it gives itself up for the sake of the truth of Being, such thinking occurs "in the freedom of sacrifice [*Opfer*]": "Sacrifice, removed from all compulsion because arising from the abyss of freedom, is the lavishing of the essence of man in the preservation of the truth of Being for beings" (GA 9: 309f.). In sacrifice, he says, there takes place a concealed thanks (*der verborgene Dank*), and thinking becomes thanking.

ende; 2. Seiendheit—Washeit: während, dauernd, ἀεί." Another important note to the 1943 version of this passage expresses more decisively the removal of *Ereignis* from beings: "In der Wahrheit des Seins west das Seyn qua Wesen der Differenz; dieses Seyn qua Seyn ist vor der Differenz das Ereignis und deshalb *ohne* Seiendes."

10. "But metaphysics is the history of Being as the pro-ceeding from the origin [*Fort-gang aus dem Anfang*]. . . . In this proceeding Being releases itself into beingness [*Seiendheit*] and refuses the clearing of what is originary in the origin [*verweigert die Lichtung der Anfängnis des Anfangs*]. Beginning as ἰδέα, beingness opens up the preeminence of beings with regard to the essential impress of truth, whose essence itself belongs to Being" (N II: 486).

The sacrifice of *Verstand* thus proves only to have prepared the way for this other sacrifice, in which the very essence of man would be expended. Originary thinking would take place as this other sacrifice. In other words, essential thinking would occur in the very squandering of the essence of man.

Heidegger continues with a passage whose mere linguistic complexity is such that I shall have to double my translation by adding much of the German text and even some commentary:

> Originary thinking is the resounding to the favor of Being [*der Widerhall der Gunst des Seins*—One could say equally, and perhaps more clearly: the echo of the favor of Being], in which [favor] that which is unique is cleared and can occur [*in der sich das Einzige lichtet und sich ereignen lässt* (The clause is—and, no doubt, would be declared by Heidegger, for essential reasons—untranslatable)]: that beings are. This resounding is the human answer to the word of the soundless voice [*der lautlosen Stimme*] of Being. The answer of thinking [Heidegger adds in a marginal note: The speechless answer of thanking in sacrifice] is the origin of the human word, which word first allows language to arise as the sounding of the word in words [*als die Verlautung des Wortes in die Wörter*]. (GA 9: 310)

Here, in the sounding and resounding of these words, everything is gathered. There is the clear night of the nothing in which man is brought before beings as such, that they *are*. But before this, first giving it its opening, there is the favor of Being. Originary thinking occurs as a resounding to the favor of Being, as the echo in which man answers the soundless voice of Being, thus originating the human word and language. Originary thinking is the sacrifice in which man squanders himself, gives himself up, by echoing the favorable yet soundless voice of Being. In originary thinking man freely sacrifices himself to the truth of Being by becoming the echo of that truth. Almost as Echo herself disappeared from sight—either dried up and turned to stone or dismembered and buried—and remained only voice.

The passage returns, finally, to calculation: "Sacrifice is the departure from beings on the path to the preservation of the favor of Being. Sacrifice can indeed be prepared and served by workings and effectings with respect to beings but is never accomplished by such. . . . Therefore, sacrifice will tolerate no calculation . . ." (GA 9: 310f.). Sacrifice is incalculable expenditure.

The Afterword thus appears to conclude by resuming, most radically and most decisively, the upward way; its draft would, it seems, draw man upward, making of him the sacrificial echo of the truth of Being, its afterword. The conclusion of the Afterword would, then, stand in contrast to that of "What is Metaphysics?" itself, which concludes with the question: Why are there beings at all and not, rather, nothing? Indeed, the respective conclusions would stand in starkest contrast, if one takes to heart what is said in the 1949 Introduction about the question with which "What Is Metaphysics?" concludes: "Through the concluding question we find ourselves led to consider that a reflection that sought to think on the way beyond the nothing to Being again turns, in the end, back to a question regarding beings" (GA 9: 381).

(c)

Heidegger's lecture course of 1935, *Introduction to Metaphysics,* was first published in 1953. From that year on, all further editions of *Being and Time* would refer to this text for the elucidation of the question of Being. And yet, remarkably, this text begins by stating immediately, without introduction, the question with which "What Is Metaphysics?" concludes: Why are there beings at all and not, rather, nothing? This question is called the first in rank, and the text of the course begins by explaining how, as first in rank, it is the broadest, deepest, and most originary of questions. The question bears precisely upon beings as a whole (*das Seiende im Ganzen*); and in much the same manner as in the overturnings in the draft of metontology and in "What Is Metaphysics?" Heidegger discusses the eruption of questioning within beings as a whole, characterizing it as an extraordinary happening by which the whole of beings comes to be opened up for the first time with a view to its ground. The question, arising in a leap (*Sprung*), opens up its own origin (*Ur-sprung*); and, as the most originary question, it is the question of questions, the question that cannot but be asked along with (*mitge-*

fragt) every question. It is the fundamental question of metaphysics (*die metaphysische Grundfrage*) (GA 40: 3–9).

If these opening pages of *Introduction to Metaphysics* were to be read solely against the background of Heidegger's initial statement of the project of *Being and Time,* they would appear strange indeed. How can it be that Heidegger does not begin with the question of Being, which in *Being and Time* not only was shown to have priority over all other questions but also, as the question of the *meaning* of Being, was made to determine the very structure and movement of fundamental ontology? How can it be that Heidegger now begins, instead, with a question of beings and that, thus beginning, he characterizes this question—the question of beings as a whole—as the most originary question? Is there any sense in which the question of beings as a whole (the question: Why are there beings at all and not, rather, nothing?) can be called more originary than the question of the meaning of Being?

In reading the beginning of *Introduction to Metaphysics,* one must, then, take into account not only *Being and Time* but even more the overturning anticipated in the analysis of conscience, openly announced in the draft of metontology, and put into play in "What is Metaphysics?" For in the overturning what is at issue is the relation of questioning to the field of beings as a whole. Only as a turn back into the ontic presupposition, only as a return to the ontic beginning, can the question with which *Introduction to Metaphysics* begins be regarded as the most originary. It is the question of questions, the question that is always asked along with (*mitgefragt*) every question, because it is the question with which questioning as such erupts within the whole of beings.

Beginning with this question, *Introduction to Metaphysics* would, then, retrace the way from the question of metontology back to the question of fundamental ontology, overturning the overturning so as to secure metaphysics as a whole consisting, at least according to *The Metaphysical Foundations of Logic,* of the two parts fundamental ontology and metontology. This is why—even without the reference to φύσις and to the historical determination of metaphysics by physics—the title of the 1935 course can be marked as ambiguous:

because, at least in its opening, it moves within the space between what the 1928 course called metontology and fundamental ontology.

Heidegger's way of introducing the question of Being into the discussion is initially quite formal, even abrupt: "But the question of Being as such [*die Frage nach dem Sein als solchem*] has a different essence and origin." Within the purview of the question of beings as a whole, the question of Being may seem to be merely a "mechanical repetition" of that question, at best, another transcendental question of a higher order. And yet, as long as the question remains undeveloped, "Being remains forgotten." Even further, the very origin of the origin, of the most originary question (that of beings as a whole), remains concealed. To the extent that metaphysics—now in its historical determination—is determined by this question, "Being *as such* is precisely hidden from metaphysics and remains forgotten, indeed so decisively that the forgottenness of Being, which itself falls into forgottenness, is the unknown but enduring impetus for metaphysical questioning" (GA 40: 19–22).

Everything depends, then, on the transition to the question of Being, even if it cannot be simply a turn away from the eruption of the question of beings as a whole. And yet, in the text the transition occurs very quickly, all too easily, as Heidegger will later realize.

Everything hinges on the addition to the question, or rather, on what would seem to be merely a superfluous addition: Why are there beings at all?—and not rather nothing? The addition ("and not rather nothing?") would seem to say nothing, and, in saying, i.e., speaking of, nothing, it would seem to run counter to logic, turning nothing into something in speaking about it. *Verstand,* if it were admitted, would stand ready to condemn such discourse. And yet, Heidegger notes, in asking this question of beings, one stands within a tradition which from its beginning has set the question of nothing alongside that of beings (GA 40: 22–27). Indeed, he continues, if one were simply to begin with the abbreviated form of the question, omitting the additional reference to nothing, that is, if one were simply to ask "Why are there beings at all?" such a questioning would advance immediately toward a ground, simply extending the method of questioning practiced in everyday life. To ask simply "Why are there beings at all?" is to ask about another, higher kind of being that would be the ground of beings as a whole. On the other hand, if the reference to nothing is retained in the question, then one is prevented from beginning with unquestionably given beings and from thus proceeding to another being that, itself self-grounding, would ground those beings: "Instead, these beings are held out, through questioning, into the possibility of not-being [*des Nichtseins*]. . . . Insofar as beings come to waver [*Schwanken*] between the widest and hardest extremes, 'either beings—or nothing,' the questioning itself loses all firm foundation" (GA 40: 30, 32). Here questioning would resume the encounter that "What Is Metaphysics?" set in the clear night of the nothing of anxiety. Questioning comes itself to be caught up in the wavering, the hovering between beings and nothing—or, as Heidegger proceeds to formulate it introducing the same slippage as in the earlier text: "Between not-Being and Being [*zwischen Nichtsein und Sein*]" (GA 40: 30). And so, "unexpectedly we are speaking here of the not-Being and Being of beings"—that is, unexpectedly (*unversehens*) the transition has been made back to fundamental ontology. Now the formulations rejoin those of *Being and Time*, rejoin the upward way. Now Heidegger does not hesitate to trace directly the line leading from the question of beings over to the question of Being. In interrogative form: "How shall we be able to inquire [*erfragen*] into, not to say find, the ground for the Being of beings, if we have not sufficiently grasped, understood, and comprehended [*gefasst, verstanden und begriffen*] Being itself?" (GA 40: 35). The question of beings as a whole leads over to the understanding of Being, to the necessity of developing that understanding.

And yet, it is precisely this transition, that is, the casting of it as a transition to *understanding,* that is the principal focus of Heidegger's later critique of *Introduction to Metaphysics*. This critique is presented in an undated 2½-page text entitled "Zur Kritik der Vorlesung," first published in 1983 as an appendix in the reissue of *Introduction to Metaphysics* in the *Gesamtausgabe*. The critique is addressed solely to that opening part of the course that I have just attempted, in its very broadest lines, to reconstitute. The critique consists of five numbered comments (GA 40: 217–219).

The first is a single sentence criticizing the very beginning of the course: "The beginning with the question 'What are beings as such [*Was ist überhaupt Seiendes*]' . . . not historically essential enough." One cannot but notice that this is not in fact exactly the question with which the 1935 course began; in the course it was a question of "why" rather than of "what," even though Heidegger moved on rather quickly to the Greek determination of beings as φύσις (as indeed the critical comment notes). Why is the beginning not historically essential enough? The comment does not say but only refers to " 'Leibniz'—*ens creatum*—Christian-theological question!": just as, reflecting on the concluding question of "What Is Metaphysics?"—the same question—the 1949 Introduction asked whether, in the end, this is merely the metaphysical question posed by Leibniz concerning a highest cause or whether the question is posed in an entirely different sense (GA 9: 382). One might suppose that in calling the beginning "not historically essential enough" Heidegger means that it does not break sufficiently with the historical-metaphysical determination of the question of beings; also, perhaps, that the very turn to beings turns too decisively away from the dispensation (*Geschick*) that constitutes the essence of history.[11] But Heidegger does not say.

The second comment refers to the "transition to 'Being,' " calling it "too thin and too artificial." The reference is to the discussion that proceeds from the first question to the wavering between Being and not-Being. What is impossible here, Heidegger now says, is that "Being is taken for itself [*für sich*]—that is "without previously saying in an originary way *die Wesung selbst!*" In other words, the course proceeded as though it were simply a matter of grasping Being—for instance, of projecting upon it, understanding it—without any consideration being given to its essential unfolding, its way of coming into such proximity as to allow anything like understanding. Indeed, Heidegger grants in the critical comment that

11. "We call the sending that gathers [*versammelnde Schicken*], that first brings man onto a way of revealing, dispensation [*Geschick*]. It is from this dispensation that the essence of all history [*Geschichte*] is determined" (VA 32).

"the wavering between Being and not-Being is essential." And yet, prior to concentrating on the wavering (as did the lectures), one must ask "how the wavering is to be experienced, how it touches us and lets us waver." Critical procedure, understanding of Being (*Seinsverständnis*), and critique of the understanding of Being—the latter by way of that *Vor-frage*, the question of Being, now declared to be no *Vor-frage* at all—none of this suffices to bring one into proximity to Being, to that wavering between Being and not-Being that belongs to *die Wesung des Seins*.

The third comment proposes, then, a leap over the methodic transition: "Questioning could leap immediately" from the beginning to the point where it is demanded that "we would have to understand Being." Then, Heidegger asks: "Is this demand compelling and to what extent?—a constant demand for founding the understanding of Being?"

The fourth comment is still more direct. Though the course left the matter less than explicit, the question of Being as it comes to be enunciated in the form "How does it stand with Being?" [*Wie steht es mit dem Sein?*]" (GA 40: 36f.) ought to make it questionable "that Being is to be grasped properly and immediately." Heidegger continues:

> This question therefore in the whole of the attempt to shake [*Versuch der Erschütterung*] the 'distinction' and *not* simple *progress to its other side*. For the draft [*Zug*] of the whole goes from understanding of Being to *happening of Being* [*vom Seinsverständnis zu* Seinsgeschehnis]—thus the *overcoming of the understanding of Being to this extent decisive*.

It is a matter, not of movement across the distinction that would mark the separation of understanding from Being, but rather of shaking this distinction, making it tremble so violently that it is transformed into a mark of the happening of Being. It is a matter of overcoming the understanding of Being, not by going beyond understanding to Being but by going beyond understanding of Being to happening of Being.

The final comment only confirms what has been said. *Introduction to Metaphysics* remains "stuck at the halfway point," not moving finally "from understanding of Being to happening of Being." The course "does not escape the fetters of understanding of Being," because it does not succeed in arriving at what is essential: *die Wesung des Seins selbst.*

Thus the call for the release from understanding. *Introduction to Metaphysics* remained fettered, even if loosely. There understanding was still inscribed, even if openly, indeed even more openly than in earlier texts, more exposed to all that would efface it. Indeed, its effacement has begun; and that is perhaps one of the reasons that Heidegger begins at that distance from understanding that *The Metaphysical Foundation of Logic* had laid out as the overturning into metontology, even if from the perspective of the critique that distance is so insufficient that one can, simply and with impunity, leap over it. The effacement has only begun, for what will finally bring it to completion is the distance of understanding, not from beings as a whole, but from Being. Or, rather, it will no longer be even a question simply of distance—as if beyond understanding there were Being—but, rather, of the withdrawal of the very space of understanding into *die Wesung des Seins selbst.* Beyond understanding there is nothing until Being is granted. Understanding will always have been exposed to such wavering between Being and nothing—that is, it will always have called for a displacement toward its beyond, a displacement that cannot but produce finally its utter effacement.

Thus the sacrifice of understanding, its sacrifice in the interest of that sacrifice in which the very essence of man would be expended for the sake of the favor of Being, of *die Wesung des Seins selbst.* Essential, originary thinking could be born only from out of the ashes of such sacrifice.

(d)

Heidegger has called it the freedom of sacrifice. He would call it, also, freedom as such, self-expending ek-sistence into the truth of Being, into the beyond. *Sacrifice* would name especially the negativity, the self-abandonment that would be put in force with such resoluteness (*Entschlossenheit*) that no reserve would remain this side of truth, not even a reserve of ignorance, of folly, of madness, of evil, only the trace of an errancy essentially connected to truth.

For in his lecture "On the Essence of Truth" (first presented in 1930, published in 1943) Heidegger rethinks the essence of truth—that is, rethinks both essence and truth—as including untruth, both in the form of concealing (i.e., as the mystery, the nonessence) and as errancy (the counteressence). In other words, he extends the domain of truth to include its opposites, while rigorously excluding the possibility of any *Aufheben* that would surmount the opposition. And yet, at the same time, such a move cannot but repress whatever, though outside truth, might be irreducible to an opposite—even a nondialectical opposite—of truth.[12]

Leaving, then, only the trace of errancy. No reserve of ignorance, of folly, of madness, of evil. Nothing that could release a reversal in which the freedom of sacrifice would become the sacrifice of freedom.[13]

Is such resolute thinking of the essence of truth sufficient to render reversal unthinkable? Or will there always remain the threat of an uncontrollable reserve, the threat of its disruptive return? Would not such a threat dictate the prudence of keeping understanding in reserve, of limiting its sacrifice?

In any case, if understanding is to be sacrificed, then it will no longer be possible to regard truth as correlative to understanding. Truth can no longer be taken to occur in understanding; it can no longer be taken to have its locus in judgment, granted that the effacement of understanding (both *Verstehen* and *Verstand*) cannot but produce, at least, a radical displacement of judgment.[14]

---

12. "The insistent turning toward what is readily available and the ek-sistent turning away from the mystery belong together. They are one and the same. . . . Man errs. Man does not merely stray into errancy. He is always astray in errancy, because as ek-sistent he in-sists and so already is caught in errancy" (GA 9: 196).

13. The thesis that "the essence of truth is freedom" developed in "On the Essence of Truth" (GA 9: 186), is elaborated as follows in "The Question Concerning Technology": "For man becomes free only insofar as he belongs to the domain of dispensation [*Geschick*] and so becomes one who listens, but not a slave. The essence of freedom is originally not connected with the will or even with the causality of human willing. Freedom governs the free [*das Freie*] in the sense of the cleared, i.e., the revealed. It is to the happening of revealing, i.e., of truth, that freedom stands in the closest and most intimate kinship" (VA 32f.).

14. Already in *Being and Time* Heidegger's analysis of truth attempts to undercut the thesis "that the 'locus' of truth is assertion (judgment)" as well as the thesis "that Aristotle, the father of logic, . . . assigned truth to the judgment as its originary

But if truth does not occur in understanding, neither can it occur in intuition (sensible or categorical), since, even in *Being and Time,* intuition is shown to be outreached by understanding and to be irreducibly correlative to that very sense of Being (*Vorhandensein*) that Heidegger undertakes to limit and to displace (see SZ 147; also GA 21: 114–125). The effacement of understanding—along with all the ruptures and displacements that it would introduce into the complex of traditional determinations—would appear to close all possibility of regarding truth as correlative to anything like a human power (*Vermögen*), capacity, or act of apprehending.

But if truth does not occur in any such correlation, where is its locus to be found? Where does truth happen?

In "The Origin of the Work of Art," also dating from 1935, Heidegger addresses this question, even though in this text a trace of understanding still remains, most notably, in his attempt to retain projection by radically recasting it as projection of openness (GA 5: 59). At a very decisive point in this text, Heidegger announces, without further commentary, five ways in which truth can occur, five places where truth can happen:

> One essential way in which truth establishes itself in the beings it has opened up is truth setting itself into work. Another way in which truth occurs [*west*] is the act that founds a state [*die staatgründende Tat*]. Still another way in which truth comes to shine forth is the nearness of that which is utterly not a being but the being that is most of all [*das Seiendste des Seienden*]. Still another way in which truth grounds itself is the essential sacrifice. Still another way in which truth becomes is the questioning of the thinker, which, as the thinking of Being, names Being in its questionableness [*Frag-würdigkeit*]. (GA 5: 49)

locus . . ."(SZ 214). Heidegger's approach is to show that truth as it occurs in judgments is founded on truth as uncovering (*Entdecken*) (adapting here Husserl's intentional analysis of truth in the *Logical Investigations*); and that truth as uncovering is founded on truth as disclosedness (*Erschlossenheit*). Nonetheless, disclosedness remains, in *Being and Time,* intrinsically connected to understanding (as *Verstehen*), though to an understanding openly inscribed, displaced.

One would need to consider whether the effacement of understanding would produce an effacement of every form that judgment has been shown to assume from Aristotle on. In particular, one would need to ask whether what Kant calls the judgment of the sublime (in which the primary operation involves imagination and reason, not understanding) would not resist simply being effaced in the effacement of understanding, though indeed displacement would be inevitable. I have discussed these issues somewhat in *Spacings—of Reason and Imagination,* chap. 4.

"The Origin of the Work of Art" discusses only the first of these five ways, the way of art or, essentially, of poetry.[15]

Let me focus on two sets of questions concerning Heidegger's five ways.

The first question is whether they are indeed five ways. There is, first, the way of poetry, and then, second, the act that founds a state, the way of the political, one may say. But what about the other three? As the Afterword to "What Is Metaphysics?" makes explicit, essential sacrifice is preeminently that self-expending from which originary, essential thinking is born. If one agrees that "that which is utterly not a being but the being that is most of all" can be nothing other than Being itself,[16] then what is announced as if it were a third way, that of the nearness of Being, serves only to name that to which one would give oneself up in the essential sacrifice in which thinking is born; it serves only to name that *Wesung des Seins* that, in its nearness, would leave no space of—no space for—understanding, requiring thus the sacrifice of understanding. But, then, in turn, what is announced as if it were a fifth way, questioning as the thinking of Being, only names what is born out of essential sacrifice to the nearness of Being. What Heidegger announces are three ways, three places where truth occurs; the places of those same three that in *Introduction to Metaphysics* (also from 1935) he called the genuine creators: the poet, the statesman, the thinker (GA 40: 66).[17] What are announced as if they were the third, the fourth, and the fifth ways, could, then, be regarded as articulating the moments of a single way, that of thinking—that is, as a topology of the place where truth occurs in relation to thinking. And yet, one

15. This way as well as the full context of the passage just cited will be discussed below in chapter 7.

16. F.-W. von Herrmann, *Heideggers Philosophie der Kunst* (Frankfurt a.M.: Vittorio Klostermann, 1980), 245–247.

17. In an earlier version of "The Origin of the Work of Art" that Heidegger presented in Freiburg in 1935 (the version published in *Holzwege* was presented in Frankfurt the following year) he distinguishes only three ways in which truth can occur: in the work of art or poetry, in the act that founds a state, and in the questioning and saying of the thinker. He continues: "Each origin is unique, and none can replace the others. Correspondingly, work, act, and concept are essentially different. . ." [*De L'Origine de l'oeuvre d'art* (Première Version), ed. Emmanuel Martineau (Authentica, 1987), 44].

could then also read the enumeration in reverse, noting that the way of poetry would also, according to Heidegger, be linked to the nearness of Being and, presumably, to something like sacrifice.

But what about the other way, the act of founding a state, the way of the political? The other set of questions on which I want to focus concerns this way.

What about the relation of the political deed—and, in particular, of the most originary political deed, that of founding a state—to the nearness of Being. Must it be said that the nearness of Being presses upon the statesman in such a way as to leave no space of—no space for—understanding, in such a way as to call for essential sacrifice, in such a way as to require of the statesman *as* statesman utter self-expenditure for the sake of the truth of Being? Must it be said, as of the thinker, that the truth of Being exacts such resoluteness from the statesman that there could remain no reserve outside the truth, no reserve of ignorance, of folly, of madness, of evil, but only the trace of errancy? Is it unthinkable that in such a founding of a state, in the self-sacrificing deed of the statesman who would relinquish understanding in order to hearken to the truth of Being—is it unthinkable, is it impossible, that ignorance, folly, madness, evil could remain in force? And not just as errancy, linked as counteressence to the truth. But, rather, irreducibly outside the truth, inevitably threatening the very state that would be founded in truth. Sacrifice of freedom, as in tyranny.

Yet, such determinations and indeterminations would be unfolded, not by the political deed itself, but rather by thinking the political, by thinking the way in which the truth occurs in the political deed. What about political thinking in this sense? Is such political thinking broached by Heidegger? Indeed it is. One could hardly expect otherwise, considering Heidegger's own political misadventure. One could hardly expect that he would not have undertaken to think the political both during his own limited engagement (limited to the institution of the university) and after his withdrawal, after his resignation of the rectorship. And yet, granted that he did broach a thinking of the political, it is surprising that he says so little. One cannot but wonder that, asked about the network governing the contemporary world, a network inseparable from political structures, Heidegger could—even in an interview—reply: "Only a god can save us. The sole possibility that is left for us is to prepare a sort of readiness, through thinking and poetizing, for the appearance of the god. . . ."[18] One can only wonder that he refers *only* to thinking and poetizing, not to political deeds, not even to thinking the political.

And yet, there are a few texts in which he does broach a thinking of the political. In every case, it is a matter of beginning to think the move from political phenomena (institutions, leadership, war, the state) to the truth in which would open the essential space of these phenomena, the truth as it would be allowed to happen in the political deed. It is the same move that is made in thinking technology, from the array of phenomena collectively called technology to the essence of technology (*Gestell*);[19] and the two, politics and technology, are, of course, not just formally parallel, since the political has never been thought without essential reference to τέχνη. Furthermore, Heidegger suggests that technology especially provokes a rethinking of essence (though, of course, such a rethinking is in play in his work at least from the time of "On the Essence of Truth"): "It is technology that demands of us that we think in a different sense what is usually understood by 'essence.'" And he adds: "If we speak of the 'essence of a house' and the 'essence of a state', we do not mean a generic type [*das Allgemeine einer Gattung*], but rather the way in which house and state hold sway, administer themselves, arise, and decay [*walten, sich verwalten, entfalten, und verfallen*]" (VA 38). To think, in this sense, the essence of the state would presumably constitute originary political thinking.[20]

One text that broaches such political thinking is the rectoral address "The Self-Assertion of the German University." Not that

18. "Nur noch ein Gott kann uns retten: Spiegel-Gespräch mit Martin Heidegger am 23. September 1966," *Der Spiegel* (31 May 1976), 209.

19. "We question concerning *technology* and in so doing would like to prepare a free relationship to it. The relationship is free if it opens our Dasein to the essence of technology. If we respond to this essence, then we shall be able to experience the technological in its delimitation" (VA 13).

20. In the sense that, in the "Letter on Humanism," Heidegger refers to originary ethics.

this text would simply submit the university to politics; on the contrary, the rectoral address affirms what is explicitly said in a later, related text: the university is to be thought in reference to that knowledge with which it is entrusted and "cannot be determined on the basis of 'politics' or any other kind of establishment of goals" (SU 29). Thus, the rectoral address undertakes to think the institution of the German university by thinking the essence of the university. Thus, again in the later text (though readable in the rectoral address itself), Heidegger says: "The core of the rectoral address . . . is the exposition of the essence of knowledge and science, on which essence the university is grounded and on which ground it is to assert itself as the German university in its essence" (SU 27). In that exposition of knowledge and science, Heidegger brings into play the resources of his thought, especially as reshaped around the end of the Marburg period. One hears, for example, echoes of the overturning, especially of the formulations in "What Is Metaphysics?"—one hears them in the determination of the essence of science expounded in the rectoral address: "Science is a standing-firm, in questioning [*das fragende Standhalten*], in the midst of constantly self-concealing beings as a whole" (SU 12). It is in reference to science as thus determined that the German university is to be defined as the institution that on the basis of science undertakes to be in education the leader and guardian of the destiny of the German people (SU 16f.). Thus, the German university is to be thought from out of the essence of science; and this requires, Heidegger later says, that the institution be thought back to the essence of truth itself in order that there be the possibility of renewing the university from out of the essence of truth itself (SU 22). The resoluteness that such renewal must involve will require sacrifice: academic freedom must be driven out of the German university, because it is not genuine freedom, is merely negative, because it is not that highest freedom in which one gives the law to oneself (SU 15). The irony could hardly have been more bitter: Heidegger himself tells how the National Socialists were eventually to prohibit the mention of his name in newspapers and magazines as well as the publication of new editions of his works (SU 42); and eventually he was to be declared utterly dispensable to the university and ordered to work on fortifications on the Rhine.[21]

Another text that broaches political thinking is "Overcoming of Metaphysics," a composite of texts from the period 1936–1946. Here Heidegger addresses the question of the world wars and undertakes to think them "as results of the destitution of Being [*Folgen der Seinsverlassenheit*]" (VA 92). Under the sway of such destitution, there remains only the errancy in which beings are made use of in order to install some kind of certainty and order. The emptiness of Being, the emptiness brought by the destitution, must be filled; since it cannot be filled by the emptiness of beings, there remains only—in order to evade it—incessant organization of beings with respect to the possibility of order, which would provide security of form to aimless activity (VA 95). For such ordering and ascertaining, leadership is required, a *Führer*, for whom all forms of government (*Staatsformen*) are merely instruments of leadership (VA 93, 97). Thus, again, it is a matter of attempting to think back from various political phenomena to the truth—in this case the destitution of Being—that opens the space of these phenomena.

Still another text that broaches political thinking is the course of 1942–1943 entitled *Parmenides*. Here it is a matter of attempting to recover (*wiederholen*) the political by way of a reflection on the Greek πόλις, that is, by attempting to think the essence of the πόλις, the truth of the πόλις. Hence: "The essence of the Greek πόλις is grounded in the essence of ἀλήθεια." More specifically: "Πόλις is the πόλος, the pole, the place around which turns in a peculiar way everything that appears to the Greeks with respect to beings" (GA 54: 132). Πόλις, Heidegger says, is neither city nor state nor city-state but the place of the unconcealment of beings, a "where" betaken by the Being of beings in its covering and uncovering, a "where" in which the history of Greek humanity is gathered (GA 54: 142).

Thus, in these texts, these fragments of a political thinking, these echoes of an unsounded original, it is rigorously a matter of the step back from the political phenomena to the essence, to the

---

21. "Spiegel-Gespräch," 204.

truth of Being that opens the space of the phenomena. The question, which would only become more pressing if these fragments were developed and which is perhaps broached in deed by the bitter ironies of Heidegger's political misadventure—the question is whether it is not the political that, most of all, resists the move to the essence, that resists the single move beyond to the truth of Being, which would only betake—and, in a rigorous, though nondialectical, sense, appropriate—a place in which to gather beings into a history. The question echoes that of Plato's Πολιτεία: whether the essentially thought πόλις—in the case of Plato the πόλις thought back to the determination of Being as εἶδος—is not inevitably threatened by disruption from below, from outside. It is a question of whether with respect to politics there is, perhaps most of all, need of the doubling return from the beyond of the truth to the place of history and of beings, of a return that would forestall the appropriation of everything to the truth, that would grant the space outside from which could arise ignorance, folly, madness, evil. There would then also, it seems, be need of prudence, need of understanding as that prudence and that judgment that would exercise vigilance at the limit of truth.

SEVEN

Poetics

Art, too, is a way in which truth happens. If such happening should prove to be essentially poetic, then to think art would be to think the poetic, to think poetry. Poetics.

(a)

Poetics.

The title translates—or, rather, reinscribes—the title of the text by Aristotle: Περὶ Ποιητικῆς.

Poetics would be, then, a discourse concerning poetry. Or, rather, in the case of Aristotle it would concern a series of forms which, though gathered under ποιητική, correspond only quite roughly to what one would today call poetry. Indeed, Aristotle's list cannot but seem somewhat heterogeneous: epic poetry, tragedy, comedy, dithyrambic poetry, most flute-playing and harp-playing (1447 a 13–16). A rather odd assortment from the standpoint of modern aesthetics: a bit of poetry, a bit of drama, a bit of music. Also, perhaps, a warning against too easily assimilating poetics (first of all, Aristotle's) to aesthetics, a mark of their heterogeneity.

Heidegger will radicalize a connection already evident in Aristotle's enumeration: the connection with language, quite direct except in the musical forms. Not only poetics but also poetry is a form of discourse, so that poetics would be a discourse on discourse, language folded back upon itself, added to itself. To the extent that poetry is essentially narrative, bound to a story, a plot (μῦθος)—the most essential element in the constitution of tragedy, according to Aristotle (1450 a 38–39)—poetics would be a λόγος concerning μῦθος, a mythology. It would be a theoretical discourse (θεωρία) concerning poetical discourse, a theory of poetry.

Heidegger will radicalize also the question of such addition of discourse to discourse. He will ask: What occurs in the space between these two discourses? What is the relation of thinking to poetry? He will radicalize these questions beyond the closure of aesthetics, at a limit where the very determination of thinking as theory and, hence, of poetics as theory of poetry can no longer remain simply intact. Poetics will no longer be bound to recover a sighting in advance, proceeding thus to an essence of poetry that would be had in common by all poetry, essence as τὸ κοινόν; rather, it will attend to such essence as is poetized when, as with Hölderlin, the poet poetizes the essence of poetry. Effacing itself before the poem, poetics would listen and respond to what speaks in the poem, to the speaking of language in which it is said what poetry is (GA 4: 7f., 33f.).

For Aristotle, too, it is a matter of saying what poetry is. Poetics is a discourse concerning poetry itself (the first words of Aristotle's text: περὶ ποιητικῆς αὐτῆς); poetics is to say what poetry itself is, before then going on to speak of its various forms (τε καὶ τῶν εἰδῶν αὐτῆς). Indeed, this is how Aristotle's text begins, according to nature (κατὰ φύσιν), taking first things first, saying, first of all, what poetry itself is, saying what not only is common to all those forms enumerated but also constitutes them as poetry, determining them and in that sense preceding them, the a priori of poetry.

Aristotle's text says it in one word: μίμησις.

This word, too, comes to be reinscribed, the name carried on. As such, it names that determination that has come to govern the theory of poetry and of art in general ever since Aristotle. Not that opposition cannot be found. Not that this determination is just emptily and dogmatically repeated in the history of the theory of art. And yet, even where the mimetic determination of art is most vigorously opposed, it is almost invariably a matter of rejecting a false mimesis for the sake of recovering genuine mimesis in its art-determining form. This gesture assumes one of its most subtle and complex—though still unmistakable—forms in the *Critique of Judg-*

ment. For example, in rethinking art as the product of genius, Kant writes: "Everyone is agreed that genius is to be wholly opposed to the *spirit of imitation* [*Nachahmungsgeiste*]."[1] And yet, in the same context he also writes: "Nature is beautiful if it also looks like art; and art can only be called beautiful if we are conscious of it as art while yet it looks like nature [*als Natur aussieht*]."[2]

The relation between Heidegger's poetics and the determination of art as mimesis will prove to be at least equally complex. Heidegger's opposition is explicit, for instance in "The Origin of the Work of Art" where he speaks of the "opinion, which has fortunately been overcome, that art is an imitation and depiction of reality [*eine Nachahmung und Abschilderung des Wirklichen*] (GA 5: 22). His opposition to mimesis is equally explicit in deed: at a strategic point in this same text he takes a Greek temple as his example of a work of art—chooses it, as he says, intentionally (*mit Absicht*)—precisely because it is not mimetic, or at least not representational (*nicht zur darstellenden Kunst gerechnet wird*) (GA 5: 27). The question will be whether there is also in play in Heidegger's poetics a more originary sense of mimesis. Is Heidegger's opposition to mimesis in its traditional forms also matched by a recovery of a more originary mimesis? Or rather, since Heidegger does not thematize any such recovery, can his opposition to mimesis be shown to have as its other side an unmarked recovery of mimesis? Can Heidegger's poetics carry on the name *mimesis?* Can one hear an echo of mimesis rebounding from that limit that marks the end of metaphysics and of aesthetics?

The formal structure of Heidegger's poetics is to be different from Aristotle's. Rather than outlining what poetry itself is and then narrowing the focus to the specific forms of poetry, Heidegger's discourse on poetry is to expand beyond poetry; it is to be extended in several directions. Furthermore, it will not be a matter of first determining what poetry is and only then extending the discourse beyond poetry; rather, only by way of these extensions will Heidegger's discourse come to determine what poetry is.

1. *Kants Werke: Akademie Textausgabe* (Berlin: Walter de Gruyter, 1968), 5:308.
2. Ibid., 5:306.

One such extension is in the direction of *art as such*. For "The Origin of the Work of Art" will come eventually to declare that "*all art . . . is essentially poetry*" (GA 5: 59). The discourse on poetry will expand into a discourse on art as such.

Another such extension is in the direction of *language as such*. For "The Origin of the Work of Art" will also declare that "Language itself is poetry in the essential sense" (GA 5: 62). Expanding into a discourse on langauge as such, Heidegger's poetics, even in its theoretical language—or, rather, as thinking—will be drawn toward a discourse of poetry on poetry.

Ποιητική is derived from ποίησις, which Heidegger translates as *Hervorbringen* (bringing-forth). Aristotle himself makes the connection at the very beginning of the *Poetics* by referring to the way that plots are to be brought forth, made, constructed. For the Greeks ποίησις included not only poetic (i.e., artistic) bringing-forth but also handicraft production (τέχνη), so that to think poetry as ποίησις would be to think it in a certain reference to handicraft: whether one makes an artifact or an epic poem, it is a matter of bringing something forth into manifestness (*Hervorbringen in die Offenbarkeit*) (see VA 19).

In this connection one should recall Heidegger's analysis (already developed in the late Marburg courses)[3] of the interpretation of τέχνη (hence, of ποίησις) that comes into play at the commencement of metaphysics. The crux of the interpretation lies in the role assigned to a certain looking in advance: in the forming of a vase out of clay, for example, the potter envisions in advance the look of what is to be produced, only then forming the artifact following the guidance of the anticipated look. Heidegger stresses that such vision in advance forms the very center of the structure of making. Later, in the "Letter on Humanism" Heidegger draws upon this analysis in his attempt to rethink θεωρία and its relation to ποίησις, in his effort to break with "the technical interpretation of thinking," to break with the determination of thinking, of θεωρία, as consisting essentially in such anticipatory vision merely taken in

---

3. GA 24: 150. See above, chap. 4 (a). Heidegger retains the analysis in, for example, "The Thing" (1950) (VA 166).

independence of any forming of an artifact. For Heidegger it would be a matter of liberating thinking from ποίησις in this specific and historically determining form (GA 9: 313f.).

Poetics, too, a theoretical discourse, would require such liberation. It would need to be twisted free from theory, to be transformed into a discourse that, as such, would transgress the limits of the classical concept of theory.[4] But also, such poetics at the end of metaphysics would undertake to think poetry outside the classical determination of ποίησις as production (*Herstellen*). For Heidegger this will require thinking the ποίησις of poetry as: bringing forth into manifestness (*Hervorbringen in die Offenbarkeit*).[5]

(b)

"The Origin of the Work of Art" begins circling, begins by circling.

The first of the circles joins artist and work of art: on the one side, the work of art is ordinarily taken to arise through the activity of the artist, so that the artist would be the origin of the work; yet, on the other side, the artist is what he is only by virtue of the work, so that the work would be equally the origin of the artist as artist. Hence: "The artist is the origin of the work. The work is the origin of the artist" (GA 5: 1).

---

4. It is not difficult to show how the determination of ποίησις as production governed not only θεωρία in general but also the specific θεωρία about art that came to be called *aesthetics*. If the vision of the look (the ἰδέα) is what forms the center of the structure of ποίησις, then in *artistic* ποίησις the vision (the insight) of the artist will be primary. The actual forming of the work of art will be secondary; the work of art will be only a means to the vision. Such an aesthetics is found in one of its more extreme forms in Schopenhauer. Let me cite three passages from *The World as Will and Representation* (trans. E. F. J. Payne [Indian Hills, Colorado: Falcon's Wing Press, 1958]): (1) Art "repeats the eternal Ideas apprehended through pure contemplation, the essential and abiding element in all the phenomena of the world. According to the material in which it repeats, it is sculpture, painting, poetry, or music. Its only source is knowledge of the Ideas; its sole aim is communication of this knowledge" (1:184f.). (2) ". . . the nature of genius consists precisely in the preeminent ability for such contemplation" (1:185). Through the work of art the artist "communicates to others the Idea he has grasped. . . . The work of art is merely a means of facilitating that knowledge" (1:195).

5. This would be a primary point of opposition between poetry and technology: "From this Greek concept of ποίησις (bringing forth into manifestness) one should distinguish the modern concept of production, which means: productive disposal [*Herstellen in die Verfügbarkeit*] (S 130).

Heidegger's first intervention is to open this circle: "Neverthe-less, neither is the sole support of the other." Specifically, then, the work of art is not such as to be completely, essentially determined by its relation to the activity of the artist, not even if, in turn, determining the artist as artist. In a work of art there is essentially something more than its being produced by a certain kind of activ-ity, something more than its correlation with the productive artist, an excess that opens the circle.

One way of determining this excess would be to refer to the mimetic character of the work of art, taking this character as an opening toward an other, which by imitation of the other would serve to disclose that other. Hence, the very beginning of "The Origin of the Work of Art" may be regarded as opening what could be (and traditionally would be) determined as a space of mimesis, an opening by virtue of which the work of art, mimetically disclos-ing an other, would essentially exceed the circle of production.

Another way would be to refer to excess on the side of the artist, to that by which what he is *as* artist would exceed his mere produc-tive activity. Such excess has traditionally been attributed to inspira-tion, to possession by the muses; the artist would be already claimed by an other, and his being thus taken over would constitute the very condition for productive artistic activity. The excess on the side of the artist has also been thought in the concept of genius.

And yet, Heidegger does not move to such determinations, re-sisting them even at the risk of moving instead within mere tautol-ogy, merely compounding the system of circles. For what he calls the excess, both on the side of the work of art and on that of the artist, is simply *art:* "In themselves and in their correlation [*Wechsel-bezug*] artist and work *are* by virtue of a third thing, which is the first, namely, that which gives artist and work of art their names— art" (GA 5: 1). The question is whether there remains a trace of mimesis in this opening. Can mimesis be recovered within the tauto-logical origination of the work of art?

Heidegger's initial move is to enter the system of circles. He begins with the work of art and proposes to move toward the discov-ery of what art, the excessive origin, is. "The Origin of the Work of Art" will continue throughout to circle within this circle joining art and work of art; even when, in the final section of the text, the turn is made from the work of art to the artist, it turns out to lead almost immediately back to the work of art, back into the circling between work of art and art. And it is a matter, not just of moving within this great circle, but of circling within it: "Not only is the main step from work to art, as the step from art to work, a circle, but every particular step that we attempt circles in this circle" (GA 5: 3).

There can be no question here of reconstituting this circling in all its compoundings and intricacies. Instead, I shall attempt to move as economically as possible to that complex of turns within which I shall propose a certain reinscription of mimesis, a reinscription that will follow the lines of a trace of mimesis discernible in those turns in Heidegger's text. Mimesis, thus reinscribed, will serve to name the connection where Heidegger thinks, perhaps most rigorously, the necessity of the doubling return from the truth of Being back to beings.

Beginning with the work of art, moving through the traditional concepts by which the work's thingly substratum would be interpreted and yet also obstructed, turning then to a description, without theory, of a pair of peasant shoes, or rather, to the shoes as depicted in Van Gogh's painting, Heidegger shows that the painting serves to disclose what the shoes are in truth. Thus, the work of art is shown to involve a happening of truth. Art is, then, to be determined as: truth's putting itself (in)to (the) work (*das Sich-ins-Werk-Setzen der Wahrheit*)—that is, to bring out the double sense: truth's putting itself to work in putting itself into the work of art.

This determination of art prompts Heidegger to ask about the relation of art to beauty. Traditionally, it is thought that art has to do more with beauty than with truth. The question is whether, within this new determination of art in reference to truth, it is possible to recover the relation of art to the beautiful.

Heidegger asks also about the possibility of recovering mimesis in this determination of art as the happening of truth; yet he poses the question ironically, characterizing the mimetic theory of art as "that opinion, which has fortunately been overcome." If art is a matter of truth and if truth means, as it has since Aristotle, correspondence with reality, then one might suppose art to be an imitation or depiction of reality. But does Van Gogh's painting simply depict some particular actual pair of shoes, doubling in the artistic imitation something actually existing? Heidegger is emphatic: "By no means."

And yet, as Aristotle recognized in differentiating between the poet and the historian (1451 a 36–1452 b 7), artistic mimesis need not pertain to particular, actually existing things. Thus, Heidegger continues, his irony slightly more veiled: "In the work, therefore, it is not a matter of the reproduction [*Wiedergabe*] of some actually present particular being, but, on the contrary, a matter of the reproduction of the universal essence of the thing" (GA 5: 22). Art would be put forth as mimesis of essence or of universal truth, were not essence, universality, and truth so utterly in question. Heidegger invokes this questionableness: "But then where and how is this universal essence, so that works of art are able to correspond to it? To what essence of what thing should a Greek temple correspond?" (GA 5: 22). Here, then, it is a matter of opposing the determination of art as happening of truth *to* the mimetic determination, displacing the latter for the sake of the former. And yet, is it a matter of simple opposition, of simple displacement? Or do the opposition and the displacement perhaps inevitably retain a trace of that which would be opposed and displaced, a trace that would hold open the possibility of a recovery of mimesis. If truth happens in art and if it is—to borrow the phrase from von Herrmann[6]—a matter of an ontological happening, in distinction from all interaction among beings, a matter of a happening in which, in Heidegger's words, "the Being of beings comes into the steadiness of its shining [*das Sein des Seienden kommt in das Ständige seines Scheinens*]" (GA 5: 21), then can art simply no longer be determined as mimetic? Or is it possible to think mimesis ontologically? Can art be determined as mimesis of the happening of Being? Can art even always have been, beneath the interpretations given it by aesthetics, determinable as mimesis of the clearing in which Being can shine forth, as mimesis of truth as ἀλήθεια?

Indeed, truth and its happening are rethought in "The Origin

---

6. *Heideggers Philosophie der Kunst*, 94.

of the Work of Art" as ἀλήθεια, as that happening of clearing and concealing that first makes it possible for beings to come to presence; this text thus appropriates all the resources that are released by the crossing of the essence of truth and the truth of essence that is most rigorously developed in "On the Essence of Truth." Art is, then, one of the ways in which truth—as the strife of clearing and concealing—can happen. It is a way in which truth puts itself to work, becomes effective, comes into play. In art truth happens as the strife of world and earth. This is, then, precisely what Heidegger sets out to think: the artwork (its *Insichstehen*) in its relation to world, to earth, and to the strife of world and earth.

Let me attempt to sketch as economically as possible the main lines of this complex.

World, neither a totality of things nor a framework cast over them, is not anything that could come to presence in such a way that one might intuit it. It is, rather, that which first lets things be, lets them come to presence: "By the opening up of a world, all things gain their lingering and hastening, their remoteness and nearness, their scope and limits" (GA 5: 31). World is, in Heidegger's phrase, *die waltende Weite der offenen Bezüge* (GA 5: 28): the governing expanse of the open relational complex, the expanse of the connections that hold sway for a historical people. As such, world so exceeds all beings that Heidegger will say, not that it *is*, but rather that *world worlds* (*Welt weltet*), thus again venturing tautology in the domain of the excessive and originary.

Earth, on the other hand, is thought in relation to φύσις; it is thought as that which harbors such things as come forth in that emergence (*Aufgehen*) that the Greeks experienced as φύσις. Earth is that which harbors such things in such a way as to secure and conceal them. As such, earth shatters every attempt to penetrate it, withdraws from all efforts to disclose it. It is essentially undisclosable, self-secluding, closed off.

In the relation of the work of art both to world and to earth there is operative a certain reciprocity. The Greek temple belongs to a world, is set within it, while, on the other hand, it also opens up a world, lets the expanse of its connections hold sway. Heidegger thinks this reciprocal relation more precisely as *Aufstellen* (setting up). The work of art is *set up* within a world; it is set up, not in the sense of "a bare placing," but rather "in the sense of erecting a building, raising a statue, presenting a tragedy at a holy festival" (GA 5: 29f.). And yet, thus set up within a world, the work of art itself sets up that world, opens and sustains it: "Towering up within itself, the work opens up a *world* and keeps it abidingly in force" (GA 5: 30). The Greek temple does not just occupy a space but, belonging to the Greek world, opens and sustains that world: "It is the temple-work that first fits together [*fügt*] and at the same time gathers [*sammelt*] around itself the unity of those paths and connections in which birth and death, disaster and blessing, victory and disgrace, endurance and decline acquire the shape of destiny [*die Gestalt seines Geschickes*] for human beings" (GA 5: 27–28).

The similarly reciprocal relation between the work of art and earth Heidegger thinks as *Herstellen* (producing, setting forth). The work of art is, as we say, *made out of* some earthy material such as stone, wood, or color; it is thus set forth, produced, from earth. But in the work of art the material is not assimilated to a function or use, as with equipment, but rather is allowed to show itself as material: "By contrast, the temple-work, in setting up a world, does not cause the material to disappear, but rather causes it to come forth for the very first time and to come into the open of the work's world" (GA 5: 32). Thus, in being set forth from earth, the work of art is set back into earth in such a way as to set forth earth, that is, in such a way as to bring the earth into the open, the clearing, while still preserving its character as self-secluding, undisclosable. By its way of being made out of an earthy material, of being *set forth* from earth, the work of art, in turn, *sets forth* earth, brings it into the open precisely as undisclosable.

The work of art can, then, be described as involving two essential features or connections (*Wesensbezüge*): the setting up of world and the setting forth of earth, each taken in its essentially reciprocal character. These connections belong together in the work of art, and it is precisely their unity that constitutes the *Insichstehen* of the work. But how do world and earth belong together such that the setting up of world and the setting forth of earth can belong together in the unity of the work? Heidegger's answer is decisive:

world and earth belong together *in opposition:* "The world, in resting upon the earth, strives to surmount it. As self-opening it cannot endure anything closed. The earth, however, as sheltering [*als die Bergende*] tends always to draw the world into itself and keep it there. The opposition of world and earth is a strife [*Streit*]" (GA 5: 35). The opposition is a strife (πόλεμος), not in the sense of mere discord and disorder, but rather in the sense of what Heidegger calls essential strife, that is, a strife in which each draws the other forth into the very fulfillment of that other's essence. Thus world can be as world only in its opposition, its strife, with earth, and vice versa. The work of art, setting up a world and setting forth earth, instigates such strife, lets happen such a happening of truth.

Echoes of Heraclitus: πόλεμος πάντων μὲν πατήρ ἐστι (Fragment 53).

(c)

The work of art thus lets truth put itself to work. And yet, as *das Sich-ins-Werk-Setzen der Wahrheit,* art involves also another moment: truth puts itself to work in putting itself *into* the work of art. The happening of truth that is instigated by art takes place *in* the work of art. The question thus comes into focus: How is it that truth can (and, in art, must) happen in something like a work, in a being that is brought forth, created, by an artist? In Heidegger's more precise formulation: "To what extent does truth, on the basis of its essence [*aus dem Grunde ihres Wesens*] have an impulse to the work [*Zug zum Werk*]" (GA 5: 48). It is a question, then, of the *Zug zum Werk:* a question of how truth is drawn toward the work; a question of how it is so aligned as to be inclined toward the work in which it will put itself to work; a question of how truth is trained on the work (as one trains one's gaze on something) and indeed even pulled toward putting itself into the work. The necessity of the return.

In a sense this is the pivotal question of Heidegger's poetics. Its development will gather up all the resources that "The Origin of the Work of Art" has prepared and will open upon Heidegger's thinking of poetry, also upon that trace of mimesis that I have proposed to mark. And yet, in the development of this question, it will not be a matter simply of arriving at an answer with which everything will then be settled. For the question is essentially unsettling, in Heidegger's term *ein Rätsel*. In approaching it nothing could be more appropriate than to incant the opening words of the Afterword to "The Origin of the Work of Art": "The foregoing reflections are concerned with the riddle [*Rätsel*] of art, the riddle that art itself is. They are far from claiming to solve the riddle. The task is to see the riddle" (GA 5: 67).

To see it, first, in the establishing of truth in the open. It is a question of the site of truth, of the open space in which the strife of clearing and concealing can take place:

> The openness of this open, that is, truth, can be what it is, namely, *this* openness, only if and as long as it establishes [*einrichtet*] itself in its open. Hence, there must always be in this open a being in which the openness takes its stand and attains its constancy [*ihren Stand und ihre Ständigkeit nimmt*]. In occupying the open, the openness holds open the open and sustains it. (GA 5: 48)

Truth requires the open; it must be established *in the open* in order to be the openness it is. But to be established in the open is to take a stand *in a being*, in which, then, truth sustains the open. This need for coming to stand in the open is, in the case of art, the *Zug zum Werk*. Yet, how does this *Zug* arise from the essence of truth? One may say, as Heidegger does, that openness can be what it is only by establishing itself in the open, that there is need for truth to have a site, an open space, a *Da*. But this is only to reiterate the riddle: that the essence of truth prescribes, in the case of art, the *Zug zum Werk*, the establishing of truth in a being. To attempt to see further into the riddle at this level would require showing how the connection with a being is necessary for the essence of truth—that is, how there is a turn to beings different from the counter-essential turn into errancy, a turn which in closing the difference would—in a way that errancy does not—serve to reopen and sustain it, a return more akin to overturning than to errancy. Such a turn to beings would be such as to reopen the difference within a being, even though it could not but always risk falling into complicity with errancy—which is to say that art and truth would always have to be thought in connection with art and error.

Heidegger does not extend the question in this direction. In any case, it remains questionable whether such an extension would really extend toward anything that could be characterized as an answer or whether it would not again come face to face with the riddle that art is, compounding the latter with the riddle of a truth submitted to irreducible alterity.

But there is another step that Heidegger does venture toward the riddle. It is a kind of step back, a step that retracts an order that the initial step would seem to have posited. What has to be taken back is the apparent priority that truth would have with respect to the establishing of that truth at a site, in a being. In other words, it is not as though there were first a truth in itself which then only subsequently would come to be established in a being. Rather, truth and its establishment in a being *belong together:* "But truth is not in itself present beforehand, somewhere among the stars, only later to descend elsewhere among beings. . . . Clearing of openness and establishment in the open belong together. They are the same one essence of the happening of truth" (GA 5: 49). It is not a matter of truth's going over into a being that it stands over against in advance; rather, truth is nothing apart from its coming to be established in a being. It is not as though there is, first, difference, which then comes to be mediated; rather, difference first occurs precisely at the site of the happening of truth. The return is necessary for truth.

The work of art is such a site, a being that is brought forth so as to establish truth, so as to bring about truth as the strife of world and earth. Such bringing-forth (*Hervorbringen*) is a form of ποίησις. Heidegger identifies it as that creating that is properly artistic, though he insists, on the other hand, that it not be construed merely as an activity of a subject. For here too it remains a matter of excess, of art's exceeding the circle of production so decisively that all creating must remain also receptive. It would be a receiving within the relation (*Bezug*) to unconcealment, though not therefore merely passive; on the contrary, Heidegger will call it "doing in the highest degree" (GA 5: 71). It is, hence, one form of the riddle: a receiving that is also a doing in the highest degree. The question is how these are to be thought together.

It is, then, in the work of art that the riddle—the riddle that art is—is to be seen. The work of art is the being in which truth, occurring as the strife of world and earth, is to have its site. This strife is not to be resolved in the work of art nor even just housed there. Rather, it is precisely there that the strife is to be opened, instigated. But the work of art can itself release the strife only if it embodies it: "This being must therefore have in itself the essential features [or lines—*Wesenszüge*] of the strife" (GA 5: 50).

What, then, is the strife? What are its *Wesenszüge?* Heidegger says that the strife is a *Riss* and stresses by this word that the strife is not a matter simply of opposition but rather is such that the opponents belong to one another in their very opposition. He draws this out especially in the words *Grundriss, Umriss, Aufriss,* drawing, as it were, the essential lines of the strife. The opponents belong together by having a certain common ground or origin—that is, strife as *Riss* is *Grundriss.* Also, they belong together by virtue of a certain operation of measure or limit by which they are brought into an outline—that is, strife as *Riss* is *Umriss.* But as opposed they open the space of the emergence (*Aufgehen,* φύσις) of things—that is, strife as *Riss* is *Auf-riss.*[7]

These essential lines of the strife must be embodied in the created being brought forth as work of art. More precisely, the strife (as *Riss*—one could say: rift) must be *set into* that being; it must be established, set firmly (*festgestellt*) into the being that is thus to be a work of art. The question is: How does this setting (*Stellen*) occur? How does it come about? Heidegger's answer gathers up virtually all the resources that have been prepared by "The Origin of the Work of Art": truth can establish itself in such a being only if "the strife opens up in this being, i.e., this being is itself brought into the rift [*Riss*]" (GA 5: 51). What appears here to be merely an equation is not such at all but, instead, is the hinge on which the entire matter turns: the strife (rift) is set into the being (work of art)/the being is itself brought (set) into the rift (strife). It is not that these two moments are identical; nor is one the ground of the other. Rather, it is a matter of gathering up those reciprocal connections

7. Ibid., 259f.

that, earlier in the text, have been thought as *Aufstellen* (being set up in a world/setting up a world) and as *Herstellen* (being set forth out of earth/setting forth earth). Now it is a matter of thinking these together, of thinking the reciprocity that joins the work of art and the strife of world and earth: the strife set into the work of art/the work of art set into the strife. It is not a matter of explaining these settings (*Stellen*), nor of explaining one setting by means of another. The point is not to secure the settings but rather to discern and preserve their reciprocity, thus to see a bit further into the riddle that art is.

The issue of such reciprocal *Stellen* Heidegger names *Gestalt.* It is imperative not to surrender the word to its ordinary senses (for instance, by translating it immediately and without reserve as *shape* or *figure*) but rather to understand it, first of all, from its connection to *Stellen*, to understand it as what issues from that reciprocal *Stellen* by which strife is set into a being and that being, in turn, is set into strife. Such *Stellen* is, says Heidegger, a *Feststellen.* In the Addendum to "The Origin of the Work of Art," he proposes to interpret *Stellen* as θέσις, as bringing-forth,[8] hence, as a form of ποίησις. He proposes also to interpret the *fest-* of *Feststellen* as: outlined, admitted into the limit, into the boundary in the sense of πέρας. Interpreted in this sense, limit is not such as simply to exclude and block out but rather gathers in such a way as to let something be brought forth, to let it shine forth; for example, "by its contour [*Umriss*] in the Greek light the mountain stands in its towering and repose" (GA 5: 71).

It is, then, as *Gestalt* that the rift occurs within a being (the work of art) that is also, in turn, set into the rift. Hence: "The createdness of the work means: truth's being set in outline [*Festges-telltsein*] in the figure [*Gestalt*]" (GA 5: 51). The *Gestalt* that issues from the reciprocal *Stellen* as *Feststellen,* this figure of truth, is also the place of the shining of truth—that is, of the beautiful: "Beauty does not occur alongside and apart from this truth. When truth sets itself into the work, it appears [*erscheint*]. The appearing

---

8. "Stellen und Legen haben den Sinn von: *Her-* ins Unverborgene, *vor-* in das Anwesende bringen, d.h. vorliegenlassen" (GA 5: 70).

[*Erscheinen*]—as this Being of truth in the work and as work—is beauty. Thus the beautiful belongs to the self-eventuation [*Sichereignis*] of truth" (GA 5: 69). Rethought in its Platonic determination, the beautiful is τὸ ἐκφανέστατον.

Truth happens, shining forth as the beautiful, when a being is brought forth in such a way that truth (as strife, as rift) is set into that being and that being is set into truth. Such setting issues in the *Gestalt.* Through such bringing-forth, truth is set in outline, set within its limit (πέρας), in the *Gestalt.* It is not, however, as though a being were first brought forth, only then to be made object of the reciprocal setting, becoming the setting for truth and being itself set into truth. Rather, the bringing-forth and the setting are one and the same: in being brought forth, the work is set into truth and becomes the setting for truth; and, conversely, in undergoing the reciprocal setting and thus issuing in the *Gestalt,* the work is brought forth. Bringing-forth (*Hervorbringen*) is—that is, is Heidegger's translation of—ποίησις. That ποίησις that is the same as the θέσις of truth Heidegger calls *Dichtung.* It may also be called— reinscribing Aristotle's title once again—*poetry* in an originary sense. *Truth happens in art as poetry:* "*All art,* as letting the advent of the truth of beings happen, is as such *essentially poetry* [Dichtung]" (GA 5: 59). Correspondingly, all philosophy of art—to say nothing of aesthetics—must become a thinking of poetry, that is, *poetics.*

It is not, of course, a matter of simple reductionism, of reducing all the other arts to the one single art of poetry. Heidegger activates the distinction between *Poesie* and *Dichtung* in order to mark the difference between the art of poetry (one art among others) and the poetic determination belonging to all art. To say that all art is essentially *Dichtung* is to say that all art is essentially ποίησις, a bringing-forth of the work of truth, whether in words, stone, color, or sound. On the other hand, Heidegger does insist that the linguistic work of art, *Poesie,* has a certain privilege among the arts. The privilege derives from the originarily poetic character of language as such: language is what first opens up the clearing. Hence:

> Language itself is *Dichtung* in the essential sense. But since language is the happening in which for man beings first disclose themselves, *Poesie,* *Dichtung* in the narrow sense, is the most originary form of *Dichtung* in

the essential sense. . . . . Building and plastic creation [*Bauen und Bilden*], on the other hand, always happen already, and happen only, in the open of saying and naming. (GA 5: 62)

Because truth happens first of all in language, the linguistic art, *Poesie*, is the most originary form of *Dichtung*, opening the space within which the other arts happen.[9]

Poetics would think *Dichtung*. It would think—has already begun in Heidegger's text to think—the happening of truth in which a being is brought forth in such a way that truth is set into that being and that being is set into truth. Poetics thus reinscribed could also reinscribe *mimesis*. Of course, it could not be, any more than in Aristotle, a matter of simple imitation, as though the work of art were an image simply reproducing within certain limits some actually existing beings. But also it could not be a matter of imitating something universal, of representing within an individual being some universal form or truth by which beings would, in the classical sense, be determined. The work of art does not imitate any being, whether individual or universal; it does not imitate anything that would simply *be* prior to the imitation, that would be set over against the imitation, which, then, would only double something already subsisting in itself. Indeed, one could say that the work of art *imitates nothing*, though one would need to regard such imitation of nothing, not as dissolving the riddle of mimesis (relegating it perhaps to some previous thinking of art that is now overcome), but rather as posing that riddle in the most unsettling way. Need it be said, after Heidegger, that the nothing is nothing simple? Indeed, one could say even that truth is nothing as long as it has not found a setting; and even in its setting, differentiated in the mani-

9. In the 1942–43 course entitled *Parmenides* Heidegger discusses the relation between language and architecture and sculpture among the Greeks: "But the fact that in a temple or in a statue of Apollo no words are used and 'formed' as material does not at all prove that these 'works'—in what they are and as they are—do not essentially have need of words. . . . The statue and the temple stand in silent dialogue with man in the unconcealed. If there were not the *silent word*, then the gazing god could never appear as the look and formal lines of the statue; without standing in the domain of uncovering of words, the temple could never stand there as the house of the gods" (GA 54: 172f.).

fold reciprocity from the being in which it is set, it is (as differentiated from beings) still nothing.

It is, then, in the relation of the work of art to truth that a trace of mimesis is to be discerned: art as mimesis of truth. It would be a mimesis not preceded by truth, a mimesis that would take place precisely in giving place to truth, in that setting of truth into the work that is also a setting of the work into truth, that setting of truth into its limit. It would be a mimesis that would take place in and as the *Gestalt* in which truth would be set into the work, placed there, without having preceded the work and yet in such a way as to be doubled in the play of reciprocity between the work of art and the strife of world and earth. It is in this doubling—by which the Greek temple once brought into play the strife of world and earth into which it was, in turn, set—that mimesis can be rethought and reinscribed within Heidegger's poetics.

(d)

But what, then, about imagination?

Let me return to that passage near the end of "The Origin of the Work of Art" where Heidegger addresses this question,[10] citing it now in full:

> If we fix our vision on the essence of the work and its relation [*Bezug*] to the happening of the truth of beings, it becomes questionable whether the essence of poetry [*Dichtung*], and this means at the same time the essence of projection, can be sufficiently thought from imagination [*von der Imagination und Einbildungskraft*]. (GA 5: 60)

Certainly, granted the analysis of art that "The Origin of the Work of Art" has developed, one would not be inclined to think poetry as a matter of imagination in the sense of mere phantasy, of mere imagining as an entertaining of images. And yet, it is Heidegger, perhaps most of all, who has provided the means for surpassing such impoverished concepts of imagination, especially through his interpretation of the Kantian transcendental imagination, which radicalizes imagination to the point where it merges with Dasein

10. See above, chaps. 4 (c) and 5 (d).

itself. If one notes, too, that the entire discussion of poetry and of projection in "The Origin of the Work of Art" serves essentially to elaborate the opening of the *Da,* the opening of the space of truth, then it is doubly surprising that Heidegger, in effect, sets imagination aside. Even more so, if one considers the possibility that imagination, sufficiently deconstructed, would seem eminently fit to name that peculiar *active reception* that Heidegger has shown to characterize artistic creation.

Let me turn, briefly, to a later text, the 1951 lecture entitled ". . . Poetically Man Dwells . . . ." It is a text very different from "The Origin of the Work of Art," much less assimilable to the classical concept of theory. The title is a citation, words extracted from a poem by Hölderlin and marked by the ellipses as so extracted. The entire lecture is an attempt to listen to these words and, in response, to think what is said in them. A poetics in which thinking would echo what sounds forth in the poem.

In order to hear the words of Hölderlin more properly, they need to be set back into the poem to which they belong. Heidegger begins by restoring them to the two lines in which they occur:

Full of merit, yet poetically, man
Dwells on this earth.

Heidegger responds. Man earns and so merits much in his dwelling; he does so by building, taken in the broadest sense to include not only the fabrication of artifacts but also the tending of growing things. *Building,* let me note, translates for Heidegger ποίησις in the technical, not specifically poetic, sense. Full of merit, and yet, says Heidegger, man is capable of dwelling only if he also builds in another way: dwelling requires that there also be in play a poetic ποίησις.

Heidegger restores the poet's words to a still larger context:

May, if life is sheer toil, a man
Lift his eyes and say: so
I too wish to be? Yes. As long as kindness,
The pure, still stays with his heart, man
Not unhappily measures himself
Against the godhead. Is God unknown?

Is he manifest like the sky? I'd sooner
Believe the latter. It's the measure of man.
Full of merit, yet poetically, man
Dwells on this earth. But no purer
Is the shade of the starry night,
If I might put it so, than
Man, who's called an image of the godhead.
Is there a measure on earth? There is
None.

Heidegger responds. Indeed there is the realm of toil, of merits to be earned, of ποίησις in the ordinary sense.

> But at the same time, in this realm, man is allowed to look up, out of it, through it, toward the heavenly ones [*zu den Himmlischen*]. The upward look passes aloft toward the sky [*zum Himmel*], and yet it remains below on the earth. The upward look spans the between of sky and earth. This between is measured out for the dwelling of man. We call the span thus measured out, through which the between of sky and earth is open, the dimension. (VA 194f.)

So, along with his toils upon the earth, his engagement in ποίησις in the ordinary sense, man has also the capacity to look upward toward the heavenly, the capacity for a look that spans the between and sets man within its openness, the dimension.

Heidegger continues. This looking upward toward the heavenly is a *self-measuring*, that is, in this upward look man measures himself against the heavenly. Such self-measuring is not something that happens just now and then but rather is essential to man: man is man *only* as spanning the between and measuring himself against the heavenly. To Hölderlin's words "man . . . measures himself against the godhead," Heidegger responds: "The godhead is the 'measure' with which man measures out his dwelling, his abode on the earth under the sky. Only insofar as man takes the measure of his dwelling in this way is he able to be in accord with his essence" (VA 195). And yet, the self-measuring is a *taking* of measure. It is not a matter of applying a measure (the godhead) to himself as one applies a yardstick to something so as to determine its length; rather it is a matter of taking from the heavenly the very measure as such (μέτρον), the measure for dwelling in the between. Heidegger concludes: "The taking of measure is what is poetic in dwelling [*das Dichterische des Wohnens*]. Poetizing is a measuring" (VA 196). Such is, then, the other ποίησις, the poetic ποίησις. What it brings forth is measure, the meaure by which to measure man's dwelling between earth and sky, in the between. Toward the end of the lecture Heidegger will call it "originary building," the building that gauges the dimension of dwelling.

Hölderlin:

> . . . man
> Not unhappily measures himself
> Against the godhead. Is God unknown?

Heidegger, responding:

> 'Is God unknown?' Manifestly not. For if he were unknown, how could he, as unknown, ever be the measure. Yet—and this is what we must now listen to and keep in mind—for Hölderlin God, as the one who he is, is unknown, and it is just as *this unknown one* that he is the measure for the poet. . . . The god, however, is unknown, and he is the measure nonetheless. Not only this, but the god who remains unknown, must, by showing *himself* as the one he is, appear as the one who remains unknown. God's *manifestness*—not only he himself—is mysterious. (VA 197)

Hence the showing, the manifestation, that allows the poet to take the measure for dwelling: it is a showing that is itself mysterious, a showing in which the god appears *as unknown*.

Hölderlin continues:

> Is he manifest like the sky? I'd sooner
> Believe the latter. It's the measure of man.

Heidegger responds:

> The measure consists in the way in which the god who remains unknown is revealed *as* such by the sky [*Himmel*]. God's appearance through the sky consists in a disclosing [*Enthüllen*] that lets us see what conceals itself, but lets us see it not by seeking to wrest what is concealed out of its concealedness, but only by guarding [tending—*hüten*] the concealed in its self-concealment. Thus the unknown god appears as the unknown by way of the sky's manifestness. This appearance is the measure against which man measures himself. (VA 197)

Hence—without violating its mysteriousness—the structure of the showing. What shows itself, what is manifest, is the sky. It is, then, in and through that self-showing (in and through the manifestness of the sky) that the unknown God appears as unknown, appears as concealed.

Poetizing (*Dichten*) is the response to such showing. To poetize is to take from this showing a measure for human dwelling, to bring forth a measure, originary ποίησις.

The structure of the showing to which poetry is submitted may also be determined by reference to the structure of images. An image is precisely something that shows itself in such a way as to let something else appear through it. Hence, in submitting to the sights of the sky through which the concealed god appears, poetry submits to images. Thus the following, most remarkable passage:

> The poet poetizes only when he takes the measure by saying the sights of the sky in such a way that he submits to its appearances as to the alien element in which the unknown god "sends" himself. Our usual name for the sight and look [*Anblick und Aussehen*] of something is "image" ["*Bild*"]. The essence of the image is: to let something be seen. By contrast, copies and imitations are already mere variations of the genuine image which, as a sight, lets the invisible be seen and so images [*einbildet*] the invisible in something alien to it. Because poetizing takes that mysterious measure, namely, in the face of the sky, therefore it speaks in "images." This is why poetic images are imagings in a distinctive sense: not mere phantasies and illusions, but imagings [*Ein-Bildungen*] that are visible inclusions of the alien in the sight of the familiar. (VA 200f.)

Hence, again, the question of poetry and imagination. Now it is not set aside but developed in a way that is at once simple and radical. The poet would require the power to bring forth the measure for dwelling, to do so *in response,* in and through submission, to that imaging—that showing, that letting appear—in which the concealed god appears through the sights of the sky. To name that power *poetic imagination* would be responsive to the essence of poetry as poetized by the poet and as thought, in response, by the thinker. Another poetics, poetics reinscribed, translated.

EIGHT

Translating Ecstasy

(a)

Listen to what is said of ecstasy, about what is sounded within it, from it: "Under the magic of the Dionysian . . . , singing and dancing, man . . . has forgotten [*verlernt*] how to walk and speak. . . . His gestures bespeak enchantment. Just as the animals now talk and the earth yields milk and honey, so there sounds from him something supernatural [*etwas Übernaturliches*]. . . . He himself now roams about enraptured [*verzückt*]."[1] In such rapture, such ecstasy, human speech is silenced, gestures alone announcing that something else, something supernatural, sounds forth.

Listen once more to what is said of this sound of ecstasy, to the words by which Nietzsche would translate that sounding: "And now let us think of how into this world [Nietzsche refers to the world of Apollinian Greek culture] there sounded, in ever more alluring and magical ways, the ecstatic tone of the Dionysian festival; of how in these all of nature's excess in pleasure, pain, and knowledge became audible, even in piercing shrieks. . . . Excess revealed itself as truth."[2] In ecstasy, from it, there is a sounding of excess, a sounding of the depth of truth—or, rather, of its exceeding of all depth, a sounding and resounding of the abyss.

What is required for translating ecstasy, for bringing into words what sounds in it? What is required for that particular translation in which ecstasy would be carried over to the level and the language of thinking, taken up at that level? Can one think ecstasy without

---

1. F. Nietzsche, *Die Geburt der Tragödie*, in vol. III/1 of *Werke: Kritische Gesamtausgabe* (Berlin: Walter de Gruyter, 1973), 25f.
2. Ibid., 36f.

thereby violating—that is, reducing—the very excess that is sounded in it? Can one think ecstasy otherwise than by limiting the very abyss that resounds in it, bringing the abyss finally back to a ground, that is cancelling it as abyss. Would ecstasy not, then, escape thinking? Would it not remain beyond translation? Or, rather, would thinking not itself have to become ecstatic in order to think ecstasy? Would it not be required that thinking interrupt the drive to ground—that is, interrupt metaphysics—and listen to what is sounded in ecstasy?

Such an interruption is openly announced in Heidegger's text "The Essence of Language." It is announced as a retraction of the privilege of questioning and of what in Heidegger's earlier texts served that privilege. Listen: "The proper bearing of thinking is not questioning but rather listening to the promise [*das Hören der Zusage*] of that which is to come into question" (US 175). This retraction is announced as an interruption of metaphysics: from early on, questioning has been taken as the decisive feature of thinking. It has been held that thinking as such comes under the imperative that it be radical, directing itself toward the *radix*, that is, seeking out the final (and, hence, first) ground. Whence the imperative? Its source lies in the very determination of essence, in the determination of essence *as ground*. Listen, then, as Heidegger's text continues: "Insofar as all essence has the character of ground, the quest for essence is a fathoming and establishing of ground [*Ergründen und Begründen des Grundes*]. The thinking that thinks toward [*zudenkt*] essence as so determined is in its ground a questioning" (US 175). The retraction of the privilege of questioning is also a retraction of the determination of essence as ground. In short, a releasing of essence into the abyss. Also, a new imperative: that thinking first of all *listen* to what sounds from the abyss.

One will ask, then: What is it that in ecstasy sounds forth from the abyss? What is it that would be translated in translating ecstasy? The question can have no direct answer; for in asking "What is . . . ?" one asks about essence as though its determination had not been interrupted. The question can have no direct answer, for it cannot be freed from the entanglements of that redetermination of essence that can yet be no simple redetermination.

Indeed, not only the answer but also the question itself must be deferred, at least granted the interruption that would free thinking to translating ecstasy. For it is precisely questioning that is interrupted. No longer the proper bearing of thinking, it must give way to listening. Putting the question aside, interrupting the drive to essence as ground, thinking becomes ecstatic by first listening.

And so, let us listen. Let the discourse be governed not by the questioning drive to ground but by listening. Let it be a responsive discourse, tracing the shape of what is heard in listening, translating it.

Let us listen to what is said in certain texts signed by Heidegger. First, by way of preparation, to certain texts that outline a thinking of ecstasy and of the way from ecstasy to langauge and translation, to ecstasy as opening to the translation of language. Then, second, still by way of preparation, to certain texts addressed to the issue of translation, broaching an analysis of the structure of translation, drawing it back into language, back toward ecstasy. Only after these preparations will it be possible to listen with sufficient perceptiveness to the text in which, perhaps most purely, that which sounds forth from the abyss is named and translated. It is named in the simple title of the text: "Language." It will be a matter, then, of redoubling the translation of language that this text accomplishes, of echoing its translation of ecstasy.

(b)

Ecstasy is in play in Heidegger's project from the outset, namely, as *Existenz*, Dasein's standing forth into its world; in the course of *Being and Time* such ecstasy comes to be determined as the temporalizing of temporality, that is, as the complex interplay of the three ecstases of originary temporality. One needs to distinguish, then, between two moments of ecstasy, which together would constitute the essential movement that Dasein is: on the one hand, Dasein's standing out into its world, hence its worldly ecstasy; on the other hand, its standing out toward the horizonal schemata that delimit the ecstases of originary temporality, hence its temporal ecstasy.

The determination of Dasein as twofold ecstasy is linked to several strategies that interrupt metaphysics and move outside its closure. The most direct link is with the limiting of the determination of Being as presence (specifically as *Vorhandenheit*); for in ecstasy, in being outside oneself, one is not simply present either inside or outside, but rather the operation of the simple limit that would separate inside from outside, presence from absence, is disrupted. There is a link also to the more explicitly post-Nietzschean strategies that Heidegger openly broaches only in the wake of his Nietzsche lectures of the late 1930s; most notably, there is a link with the rethinking of the sensible that is required once it has been, as with Nietzsche, twisted free from its opposition to the intelligible. In this regard it is a matter, for instance, of thinking meaning no longer as idea but as arising in Dasein's worldly ecstasy, which thus becomes the locus for reconstituting, this side of the "true world" that has finally become a fable, the difference that metaphysics always referred to the opposition between intelligible and sensible.

The two moments of ecstasy, the worldly and the temporal, are of course not simply parallel. Indeed, the relation between them is so thoroughly at issue and bears so decisively on the very shape of Heidegger's project that one could almost justify taking the issue of this relation as a guiding thread for retracing the itinerary that leads from *Being and Time* to such texts as the "Letter on Humanism." In *Being and Time* the intent is clear: Heidegger proposes to ground Dasein's worldly ecstasy on its temporal ecstasy—that is, he undertakes to show that Dasein's standing forth into a world is grounded on what he calls the horizonal constitution of temporal ecstasy. The task is to show how each of the three temporal ecstases involves a horizonal schema and how these schemata, drawn together by the unity of the ecstases themselves, unfold that horizon of horizons that is called world. The task, announced in *Being and Time* almost as if it were a result,[3] is resumed in *The Basic Problems of Phenomenology*, resumed in a way that points up more decisively

---

3. "The horizonal unity of the schemata of the ecstases makes possible the originary connection of the in-order-to relationships with the for-the-sake-of [*der Um-zu-Bezüge mit dem Um-willen*]. This implies that on the basis [*auf dem Grunde*] of the horizonal constitution of the ecstatic unity of temporality there belongs to that being that is always its 'there' [*Da*] something like a disclosed world" (SZ 365).

how such a grounding is required by the very project of interpreting the meaning of Being as time; for what Heidegger sets out to show in *The Basic Problems of Phenomenology* is that the horizonal constitution of temporality not only serves to unfold world but also in this very unfolding puts into play the understanding of Being.[4] Yet at the end of the 1927 lectures the demonstration is broken off. It appears not to have been resumed in any later texts or lectures.

By the time of the "Letter on Humanism" (1946), the drive to ground worldly ecstasy on temporal ecstasy has been interrupted. In a sense the task has become that of thinking the unity of the two moments of ecstasy, of thinking them together without seeking to ground one on the other. Thus, in the Introduction added to "What Is Metaphysics?" in 1949, Heidegger prescribes that existence, identified as ekstasis, is to be thought by thinking together the moments of care (in which Dasein's worldly ecstasy is expressed in its full structure) and Being-toward-death (in which Dasein's temporal ecstasy is gathered into the extreme of its finitude) (GA 9: 374). And yet, what is now decisive is that these moments of ecstasy are thought in their unity as ontological ecstasy, as a standing out into the openness of Being. In the "Letter on Humanism" what had been called world—now placed in quotation marks so as to mark the divergence—is called "the clearing of Being [*die Lichtung des Seins*] into which man stands out" (GA 9: 350). Listen further : "Ek-sistence, thought ecstatically, . . . means standing out into the truth of Being" (GA 9: 326)—that is, as Heidegger will also say in texts of this period, standing out into Being itself.[5]

Listen, then, still further to what is said of the need that man be claimed by Being, about the *Anspruch* under which man must come

4. "*Accordingly,* we understand Being from the originary horizonal schema of the ecstases of temporality" (GA 24: 436). See above, chap. 4 (c).

5. Hence: "the truth of Being as the clearing. . . . But the clearing itself is Being" (GA 9: 331f.). Note also the discussion of "Being as the dimension of the ecstatic of ek-sistence. However, the dimension is not something spatial in the familiar sense. Rather, everything spatial and all space-time occur essentially [*west*] in the dimensionality which Being itself is" (GA 9: 333f.). That temporal ecstasy, too, is being thought in ontological ecstasy is perhaps most explicit in the following: "In *Being and Time* 'Being' is not something other than 'time' insofar as 'time' is named as the first name [*Vorname*] for the truth of Being, which truth is the essential [*das Wesende*] of Being and so Being itself" (GA 9:376).

in order to stand out into Being itself: "Only from out of this claim, 'has' he found that in which his essence dwells. Only from out of this dwelling, 'has' he 'language' as the home that preserves the ecstatic for his essence" (GA 9: 323). But then, finally, dropping the quotation marks that just now served to displace what was still called language: "Language is the clearing-concealing advent of Being itself" (GA 9: 326).

The complex begins to take shape. Claimed through language, by its sounding the advent of Being, man stands out into the clearing. This clearing is his dwelling; and, hence, almost paradoxically, in his ecstasy, in being outside himself, he is at home. Thus at home he has—even if improperly, in a divergent sense—language, which preserves his ecstasy, holds him in it. Ecstasy—thought ontologically—is thus suspended between two divergent occurrences of language. Ecstasy, hence also homecoming, occurs in and as the movement between these two occurrences of language, in and as the translation from one to the other.

(c)

The contexts in which Heidegger most directly addresses the issue of translation are those in which he is concerned with the decisive words of Greek thinking and with the translation of these words into Latin—for instance, the translation of φύσις as *natura* and of ὑποκείμενον as *subiectum*. Heidegger stresses that these seemingly unquestionable translations, in which Greek thought was handed down to the Middle Ages and then to modern philosophy, are anything but unquestionable. Listen, for instance, to what is said in "The Origin of the Work of Art":

> However, this translation of Greek names into Latin is in no way the unquestionable process that even today it is still considered to be. Rather, beneath the seemingly literal and thus faithful translation there is concealed a *trans*lation of Greek experience into a different way of thinking. Roman thought takes over the Greek words without the corresponding equally originary experience of what they say, without the Greek word. The rootlessness of Western thought begins with this translating. (GA 5: 8; cf. GA 40: 16)

What Heidegger seems to be describing here is a process of the sort analyzed in some detail in *Being and Time,* for instance, in the discussion of *Gerede,* namely, the process in which words are simply passed along and taken over without the corresponding experience of what is said in them (SZ §35). At the simplest level and in classical phenomenological terms, it is a matter of transmitting the mere empty intentions borne by words, transmitting them without the experiences, the empirical or categorical intuitions, by which those intentions would be filled and made concretely meaningful. Such translation can take place not only in the passage from one language to another but also, as in *Gerede,* in transmissions within the same language. At another level, such a process of transmission, its outcome with regard to the words that would say the Greek experience of Being, provides the point of departure for the project of *Being and Time:* the Greek experience of Being has been handed down in increasingly vacuous words that have now to be rejoined to the originary experience so as to reanimate the problematic and the language of ontology.

The translation from Greek to Latin constitutes the first and most decisive stage by which what the Greeks experienced and said came to be concealed: the rootlessness of Western thought begins with this translating. In this first and most decisive translation, the words of Greek thinking were—so it seems—passed along to Roman thought in the form of their Latin equivalents yet without the originary Greek experience of what was said in them. Subsequent translations, both between languages and within the same language, would only have furthered the separation broached by the first translation, the separation of word from experience.

And yet, the matter cannot be so simple nor the danger intrinsic to translation so readily circumscribed. For there can be no such simple separation between word and experience. It is not as though, when the experience is lost, the word would simply perdure without any essential loss, either as such or as its equivalent in another language. It is not as though the word, separated from experience, would remain like an empty shell ready to be filled again if only the relevant experience could be reawakened. Listen to what is said in Heidegger's discussion of translation in *Introduc-*

tion to Metaphysics: "For words and language are not shells in which things are packed for the commerce of those who speak and write. In the word, in language, things first come into being and are" (GA 40: 16). Even when remote from originary experience, words do not simply await the experience by which they would be renewed but rather can serve—indeed, must serve—to open the space of such experience. This is why, when "The Origin of the Work of Art" discusses how Roman thought took over the Greek words (*Wörter*), it is said to have done so not only without the originary experience but also without the Greek word (*Wort*).

Even if one could circumscribe a region of experience so essentially prelinguistic that it could be separated off from the words in which what it discloses was once said—and even in the perspective of *Being and Time* any such experience must always prove to be reinscribed in language at a more originary level—such experience could have little in common with the experience at issue in the translation of Greek thought into the subsequent history of metaphysics. For what is at issue in this translation is the fundamental Greek experience of the Being of beings in the sense of presence (*die griechische Grunderfahrung des Seins des Seienden im Sinne der Anwesenheit*). Need it be said that such experience cannot be a matter of an intuition utterly removed from the play of language? It is, rather, the experience that lets open the very space in which beings can first come to show themselves as present and, hence, as to be intuited.

Translation cannot be, then, simply a transition from word to word in which a complementary and distinct experience of what is said in the word can be either retained, lost, or recovered, either wholly or in part. Such a schema of conjunction or disjunction, preserving an essential distinction between language and experience, is inadequate to the structure of translation.

In order to prepare a more adequate schema of translation, let me recall the schema of language as such presented in Aristotle's *On Interpretation.* Heidegger has stressed how thoroughly this Aristotelian schema determined all subsequent thinking about language. How, then, it needs to be asked, does the schema determine the character of translation?

The relevant passage reads:

Spoken words [τὰ ἐν τῇ φωνῇ] are symbols of affections in the soul, and written words are symbols of spoken words. As writing is not the same for all men, so likewise speech is not the same for all. But the affections of the soul, of which these words are primarily signs, are themselves the same for all, as are also the things of which these affections are likenesses. (16 a)

What is most striking is that the very fabric of language is described here as something woven by translation: writing would translate speech, speech would translate the affections in the soul, and these affections would translate things. In each case something is carried across from one order to another. Thus, translation belongs to the very operation of language rather than being something that just occasionally supervenes upon that operation.

Let me focus on the intermediate member of the schema, acknowledging for the moment that privilege that Derrida has shown it to have enjoyed in so many complex connections in the history of metaphysics. Here it is a matter of translating affection into sound; or, taking the affection in the soul to be an intuition of meaning or of a meaningful nexus of things, it is a matter of translating meaning into sounding words. Translating the terms of such translation still further, it is a matter of translating signified into signifier in such a way that the meaning signified can, in turn, be translated from one speaker to another according to a schema whose lines have been drawn by Saussure.[6] Words would be, then, the vehicles by which meanings would circulate among speakers, translations in the service of translation, translating translation.

Translation from one language to another would merely double the translation between word and meaning. It would be a matter of translating the words of one language into meaning, envisioning the pure signified beyond the play of signifiers, and then of translating that meaning into the words of the other language.

And yet, words are not mere shells to be filled by an experience of meaning; they are not mere vehicles in which meanings would circulate among speakers. For there are no pure meanings aloof from the

6. See F. de Saussure, *Cours de linguistique générale* (Paris: Payot, 1980), 27–32.

play of words, no signifieds so essentially protected from the play of signifiers that they could govern translation from without, completely stabilizing it. Rather, from *Being and Time* on—that is, after the "true" world had finally become a fable—meaning is shown to originate within the sphere of an ecstasy that is inseparable from language, within a space whose very opening is always already linguistic—that is, within a "there" (*"Da"*) that has discourse (*Rede*) as one of its constituent moments. But in this case speaking cannot be a translating of an essentially nonlinguistic meaning into the sound of words, a translating of the nonlinguistic into language. Rather, it must occur within language, first, as a certain standing out toward what language offers as to be said; then as a translating of what is thus ecstatically received, a sounding that would translate what sounds forth in ecstasy, an ecstasy suspended between two soundings, between two divergent occurrences of language.

(d)

Let us listen, then, to "Language," to what is said in the text so entitled, to its way of saying the translating of ecstasy.

In this text there is a circling. It begins with the words: "Man speaks [*Der Mensch spricht*]." It concludes also with human speech—saying: "Man speaks insofar as he responds to language [*Der Mensch spricht, insofern er der Sprache entspricht*]." Yet, within the text what is addressed for the most part is not human speech but rather what is called the speaking of language—that is, there is operative in the text a displacement of human speech in favor of the speaking of language. It is only through this displacement that the text finally circles back to the issue of human speech, marking that displacement of human speech: man speaks insofar as he responds to language. This displacement is the ecstasy that belongs to speech. It is not only addressed but also enacted by Heidegger's text.

Anticipating the displacement, one can also sense in the opening, "Man speaks," the full compass of the text, that of the relation between man and speech, between man and language. Indeed, the first move beyond the opening poses speaking as most closely tied to being human: we are always speaking, continually, even when working or resting, even when not actually speaking or even actually listening. Speech is, then, something that belongs essentially to man; and though the text is not allowed to fall immediately into the traditional mold constituted by the words ζῷον λόγον ἔχον, it does retain the following as something of a point of departure: "In any case, language belongs to the closest neighborhood of the essence of man" (US 11). With the relation of man and language, it is a matter of displacement, of man's removal to the place of language; and yet, that very removal from his place establishes him essentially in it, in the closest neighborhood of the essence of man—both at once: ecstasy and homecoming.

The title names that on which the text would reflect (*nachden-ken*), that which it would discuss (*erötern*): language. Though traditionally such reflection requires forming a representation of what language is in general, of what is called the essence of language, this is precisely what has now to be foregone. In discussing (*erörtern*) language it is, rather, a matter of reaching the appropriate place (*Ort*), of letting oneself be suitably displaced. Instead of bringing language to ourselves, fitting it to the place of our ready-made concepts, it is required that we betake ourselves to the place of language—in short, that thinking be ecstatic.

Reflection would thus submit itself to language rather than drawing language to itself or to something else. It would reflect on language *itself,* language *as such.* One cannot but ask: How does language occur *as* language?—even though the question, a question of the proper of language, is itself improper and must be submitted to the entire course of Heidegger's text, a course that is not, first of all, a questioning. Only on that course can it then be properly answered: Language speaks (*Die Sprache spricht*). Listen, then, even if in advance:

> To reflect on language thus demands that we enter into the speaking of language in order to take up our stay with language, i.e., within *its* speaking, not within ours. (US 12)

It will be a matter of displacement from human speech to the speaking of language.

In order to reflect on language *as* language, it is also required that one forego all grounding of language on something else; this entails that such thinking must break with the determination of essence as ground and, hence, with its own determination as questioning. Moving within tautology, declaring that language is language, interrupting the question of ground, such reflection is left hovering over an abyss. But listen:

> Language is: language. Language speaks. If we let ourselves fall into the abyss that this proposition names, we do not go tumbling into emptiness. We fall upward, to a height. Its loftiness opens up a depth. The two span a realm in which we would like to become at home, so as to find the abode for the essence of man. To reflect on language means: to reach the speaking of language in such a way that this speaking takes place [*sich ereignet*—untranslatable] as that which grants an abode for the essence of mortals. (US 13f.)

Displacement into the abyss of the speaking of language, ecstasy that would listen to what sounds from the abyss and that would find there the abode of mortals. Ecstasy suspended between human speech and the speaking of language. Ecstasy as homecoming in the abyss.

Reflection on language as language must be ecstatic, must undergo displacement to the speaking of language. But where is one to find the speaking of langauge? Heidegger's text will confirm that it is found in *the spoken*—or, rather, that it can be found in the spoken provided the spoken is not reduced to a mere residue of speaking in which speaking itself has ceased, provided one can listen to the spoken as that in which speaking is gathered in such a way as to endure, that is, is sheltered (*geborgen*). In order to reach ecstatically the speaking of language, one needs to listen thus to the spoken. Heidegger's text proposes to attend to something spoken *purely*, to something that shelters an originary speaking. It is asserted—and, before one has listened, it can only, as Heidegger's text says, be asserted—that what is purely spoken is the poem.

Structurally, then, it is a matter of listening to language speaking in the poem, that is, a matter of a thinking that would circulate between language speaking and the poem, the translation, in which language speaks. Such a thinking produces, then, another translation, Heidegger's text. By circulating between this second transla-

tion and the speaking of language in the poem, still a third translation is produced, the present text. Translation upon translation
upon translation. Thinking would be inseparable from translation
in the sense of producing always a translation, spoken or written
words. Yet also, one cannot but wonder whether it would be inseparable from translation in another, more disturbing sense, namely, in
the sense that that which thinking would translate would itself be
irreducibly translational. The ever-withdrawing original would,
then, always already have been translated.

Let me, then, marking this structure, redouble Heidegger's listening to language speaking in the poem. The poem is—in
English—"A Winter Evening" by Georg Trakl, and it begins with
these words:

> Window with falling snow is arrayed,
> Long tolls the vesper bell,
> The house is provided well,
> The table is for many laid.[7]

Heidegger translates the stanza. It calls the familiar things that
belong to a winter evening: window, snow, bell, house, table. It calls
these things forth, brings them closer, yet without depriving them
of their remoteness. Calling them forth by calling to them in the
distance, the stanza—and that is to say language speaking in the
poem—also calls the *place* of those things, the place of their arrival,
the place where they may have their bearing on man.

Listen as Heidegger translates further, indeed more decisively:

> The snowfall brings men under the sky that is darkening into night.
> The tolling of the evening bell brings them, as mortals, before the
> divine. House and table bind mortals to the earth. The things that are
> named, thus called, gather to themselves sky and earth, mortals and
> divinities. The four are originally united in being toward one another.
> The things let the fourfold of the four stay [*verweilen*] with them. This
> gathering letting-stay is the thinging of things. The unitary fourfold of
> sky and earth, mortals and divinities, which is stayed in the thinging of
> things, we call: the world. In the naming, the things named are called

---

7. The translation of this and the other two stanzas of "Ein Winterabend" is,
with only minor changes, taken from Albert Hofstadter (translator): Martin Heidegger, *Poetry, Language, Thought* (New York: Harper & Row, 1971).

into their thinging. Thinging, they unfold world, in which things abide and so are the abiding ones. (US 22)

Let me say, then: the speaking of language in the first stanza of the poem calls things forth in such a way that they gather the fourfold and let it stay with them as the place of their bearing, as world. Such gathering and staying is called: the thinging of things. The speaking of language in the first stanza of Trakl's poem calls things into their thinging.

The second stanza begins:

Wandering ones, more than a few,
Come to the door on dark paths.

Heidegger's translation: these lines name other things (door, dark path) but especially they call forth those who wander toward death, mortals.

But then, with the remainder of the stanza, everything changes:

Golden blooms the tree of graces
Drawing up the earth's cool dew.

Listen as Heidegger translates:

The tree is rooted soundly in the earth. Thus it flourishes into a blooming that opens itself to the blessings of the sky. The towering of the tree has been called. It spans both the rapture of flowering and the soberness of the nourishing sap. The earth's abated growth and the sky's open bounty belong together. The poem names the tree of graces. Its sound blossoming harbors the fruit that falls to us unearned: holy, saving, gracious toward mortals. In the golden-blossoming tree there prevail earth and sky, divinities and mortals. Their unitary fourfold is the world. . . . The third and fourth lines of the second stanza call the tree of graces. They expressly bid the world to come. They call the world-fourfold here and thus call world to things. (US 23–24)

Let me say, simply: in naming the tree, the speaking of language in the second stanza culminates by calling forth the fourfold, world.

Heidegger introduces a reflection that is gradually distanced from attention to the poem. He observes, first, how each of the two stanzas, calling things and world, respectively, calls also the other—that is, how the first calls things to world and the second calls world to things. Thus, world and things, as called forth by the speaking of language in the poem, do not simply subsist alongside one another but rather interpenetrate: things bear world, and world grants things. Heidegger focuses on this space of interpenetration—that is, he offers three names for this space: *das Zwischen, die Innigkeit, der Unterschied.*

It is for me to note that something very decisive is happening at this point in Heidegger's text: having listened to the naming spoken in the poem, thinking now itself issues in its own responsive naming, a new order of translation, more distanced, more proper to thinking. It is also for me to translate or forego translating these names by which thinking calls the space where world and things interpenetrate. Let me translate only one, *Unterschied,* translate it as *difference.*

Heidegger observes that as a name for this space of world and things difference is no longer a generic concept for various kinds of differences but now, withdrawn from its usual sense, names a singular difference, something unique. Also, that which is singularly named difference does not supervene to mediate prior terms—that is, it is not as if world and things were first somehow there and then came to be joined by this differential middle. Rather, in Heidegger's words: "As the middle, it first determines world and things to their essence" (US 25).

It is, then, difference that is most properly called in such calling of things and world as Heidegger hears in Trakl's poem: "In the bidding that calls thing and world, what is properly [*eigentlich*] called is: the difference" (US 26).

This is what he hears preeminently called in the final stanza of Trakl's poem:

> Wanderer quietly steps within;
> Pain has turned the threshold to stone.
> There lie, in pure brightness shown,
> Upon the table bread and wine.

Heidegger:

> Bread and wine are the fruits of sky and earth, gifts from the divinities to mortals. Bread and wine gather these four to themselves from the simple unity of their fourfoldness. . . . The third stanza calls world and things into the middle of their *Innigkeit.* (US 28)

Again, Heidegger introduces the other order of translation, a naming more proper to thinking. The speaking of language calls the difference in that it calls each, world and things, to rest in the other—that is, it reposes each in the other. To put into repose is to still. The call that calls the double stilling Heidegger calls: *Läuten.*

Let me translate: *tolling*—so as then to translate Heidegger's words, italicized, as follows: "*Language speaks as the tolling of stillness*" (US 30).

Having thus listened to language speaking in the poem, circulating so as to produce another translation, Heidegger has come finally to name the speaking of language, to name it: *Läuten,* tolling. It is for me to note that this naming is the highpoint of Heidegger's text, highpoint in the sense determined by Heidegger's insistence, early in the text, that in falling into the abyss of language, we fall upward, to a height. This naming marks the point in Heidegger's text where the displacement from human speech to the speaking of language is enacted most decisively, marks it by declaring: "The tolling of stillness is nothing human" (US 30). Also by then, finally, turning back to human speaking, delimiting it as the responsive sounding of the tolling of stillness: man speaks insofar as he responds to language, transforming his "saying into the almost concealed, ecstatic [*rauschenden*], lyrical echo [*Widerklang*] of an unspeakable saying [*Sage*]" (US 231). Thus also will Heidegger have spoken, even as he turns finally to that very speaking.

Thus also the third translation, the one that the present text will have produced. It is for this translation to say that this naming, above all, translates what sounds forth in ecstasy. In this naming, above all, Heidegger is translating ecstasy.

Afterword

Afterword—

Another word for echo. A word that sounds after another, that sounds like it and that sounds at a certain distance from it, a certain distance in time as well as in space. The afterword may reproduce the word at a distance, from a distance, thus reproduce it imperfectly, falling away from the word. Or the afterword may add a word of its own, blending it with the original, sheltering the original and itself becoming to some extent an original. Another original after the original, doubling the original originarily in returning it.

Afterword—

After the word of Heidegger. After he has sounded the words that would have the last word, even becoming finally untranslatable: *Sein, Lichtung, Ereignis.* Resounding these words in imitation, afterwards. Wondering about what comes after these words, even after they have had the last word. About what comes after them not in some further beyond (for they will have had the last word). But about that to which one would return, would be drawn, or, rather, could not but be redrawn, after these words. The return that would double the ascent to the beyond of these words. So, after these words, descent toward things, toward the things of the earth.

Afterword—

After the word by which Heidegger would name the word itself, the very speaking of language. After the word *Läuten.* After the words of the translation: language speaks as the tolling of stillness. After the word that, in thus pronouncing the tolling of stillness, will have broken the stillness, shattered the silence with its sounding.

Human speaking will always have been such an afterword. It does not rest upon itself but upon its relation to the speaking of language, which, according to the translated words of Heidegger, is the tolling of stillness. Human speech is the afterword that breaks the silence by sounding what language has bespoken. Human speech is the echo of language.

But now, after the words of Heidegger, doubling them from a distance, mimetically—in other words, echoing the words of Heidegger after Heidegger. Now it is a matter of wondering about what comes after the word, after language, after its tolling of stillness. A matter of wondering about the afterword. Of wondering about a return from language and its speaking, a return from the tautology of *Die Sprache spricht*. Wondering whether the word of language is to have the last word. Wondering about the word with which Heidegger names human speech: *Entsprechen*. Wondering about the *Ent-*, the *re-* of *response*. Wondering whether it is the same as: reproduce. Wondering—dreaming even—about a doubling that would return from the tautology of the word and its mere afterword, that would return to discover, to recover, something indigenous this side of the tolling of stillness. An element that would blend with that tolling, as the voice of the woods around Walden Pond blended with the tolling of the church bells coming from the towns. An element that would make the afterword, the echo, human speech, to some extent original.

If there is such an element—need it be said, the return toward it will require especially that the *there is* be written with eraser in hand—it is only to be found in that which makes human speech be to an extent sensible, its sounding.

In the lecture "The Essence of Language" Heidegger speaks about the sounding of human speech, speaks toward an element that would remain withdrawn this side of the essence of language, speaks of it as if from a distance, broaching but also diverting again toward the essence what would be originary in that sounding.

Language and its sounding have, first of all, to be drawn into the end of metaphysics, displaced from the opposition that is itself finally displaced in that end: Heidegger says that he does not want to denigrate the vocal sounding of speech, declaring it something bodily, something merely sensible in speech, in order then to valorize the sense or meaning content, taken as the spiritual, as the spirit of language (*Geist der Sprache*). Rather, he says, there is need to experience what is bodily and sensible in language (both *Laut-und Schriftzug*); and there is need to grant that for language to sound ("*dass die Sprache lautet und klingt und schwingt, schwebt und bebt*"—US 205) is as proper to it as for it to have a meaning. The sensible element of language, Heidegger continues, is bespoken by the way in which the German language names regionally varying ways of speaking: *Mundarten*. In distinction from the other word (the *Fremdwort*), *Dialekt*, stemming from διαλέγειν, thus bespeaking *Auslesen*, gathering, λόγος. Heidegger says: "In dialect [*Mundart*] there speaks ever variously the region [*Landschaft*] and that means the earth. . . . The body and the mouth belong to the streaming and growth of the earth, on which we mortals flourish, from which we receive the genuineness of an indigenousness [*Bodenständigkeit*]" (US 205). In another word: *Heimat*.

To think the return from language to a sensible, indigenous element that would render human speech to some extent original thus requires that one think together: language and *Heimat*. And indeed, when Heidegger undertakes to do so, in the text "*Sprache und Heimat*," he begins precisely by breaking with language, by moving away into the return from *die Sprache:* "D i e Sprache gibt es nicht" (GA 13: 155). What is called—improperly—*language* is in its essential origin dialect. Heidegger says: "The essence of language is rooted in dialect" (GA 13: 156). The return thus announced will always be threatened by the possibility of reversal. It will always be possible—and, for essential reasons, tempting—to convert rooted-ness and indigenousness into grounding and to bring dialect, fi-nally, back to an *Ursprache* that would resound in it. Heidegger does not always evade this possibility, not even in the context of thinking together: language and *Heimat*.[1] Language would, then, bring forth

1. It is precisely in the text "*Sprache und Heimat*," in fact, in a discussion of dialect poetry, that Heidegger broaches such a reappropriation of dialect by an *Ursprache*. Dialect poetry, he says, "first unfolds the dialect itself into its own poetic essence and brings the dialect to the fullness, breadth, and clarity of its own un-spoken language. The latter reaches itself into the poetic composition and is estab-lished there as something remaining, which, even if one no longer hears it, endures as the pure echo of the *Ursprache* resounding in the dialect . . ." (GA 13: 177). Dialect is thus reclaimed by an *Ursprache*, by another language (which Heidegger is careful

(ποιεῖν) *Heimat;* precisely in its poetic essence, language would bring forth even the earth.

And yet, before the reversal language would have been itself (i.e., in its essence) already taken back into dialect. As in the dialect poetry of Johann Peter Hebel, which Heidegger read natively and with such care. The mystery of such language as that of Hebel's Allemanic poetry lies in Hebel's ability, Heidegger says, "to incorporate the language of the Allemanic dialect into the elevated and written language. In this way," Heidegger continues, "the poet lets the written language [the literary language—*Schriftsprache*] sound as a pure echo of the richness of the dialect" (GA 13: 148).[2]

Withdrawn from its essence beyond, language would be drawn back toward dialect, toward *Heimat,* toward the earth, drawn in a way that would be originary—I withdraw, here, now, this word itself into the same draft—to such an extent that it could never be simply erased by a reappropriating reversal.

After the afterwords of the word, after the echoes of language, of its essential speaking, there would be, withdrawing from their very saying: *Heimat,* earth. As—so it was said—Echo, dismembered (like Dionysus), continued to sound forth from beneath the earth.

to distinguish "from a universal world-language"); it is reconstituted as the *mere* echo of the *Ursprache,* an echo to no extent original. Echo itself is thus taken up into the reversal.

2. This passage, cited from *Hebel der Hausfreund* (1957), is repeated with only slight variations (e.g., *auffangen* in place of *einverleiben*) in two other texts of the same period, "*Für das Langenharder Hebelbuch*" (1954) (GA 13: 118) and "*Die Sprache Johann Peter Hebels*" (1955) (GA 13: 125).

Index

Absence, 93, 95, 193
Abyss: and imagination, 117; and
  death, 118; and Being, 136; of freedom, 151; and ecstasy, 190, 191, 201;
  and essence, 191
Aesthetics: and poetics, 168, 172n4,
  183; limit of, 168; end of, 170; and
  Schopenhauer, 172n4; and mimesis,
  175
Anxiety, 148, 149, 156
Appropriation, 143
Aristotle, 46, 115, 160n14, 168–171,
  174, 183, 184, 197
Art: and truth, 168, 174, 180, 185; and
  beauty, 174; riddle of, 179–182; and
  work of art, 172–174, 176–178, 180,
  183–185; and poetry, 183; and language, 184, 184n; and universal, 184
Augustine, 48
Authenticity, 131, 146

Beautiful, 174, 182, 183

Circling: and nonphilosophy, 17; and
  meaning, 98; of imagination, 142n3;
  toward Being, 149; and art, 172, 174,
  180; and language, 199
Circumspection, 83
Clearing: as *Lichtung*, 13, 41; and thinking, 31–32; and echo, 34, 42; beyond
  of Being, 34, 35, 36, 40; and Being,
  34–36, 41, 72, 194, 194n5; and temporality, 35; and questioning, 37; and
  Parmenides, 38, 39; and *Ereignis*, 71;
  and time, 71, 72; and *Da*, 121; and
  ἀλήθεια, 140n; and origin, 151n10;
  and art, 175, 176, 179; and truth,
  180; and language, 183
Coincidence: of questioner and questioned, 19, 26, 50n14; not identity,
  19; and thinking, 24; of owness and
  alterity, 122, 130, 132, 133, 137; of
  being and nonbeing, 123–124, 130,
  133, 134, 136; and doubling, 134
Concealment: and thinking, 42, 43; and
  temporality, 62, 69; and things, 87,
  88; and truth, 176, 179; and earth,
  176; and God, 188, 189

Conscience, 146
Contradiction, 123

Da: and Dasein, 92, 121, 143n4; Being
  of, 141; and poetry, 186; and space,
  199
Death: and end, 34; analysis of, 45,
  57n, 92, 92n; of Dasein, 50–51; as
  possibility, 51, 52, 57, 92; and presence, 52; and time, 61; and birth, 67,
  79; and projection, 93; and man,
  118, 122; and abyss, 118; and excess,
  118; as death, 121, 136, 137; proper
  to man, 122, 135; and imagination,
  122, 133, 134; and contradiction,
  123; and owness, 124, 127, 134; and
  alterity, 124, 133, 134; and existence,
  124, 130; end of Dasein, 125; and
  perishing, 125, 135; and possibility,
  126–133, 136; analysis of 126–127,
  129, 130, 131, 135, 136, 138; Being-
  toward-death, 126, 129, 130, 131,
  133, 135; as impending, 127, 129;
  and actuality, 131, 132; and afterlife,
  133; and Being, 135; and nothing,
  135, 136; and language, 137; and sacrifice, 139
Decentering, 91, 92, 93, 143
de Launay, M., 45
Derrida, J., 19, 21, 33n, 42n, 79, 81,
  198
Destruktion, 11, 18
Difference: and Dasein, 27, 53; and beings and Being, 28, 179; in sense, 86;
  ontological, 103; and truth, 180; and
  space, 204; and essence, 204
Dionysus, 3, 209
Disclosedness: *Erschlossenheit*, 26, 79,
  141, 142n4; and Dasein, 35, 62, 66,
  84, 85, 89, 91, 92, 131, 132; and the
  sensible, 79, 84, 85, 94, 96; space of,
  79, 95; and sight, 82, 83; and care,
  84; and self-presence, 91, 93; and
  temporality, 96; and death, 129; and
  limit, 139; and truth, 139; and understanding, 141, 142, 161n; and discoveredness, 142, 142n4; constitution of,
  143n4

JOHN SALLIS is W. Alton Jones Professor of Philosophy at Vanderbilt University. His previous books include *Delimitations: Phenomenology and the End of Metaphysics, Spacings—Of Reason and Imagination, The Gathering of Reason, Being and Logos,* and *Phenomenology and the Return to Beginnings.*